IMAGES
of America

LAKE PLEASANT AND SPECULATOR IN THE ADIRONDACKS

ON THE COVER: The Sturges House was built by Dave Sturges, son of Aaron Sturges, a shoemaker from Connecticut who came to Speculator in 1832. Dave was a guide for his father at Lewey Lake when he was 16 years old. Dave started with a two-story hotel in 1858, added on a three-story addition, and built an annex across the road. At the Sturges House, Dave had a croquet playing area and had guides for the sportsmen. The Sturges House stood where the present bank, Speculator Post Office, and Charlie John's Store are now. In 1942, the Sturges House burned down. (Historical Society of Lake Pleasant and Speculator Collection.)

IMAGES
of America

LAKE PLEASANT AND SPECULATOR IN THE ADIRONDACKS

Anne A. Weaver and Beverly Hoffman

ARCADIA
PUBLISHING

ISBN 978-0-7385-7251-2

Published by Arcadia Publishing
Charleston, South Carolina

Printed in the United States of America

Library of Congress Control Number: 2009936093

For all general information contact Arcadia Publishing at:
Telephone 843-853-2070
Fax 843-853-0044
E-mail sales@arcadiapublishing.com
For customer service and orders:
Toll-Free 1-888-313-2665

Visit us on the Internet at www.arcadiapublishing.com

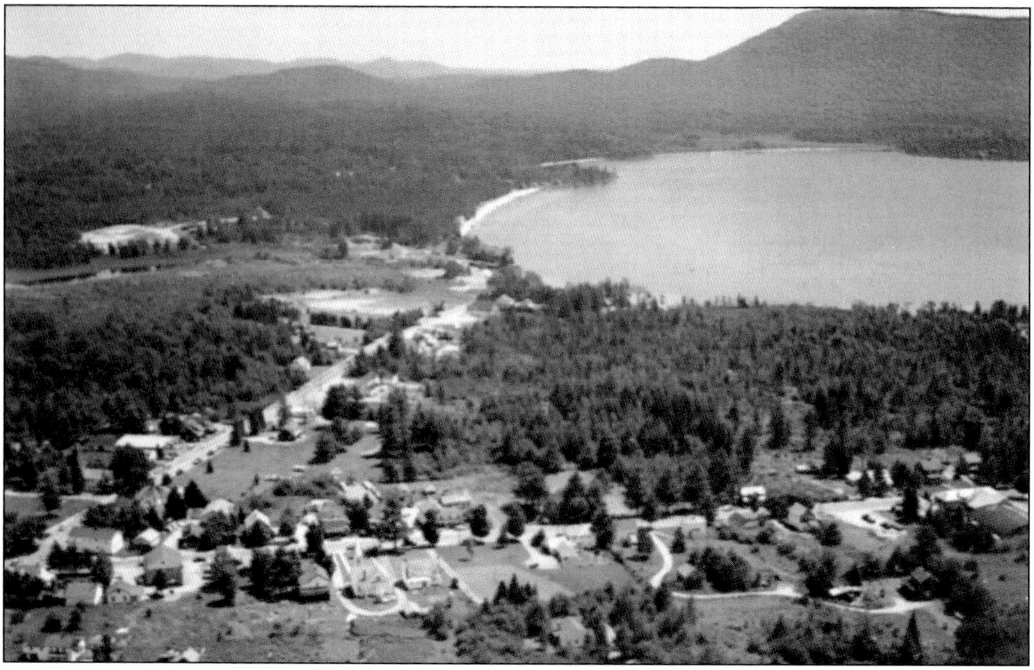

This is an aerial view of the village of Speculator looking south toward Speculator Mountain in the 1960s. We would like to dedicate this book to all those who came before us and helped make Speculator and Lake Pleasant the wonderful communities they are today. They have stoically faced the elements of weather, poor farming soil, poor economic times, wars, poverty, and so much more, yet they believed in this area and continue to live here. Our grateful thanks go to them all. (Historical Society of Lake Pleasant and Speculator Collection.)

Contents

Acknowledgments

We would like to thank those who have told stories and given photographs to us throughout these several years that we have been historians. A special thanks goes to Arthur and Lila Tefft, who came to Speculator from Connecticut to stay and photograph the history of our area for many years. A special thanks also goes to the Historical Society of Lake Pleasant and Speculator for allowing us to use their collection. Photographs in this book came from the historical society's collection unless otherwise noted. We would like to thank the following who have donated many photographs to us: Esther Hoover, Susan Kraus, Lila Morris, Cal and Joan Morrison, John and Jo O'Connell, Gertrude Peck, Ed and Marie Perkins, Tom and Marge Perkins, Margery Peters, Letty Rudes, Barbara Schoonmaker, Elizabeth Taft, Jo Weaver, Peter Weaver, and William Weaver. We also want to thank our past county historians, Paul Wilbur, Ted Aber, and Stella King, and to our present county historian, Bill Zullo, and to our past town historian, Ernie Virgil.

INTRODUCTION

Evidence of Native Americans has been found in arrowheads and spearheads near the lakeshores. However, many historians believe our area of Lake Pleasant and Speculator was the hunting and fishing grounds of the Native Americans living in the Mohawk Valley. The first settlers arrived around 1795; this area was then a part of the Town of Mayfield in Montgomery County. The inexpensive land was offered by New York City landowners to induce settlement. The heavily forested majestic mountains, the abundant game for food and furs, and the numerous lakes and streams full of fish awaited these first settlers.

A few hardy pioneers came to the wilderness, cleared the land, and built self-sufficient farms. They built gristmills and sawmills for local use. All seemed good except for the heavy snows, and the lack of good roads meant they were isolated in the winter and spring.

A short, cool summer-growing season meant adapting their farming to crops that would survive to feed themselves and their livestock. Sheep did well on the rocky hillsides, and cloth was manufactured in many homes. Wild animals such as wolves, coyotes, bobcats, and mountain lions had to be dealt with. Apple orchards were planted with some success.

A few mills to craft woodenwares and tools were built. Some found income from shingle making, and nearly every building was roofed with these wooden shingles. Small dairies supplied butter, cheese, and milk to neighbors and later to the logging camps and large hotels.

Still development was slow and deprivations numerous. Many left to be closer to their families, where farmland was richer and jobs that offered a steady income could be found.

Several small settlements, separated by distance and a lack of passable roads, soon became separate towns. The large area was impractical to govern, and the Montgomery County courthouse was 60 miles away. In 1805, the Town of Wells was established, which included the area of Lake Pleasant.

In 1812, the Town of Lake Pleasant was established with about 300 residents. It was a large area with scattered settlements and far-reaching boundaries. It extended north indefinitely and to the west to the Herkimer County line. Hamilton County became a provisional county in 1816, but since it lacked a sufficient number of residents, it was counted with Montgomery County until 1837.

Lake Pleasant later gave up some of its land to other towns such as Morehouse in 1835, Arietta in 1836, Long Lake in 1837, Gilman from 1839 to 1860, and Indian Lake in 1858. The Town of Gilman stretched over 40 miles from Wells to Long Lake and was soon recognized as impractical, and the land was annexed to neighboring towns.

Gradually settlement continued, and two small communities developed, about 4 miles apart, near the lake called Lake Pleasant. In 1844, Hezekiah Sage sought to develop a town called Sageville at the "head" of the lake. The county buildings were to be located here and there was already a hotel, store, and a few houses. In 1897, Sageville was changed back to Lake Pleasant.

The small settlement at the foot of the lake was Lake Pleasant until 1864 when Joel Newton built a small store and hotel in the center of the town and secured a post office with the name Newton's Corners. At that time, Page Hill and Page Street were included in Newton's Corners.

Joel Newton's structure burned in 1870, and in 1872 the Newton's Corners Post Office was reopened in Satterlee's store. Henry Dunning built a hotel in 1882 where Newton's had been and the post office moved there, and in 1896 the community received a new name, Speculator, after the prominent mountain seen across the lake.

Growth escalated between the 1880s and early 1900s. Whole families spent their summers enjoying the mountain hospitality and fresh air. Several more large hotels were built to accommodate them and eventually more stores, homes, and summer cottages were built.

In the beginning, small sawmills provided lumber for local use. After the Civil War, a growing nation needed lumber, and large lumber companies were formed and mills were built near the Glens Falls area. At first logging was prevalent along the Upper Hudson River as rivers were used to float the logs to the mills.

Later logging operations moved into Lake Pleasant, and the Sacandaga River was used to float logs to Glens Falls as the State of New York designated rivers as public highways for moving logs. Eventually as the roads were built and improved over the years, trucks transported logs.

There were a few small logging operations in this area that sold their logs to the larger companies. Many local farmers found winter employment with these small companies as well as supplying the companies with potatoes, meat, and dairy products and hay and feed for the horses.

The lumber companies bought large parcels of land for their timber. Some of this land was later abandoned and became state land. This was the beginning of the Adirondack Park as designated in 1892. Some of the land is still owned by the large lumber companies, and the logging industry is still carried on today.

Around the 1850s, city sportsmen began to come to the mountains to hunt, fish, and enjoy expeditions into the deep woods. They hired local men who knew the area to be their guides. The guides provided food and crude lean-tos for shelter. Hunting shanties were later widely used.

With these sportsmen came their whole families to use the many hotels and boardinghouses in Lake Pleasant and Speculator. Private summer camps and cottages were built and along came the established family and children camps. Camps such as Camp-of-the-Woods, Camp Setag for girls, Kamp Kun-ju-muk for boys, the YMCA Camp Agaming, and Deerfoot Lodge for boys were established around the shores of the local lakes.

In 1925, a few ambitious and industrious business leaders felt they needed to update and modernize their facilities. Speculator was a "booming mecca" for tourists. With the support of the voters, the Village of Speculator was "incorporated" with a mayor and two trustees, which later changed to four trustees. The village purchased the small water system of Dexter Slack and expanded it. The village had a generating plant and waterwheel installed at Christine Falls, and by 1926 they had electricity.

This was the year Gene Tunney arrived to train for the heavyweight championship fight. At least 10 other boxers followed him to train in Speculator.

The Town of Lake Pleasant and the Village of Speculator continue to rely on tourism today. The town is surrounded by the New York State Preserve, which offers many recreational activities for the young and the old. The Village of Speculator is the center of activities such as hiking, swimming, fishing, downhill skiing, tennis, basketball, and so much more.

One

EARLY YEARS

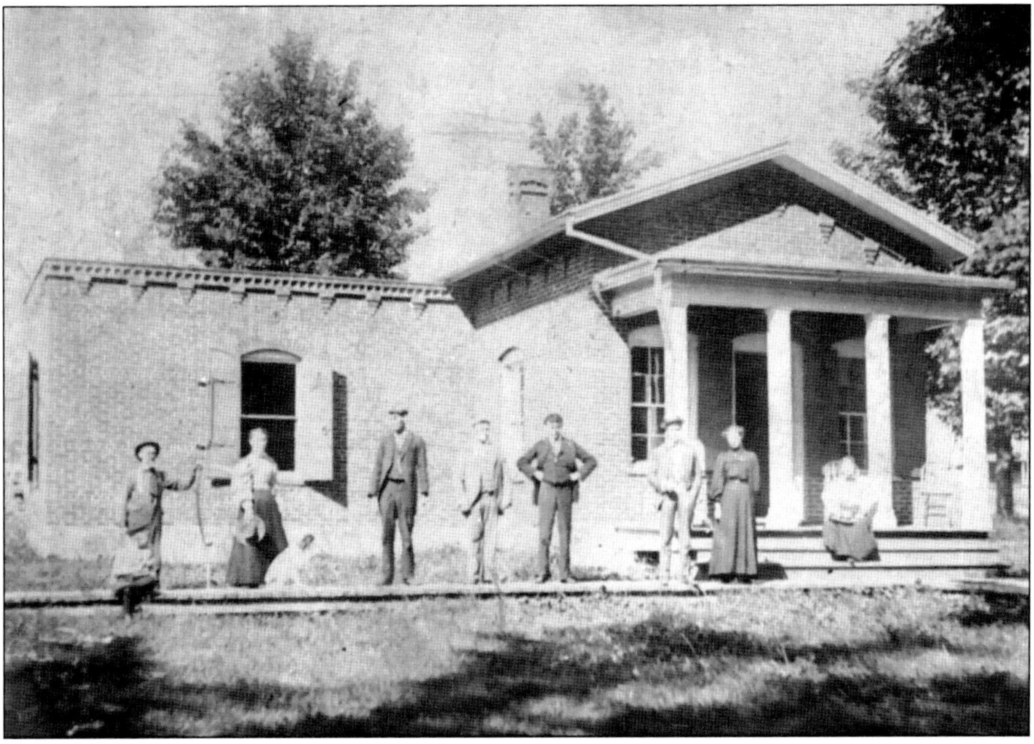

The Town of Lake Pleasant was established in 1812 and was the second town after Wells to become part of Hamilton County (established 1816). Hamilton County was at first a provisional county because of its small population and so remained attached to Montgomery County until 1836. The county clerk's office was built after the county jail and courthouse.

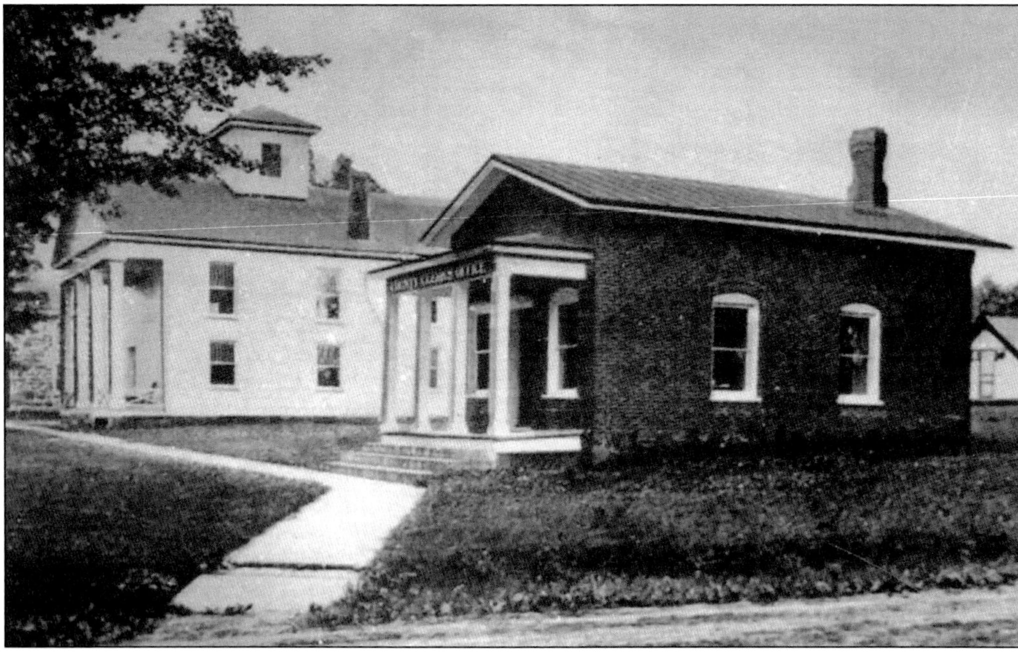

Lake Pleasant was chosen as the county seat, and a Colonial-designed wooden courthouse was built in 1843. The county clerk's office was built soon after. They are located on a knoll at the head of Lake Pleasant with a view of both Lake Pleasant and Round Lake (later Sacandaga).

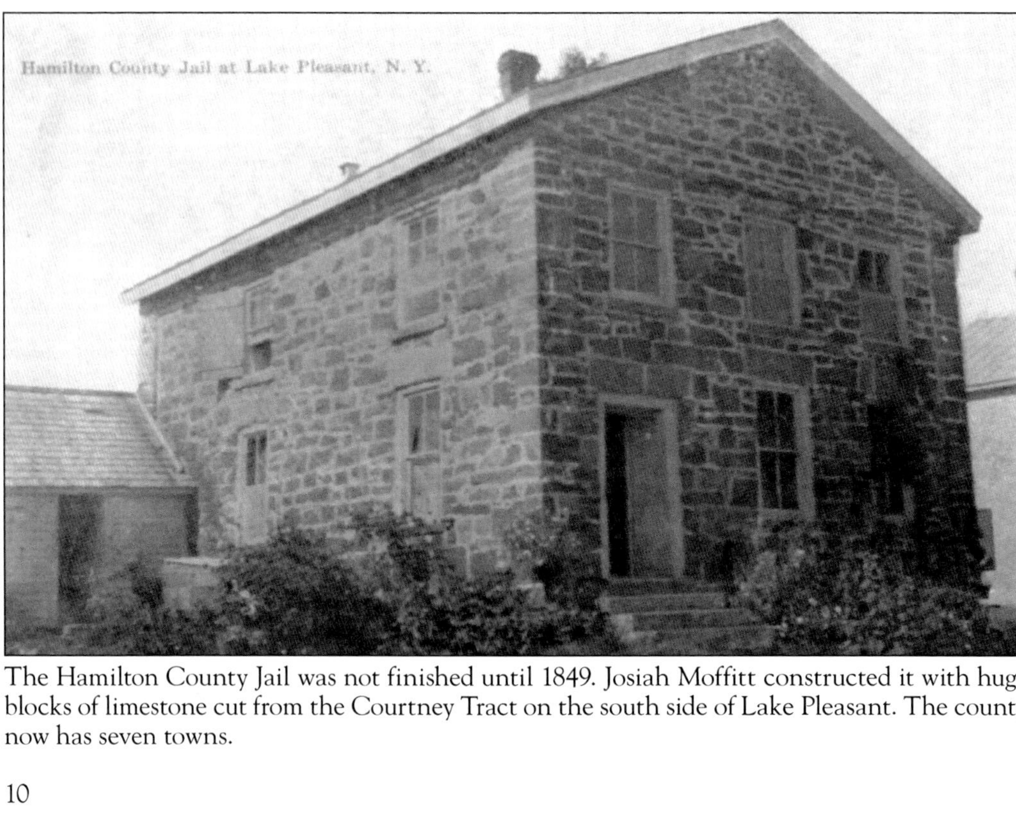

The Hamilton County Jail was not finished until 1849. Josiah Moffitt constructed it with huge blocks of limestone cut from the Courtney Tract on the south side of Lake Pleasant. The county now has seven towns.

Over the years, the county has had a long line of sheriffs. Good-natured Frank "Pants" Lawrence was quite popular and served for 12 years in the early 1900s. He was also a much sought after guide.

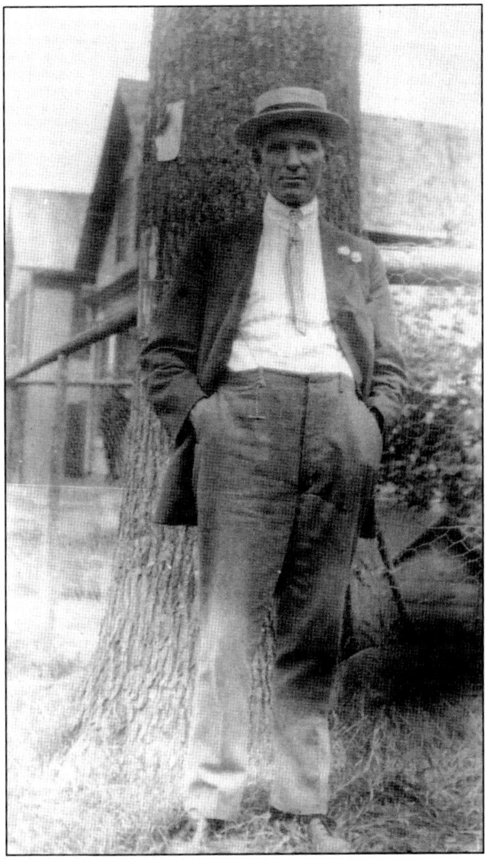

Pictured is the bridge over Lake Pleasant with Nesbit cottage beyond the bridge, an old barn on the right, and pleasure boats on Sacandaga River.

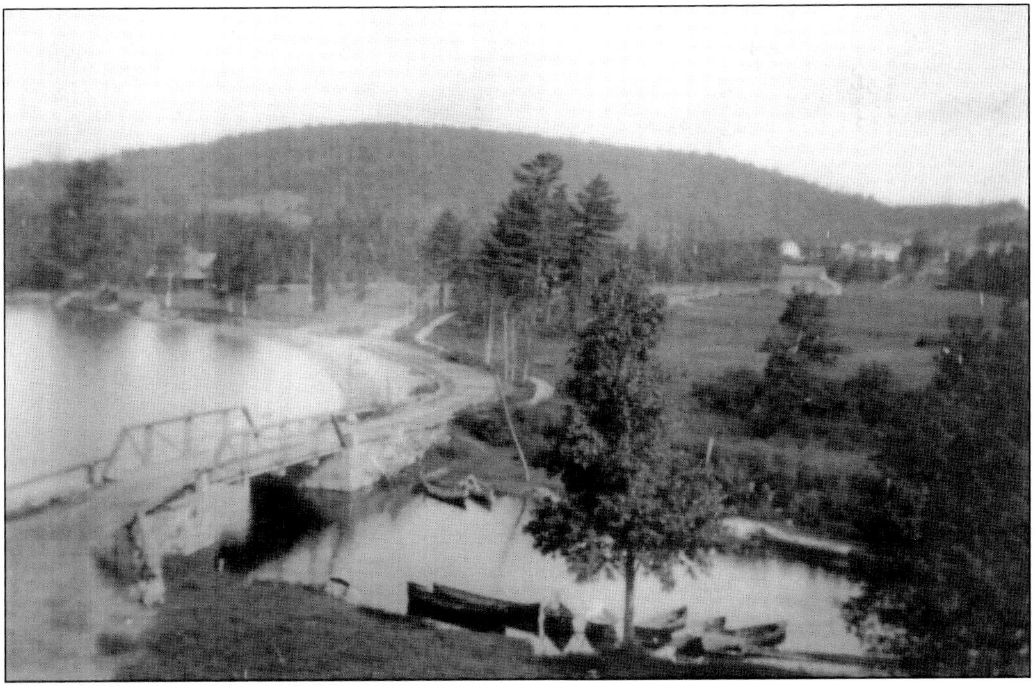

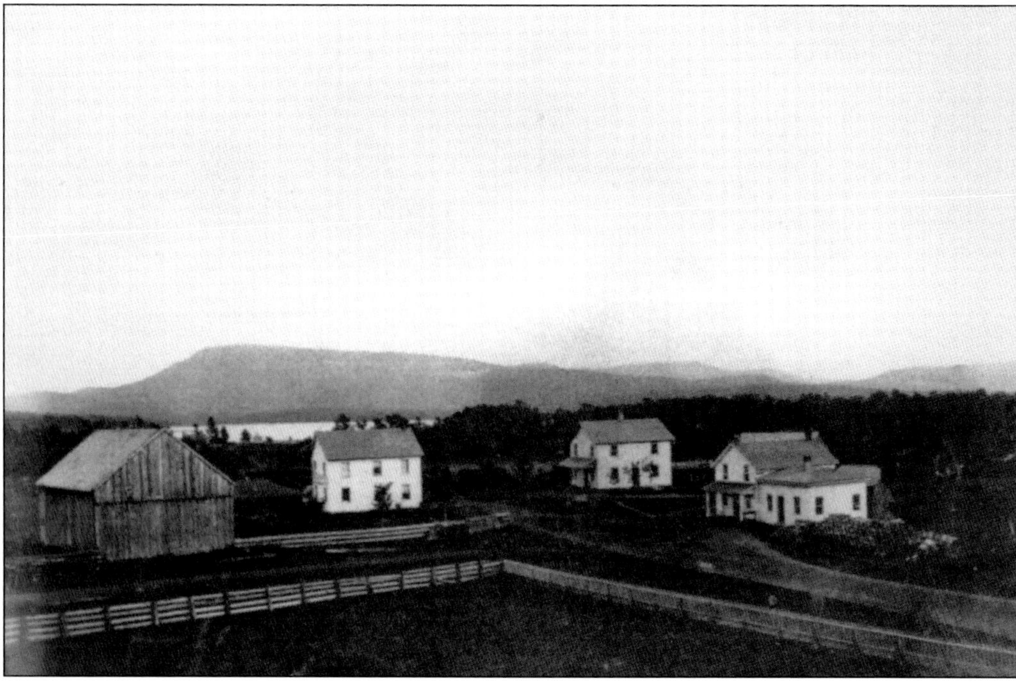

Newton's Corners around the 1880s had the Toles Satterlee's store on the right. On the left is Henry B. Slack's store and barn. The other building is Orrin Dunning's store and hotel. In the background is Lake Pleasant and Speculator Mountain.

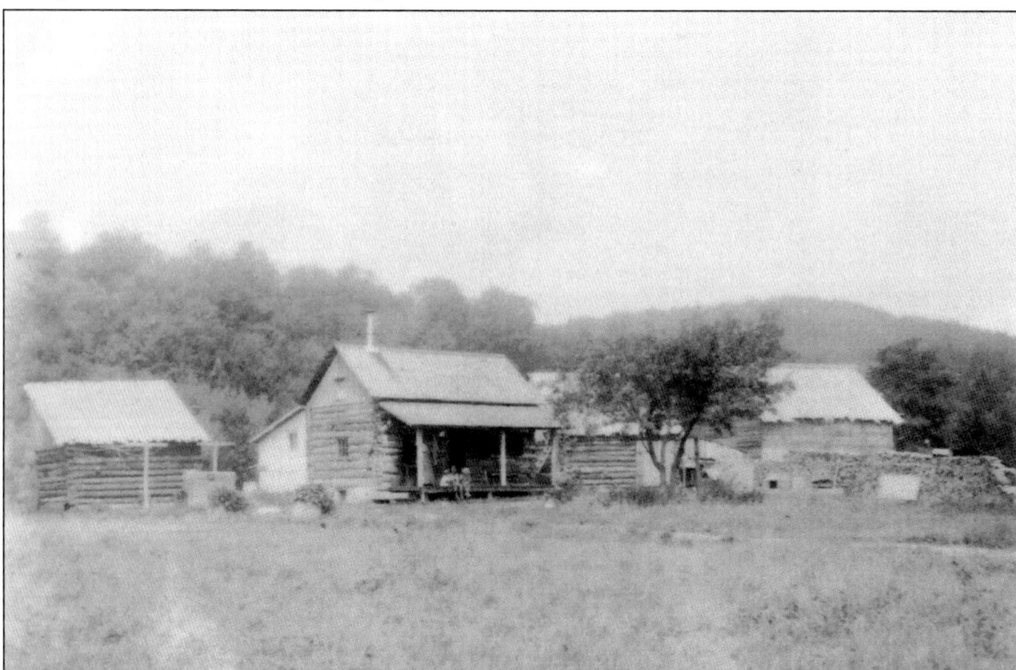

The Henrietta Abram's farm was located over the crest of Nathan Page's Hill. It was typical of many early, self-sufficient farms.

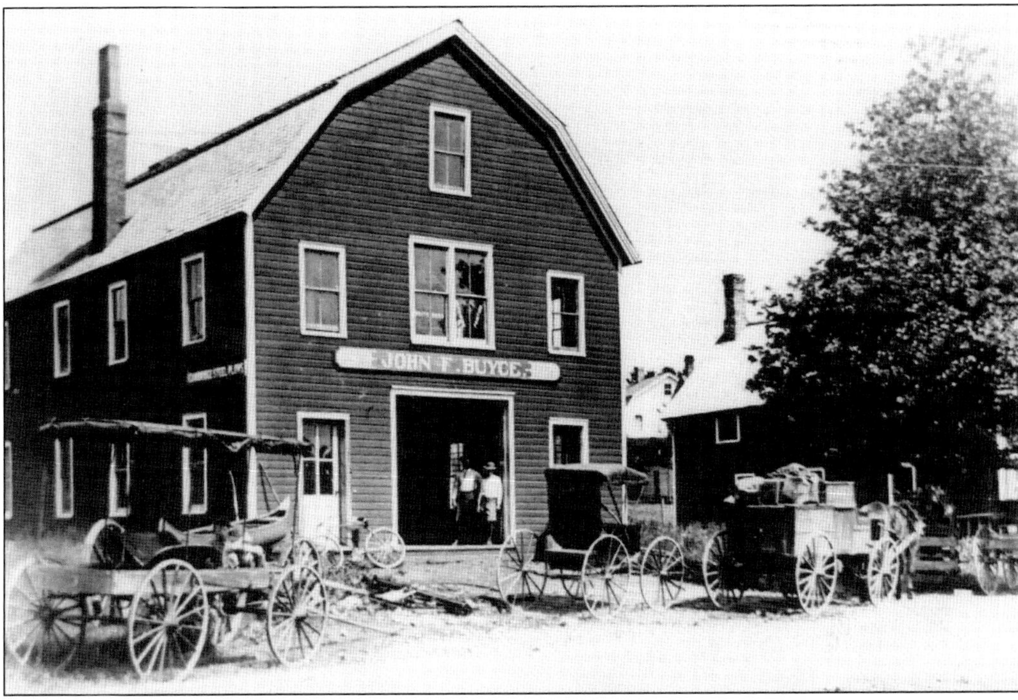

John F. Buyce's blacksmith shop advertised John Buyce as "Practical Horseshoer, Blacksmith, and Wheelwright." His letterhead reads, "Builder of fine pleasure and hunting rowboats of any size or style." This new three-story shop was built in 1908. His brother, Alvah, worked here too.

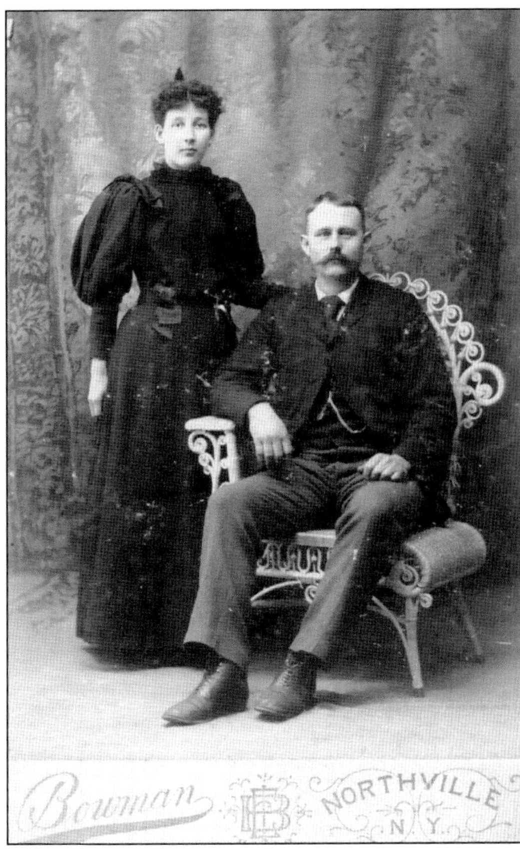

John F. Buyce married Jennie Slack, but Jennie died young and left John to raise their 14-year-old son, L. Milton, alone.

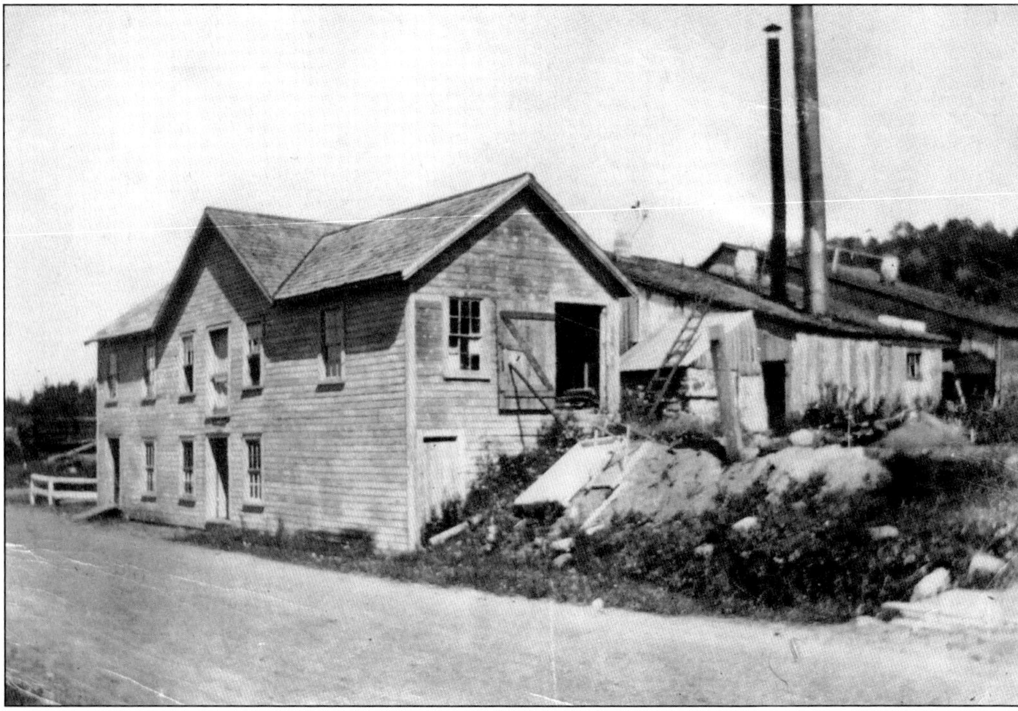

Asa Aird sawed lumber for many of the homes, hotels, and summer cottages around Lake Pleasant. He had an old up-and-down saw before changing to a circular one. The sawmill was located on Route 8 in the Airdville area.

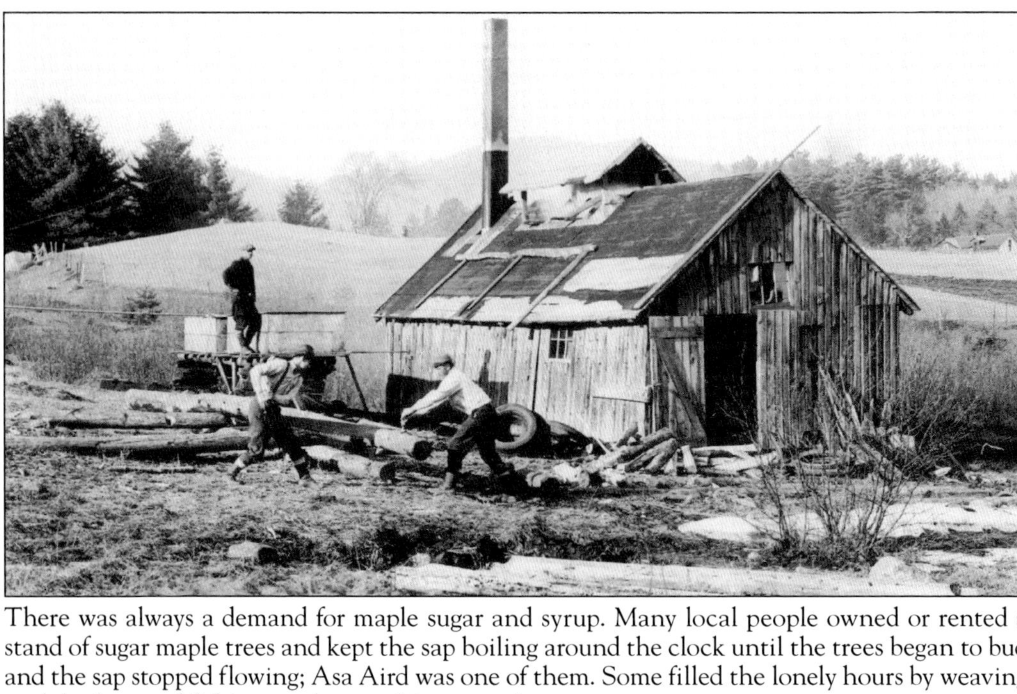

There was always a demand for maple sugar and syrup. Many local people owned or rented a stand of sugar maple trees and kept the sap boiling around the clock until the trees began to bud and the sap stopped flowing; Asa Aird was one of them. Some filled the lonely hours by weaving pack baskets and fishing creels or making snowshoes.

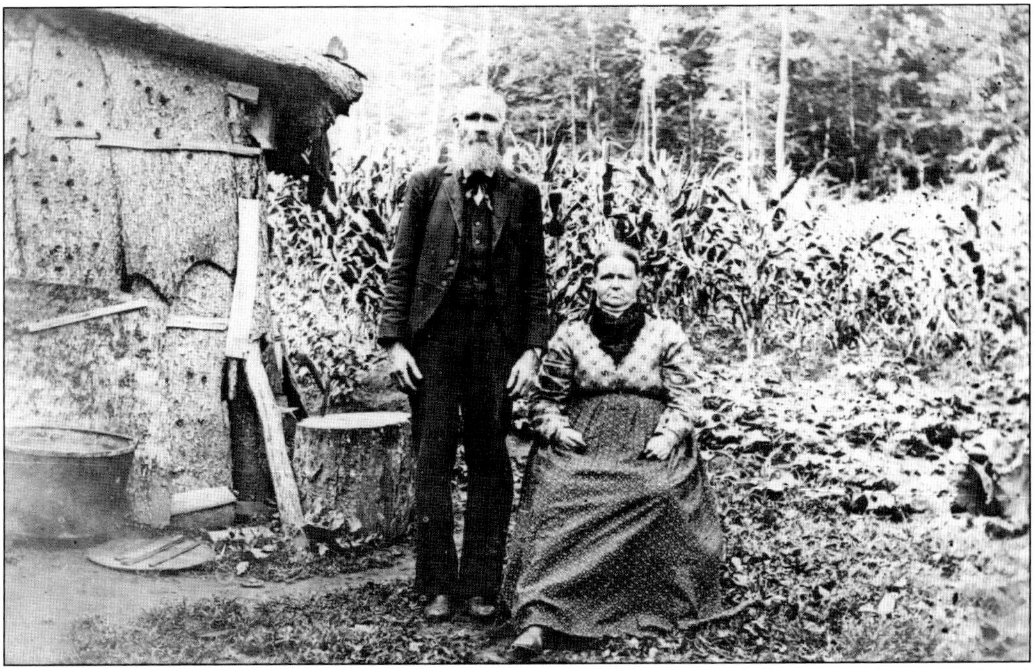

Alonzo Wilbur was a Civil War veteran and with his wife, Elizabeth Dunning, he owned and operated the Wilbur Hotel at Newton's Corners. They were instrumental in getting the Speculator Grace Methodist Church built.

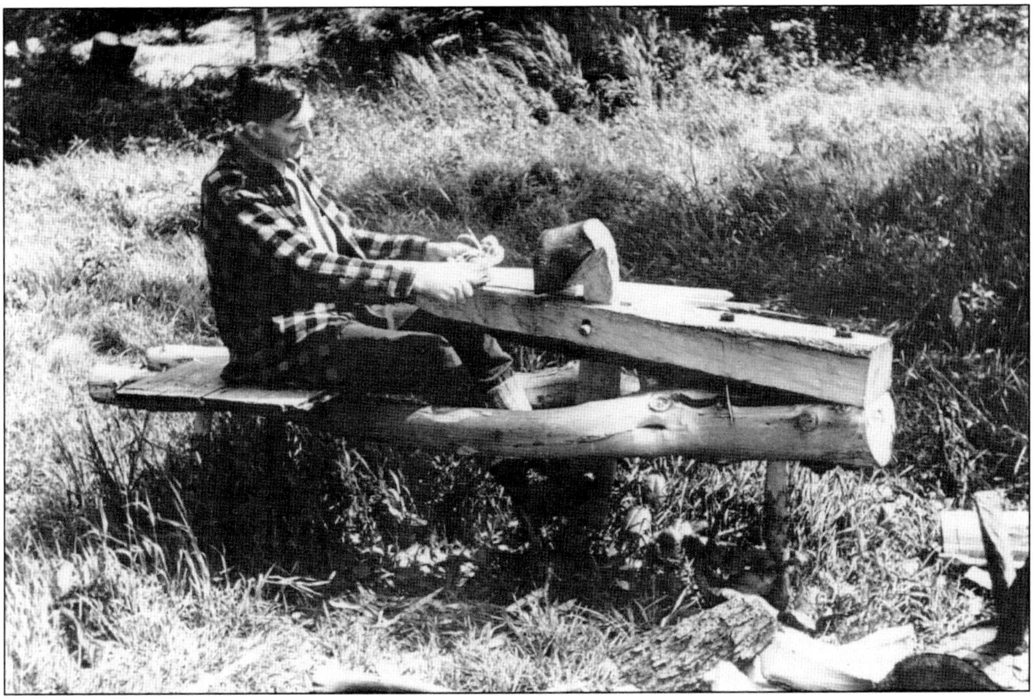

Making shingles by hand was a profitable occupation in the early years of Lake Pleasant. A drawshave is used to shape the thin wood. Most of the local homes and barns had wooden shingle roofs. Jim Lawrence was a forest ranger that traveled the woods with his horse carrying his provisions.

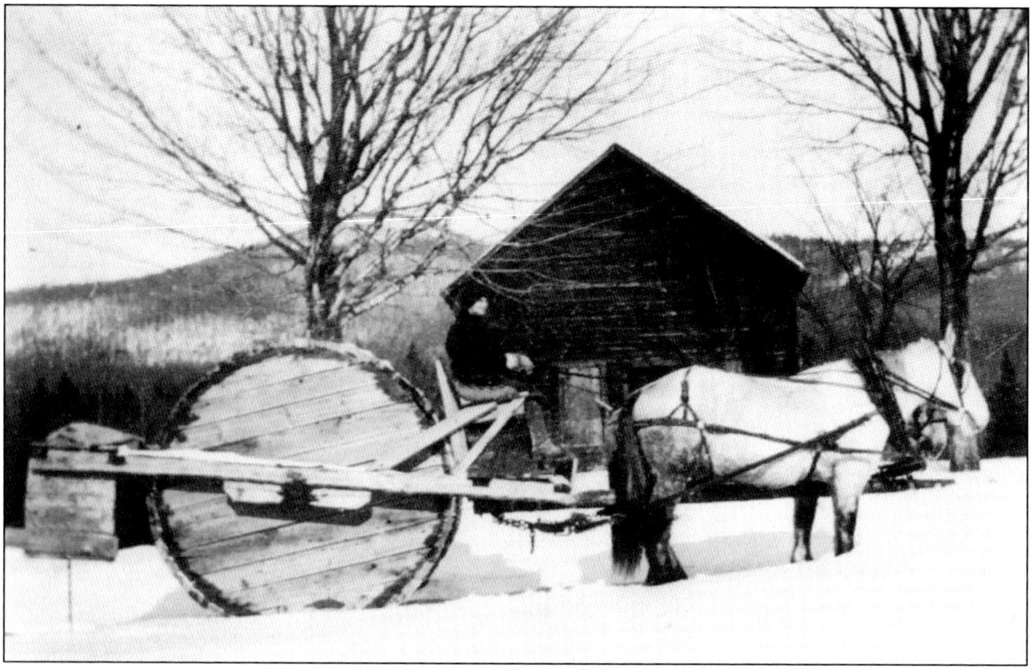

Large wooden rollers were constructed to pack down the roads so they would be wide enough to travel over. Most rollers also had a box used for carrying sand.

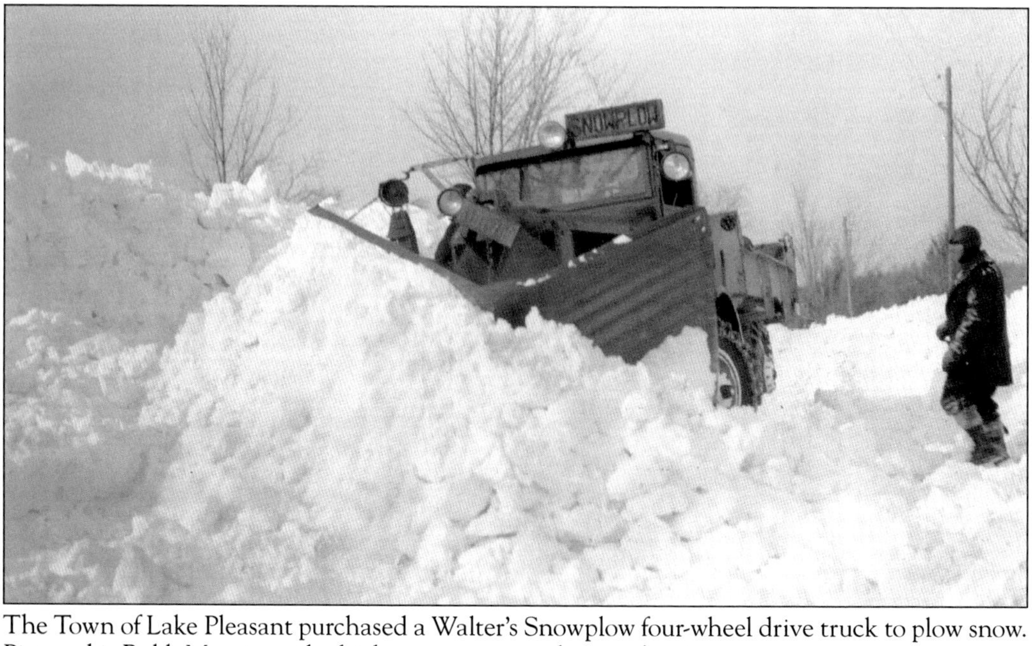

The Town of Lake Pleasant purchased a Walter's Snowplow four-wheel drive truck to plow snow. Pictured is Robb Morrison, the highway superintendent at the time.

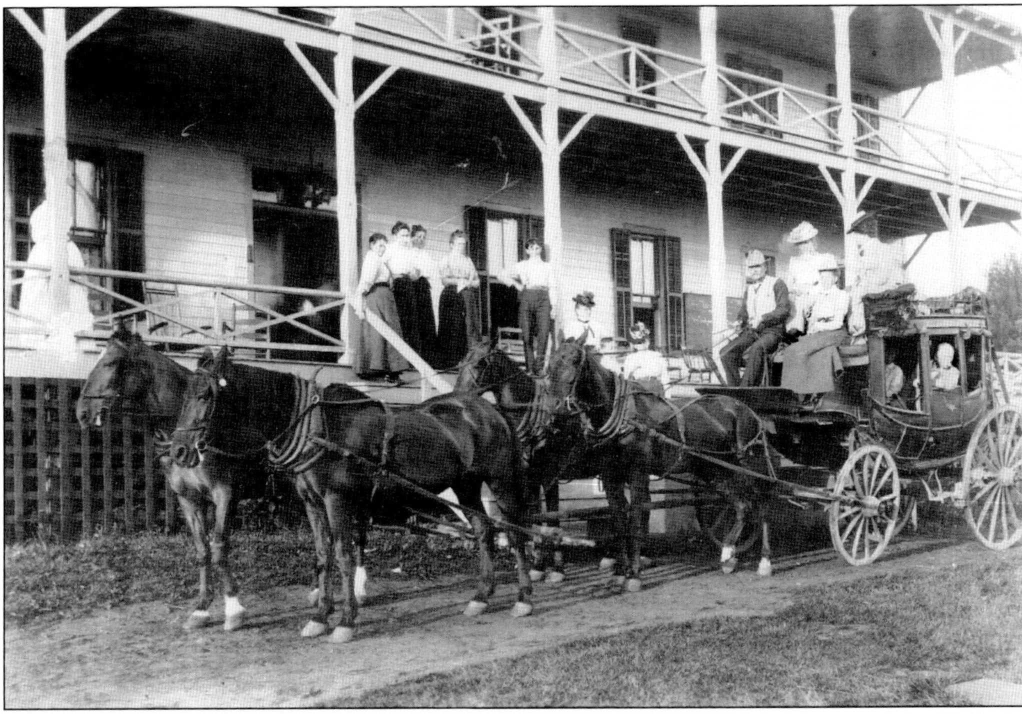

With an increase in travelers to the mountains, the roads saw improvements. The Tally-ho stagecoach ran from the train station in Northville to the hotels in southern Hamilton County. It usually stopped in Wells for dinner as a rest for both the passengers and horses.

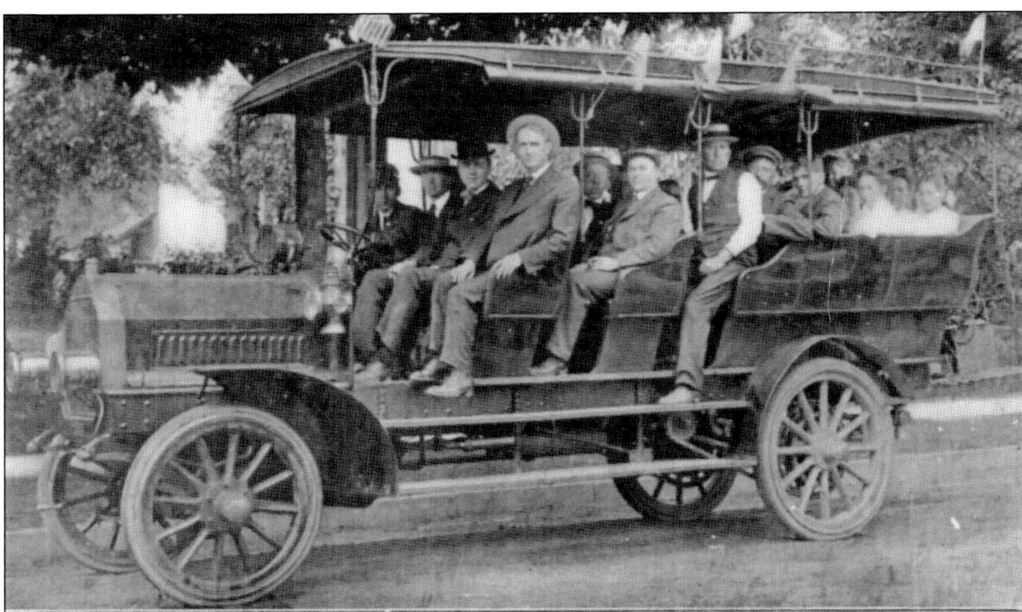

John Ostrander and Edward Call bought a 1907 White's Automobile Stage, a horseless stagecoach. It was quite unsuccessful on the rutted and muddy roads.

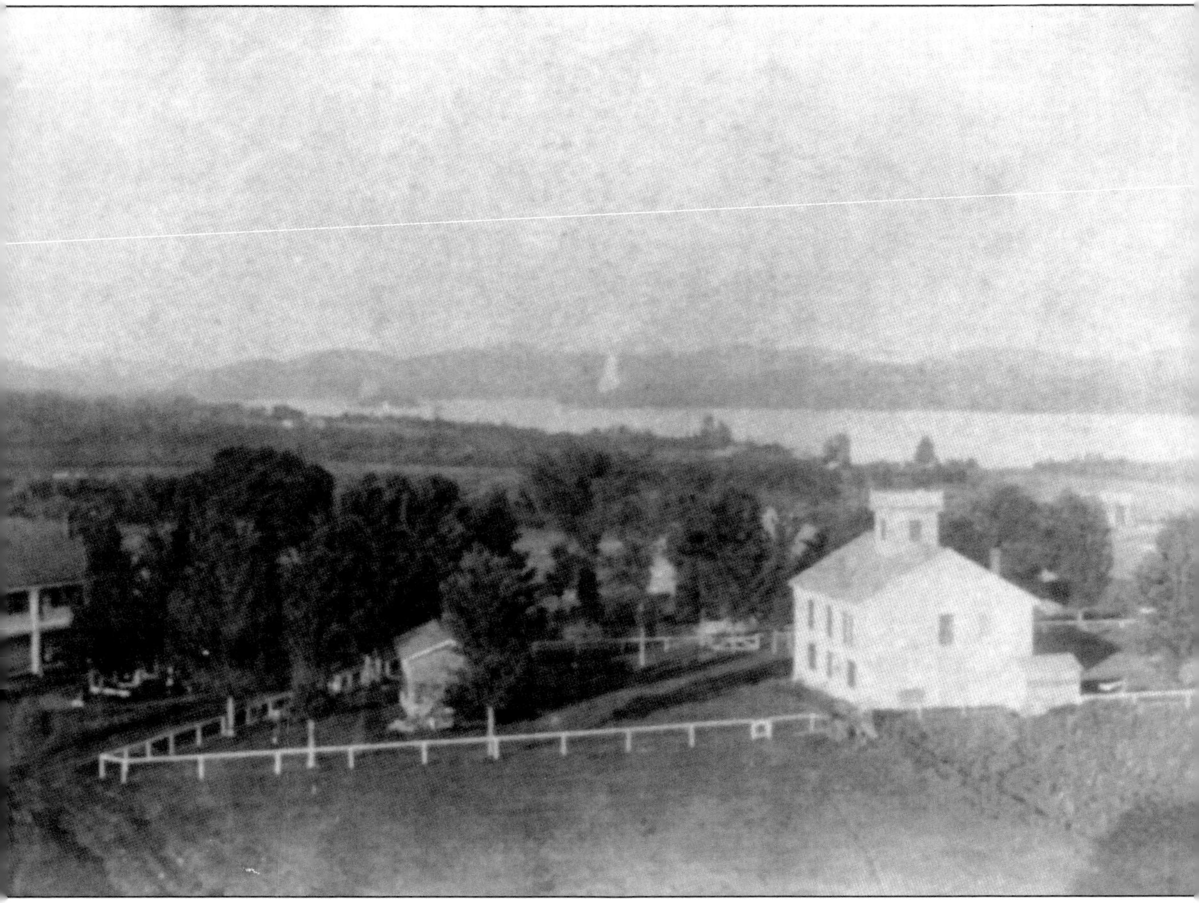

This is the back view of the county clerk's office and courthouse in Lake Pleasant. To the left is the Lake Pleasant Inn, owned by Joseph D. Morley in 1900.

Two

Hotels and Boardinghouses

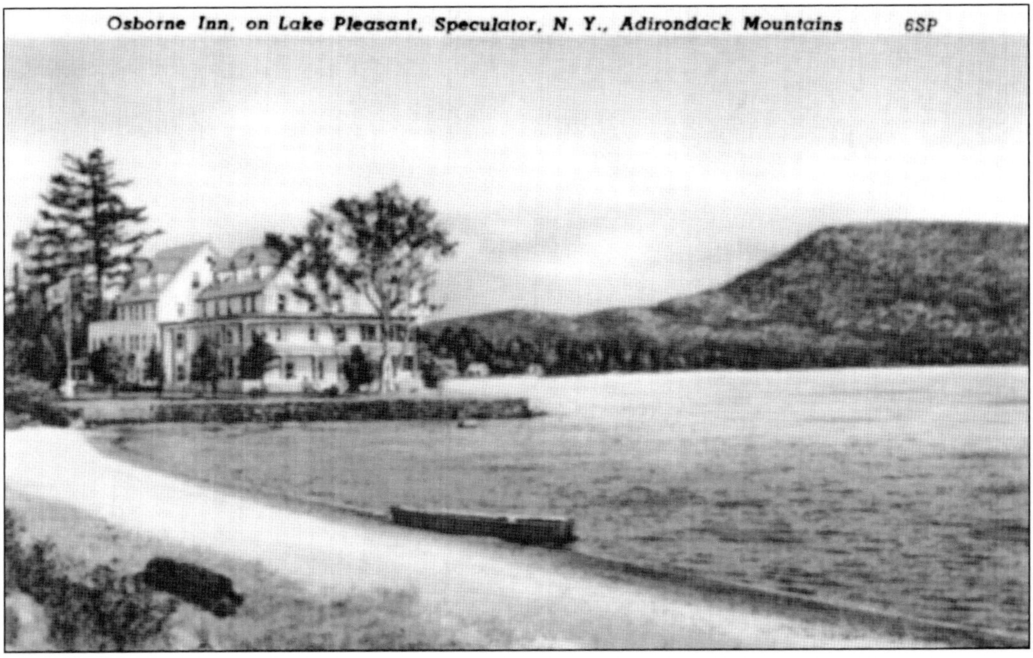

Will and Nora Osborne built this statuesque hotel on the edge of the outlet of Lake Pleasant. Always popular, it gained its greatest recognition in the 1920s and 1930s when the Osborne family was host to the prizefighters and the wealthy guests who came to watch them train.

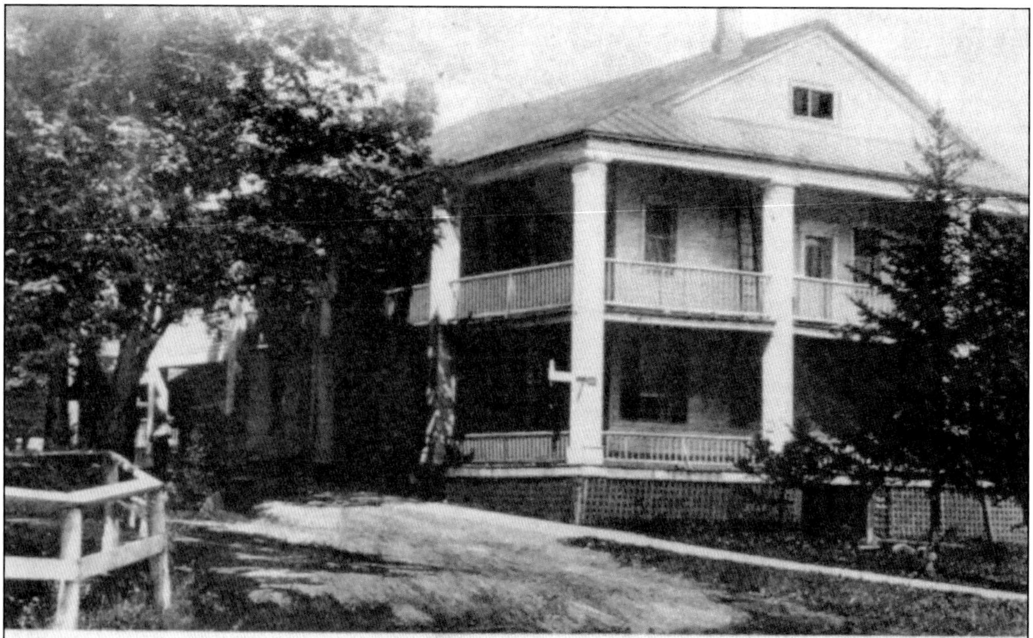

Lake Pleasant Inn, Built in 1840, Lake Pleasant, N. Y.

The Lake Pleasant Inn was built about 1840 by Hezekiah Sage across the road from the land that had been purchased to construct the county courthouse complex. In 1844, Sage was granted a post office under the name of Sageville. Proprietors have included John C. Holmes, Stephen Andrews, and J. D. Morley.

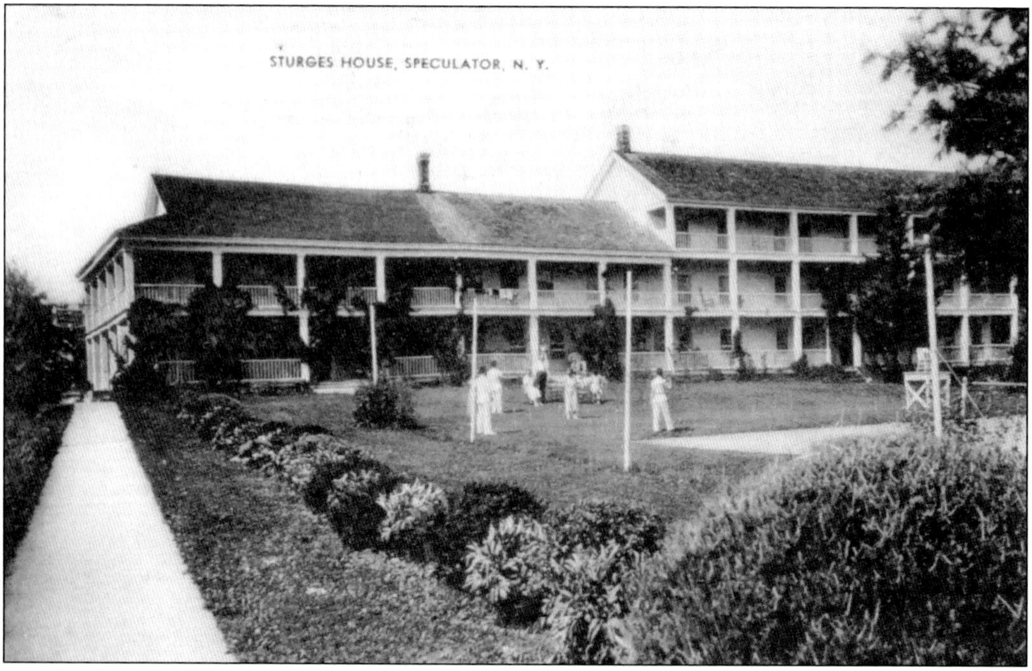

Dave Sturges started building this hotel in 1858. At first it was a large two-story hotel, but it soon acquired an even larger three-story addition. Dave married Irene Holmes, daughter of John C. Holmes, proprietor of the Lake Pleasant Inn. The Sturges House burned in 1942.

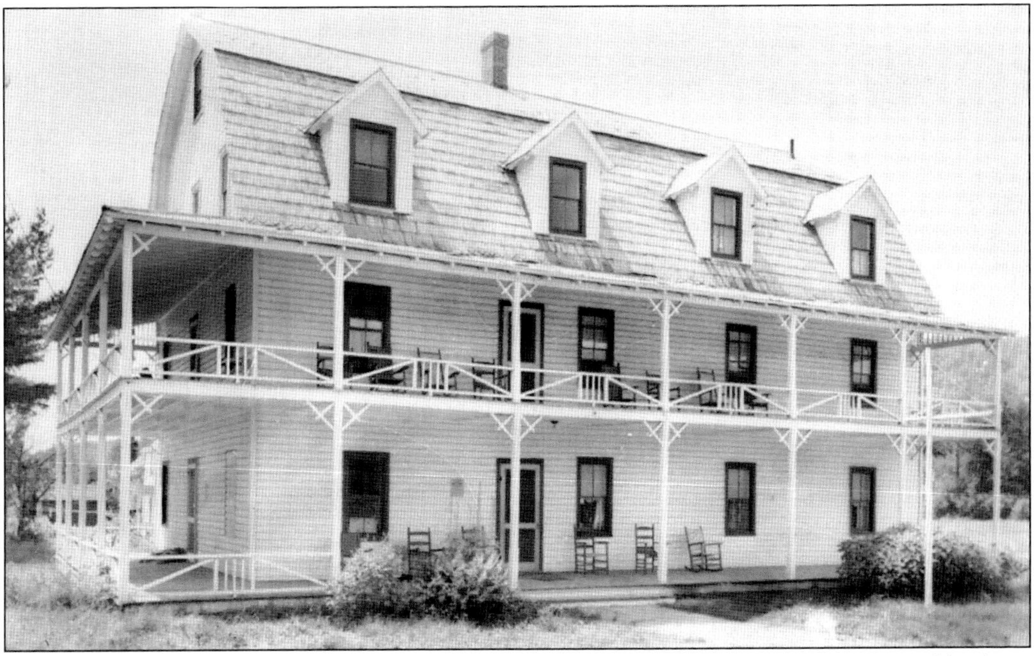

Around 1900, Dave Sturges saw a need to accommodate even more summer guests and built an annex across the road from the Sturges House. Whole families came to stay all summer to escape the city heat and pollution. Dave was an amiable host who arranged games and excursions and hired musicians for dance parties.

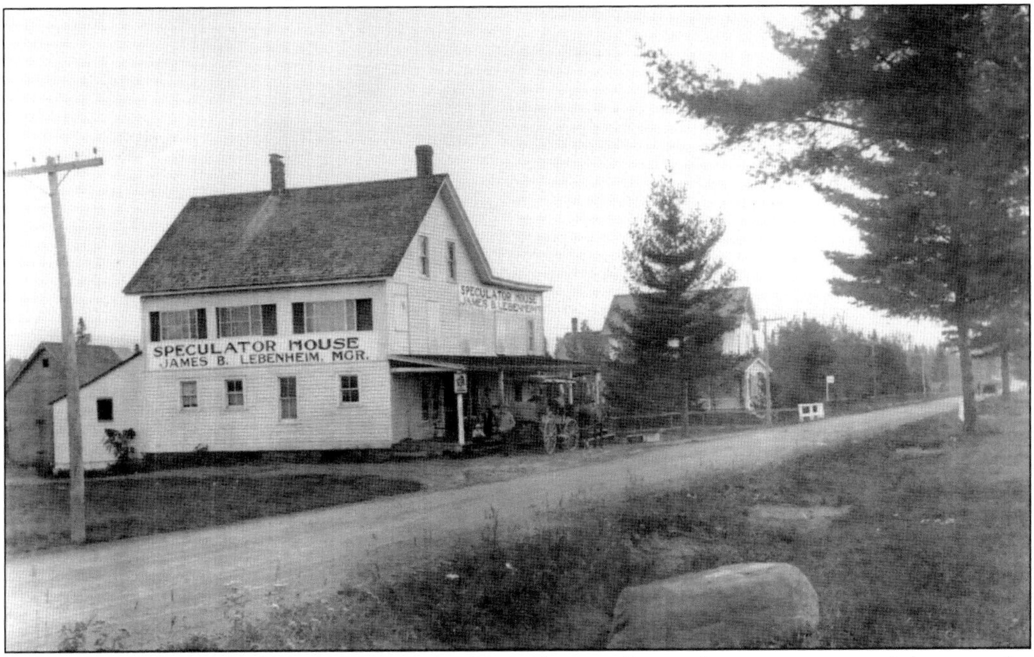

The date that the Speculator House was built is unknown, but perhaps it was around the time the name Newton's Corners was changed to Speculator in 1896. William Cochrane was proprietor in 1905, James Leibenheim in 1915, Kate Jettie and Patrick Wallace in the 1925 era, Sam Lawrence for an unspecified amount of time, and lastly Halsey and Agnes Page with Mildred Aird.

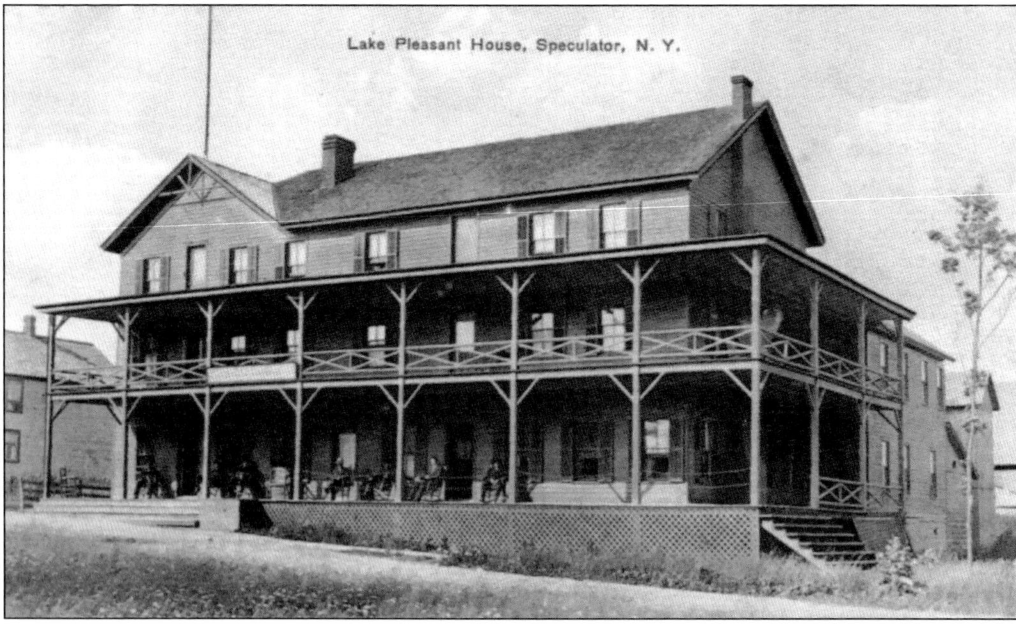

The Lake Pleasant House was built in 1888 by Edgar and Anna Dunning in Newton's Corners with a beautiful view of Lake Pleasant. Lee Fountain ran it as a store and hotel and also had a workshop out back where he made his famous rustic furniture. Later the hotel became best known as the Brook's Hotel when Nora Brooks ran it. French Louie, a legendary Adirondack hermit, was a frequent visitor and spent his last night here.

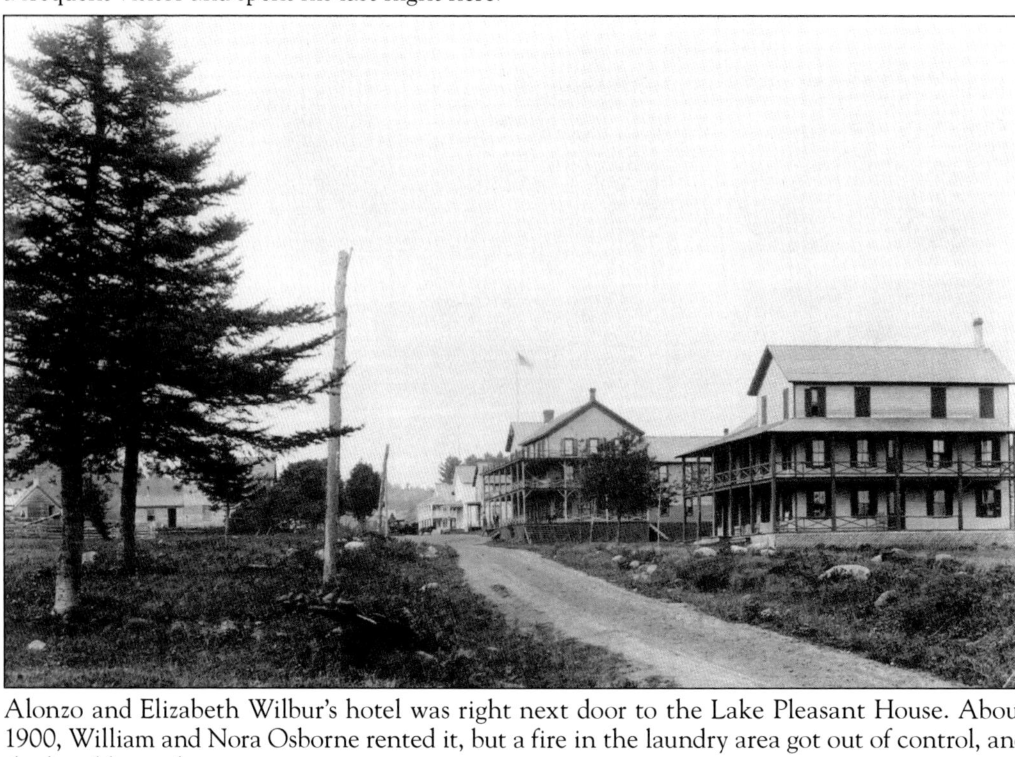

Alonzo and Elizabeth Wilbur's hotel was right next door to the Lake Pleasant House. About 1900, William and Nora Osborne rented it, but a fire in the laundry area got out of control, and the hotel burned.

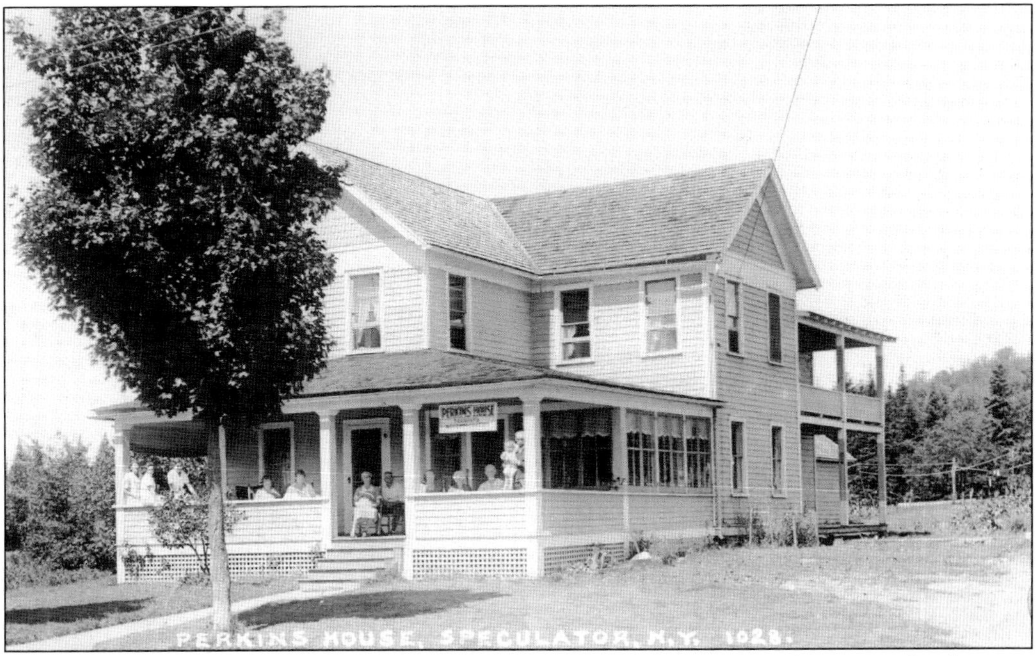

George and May Perkins built this boardinghouse before 1900. George Perkins was a lumberman and his wife ran the boardinghouse. Later their son, Ashley, and his wife, Henrietta, continued running it for many years.

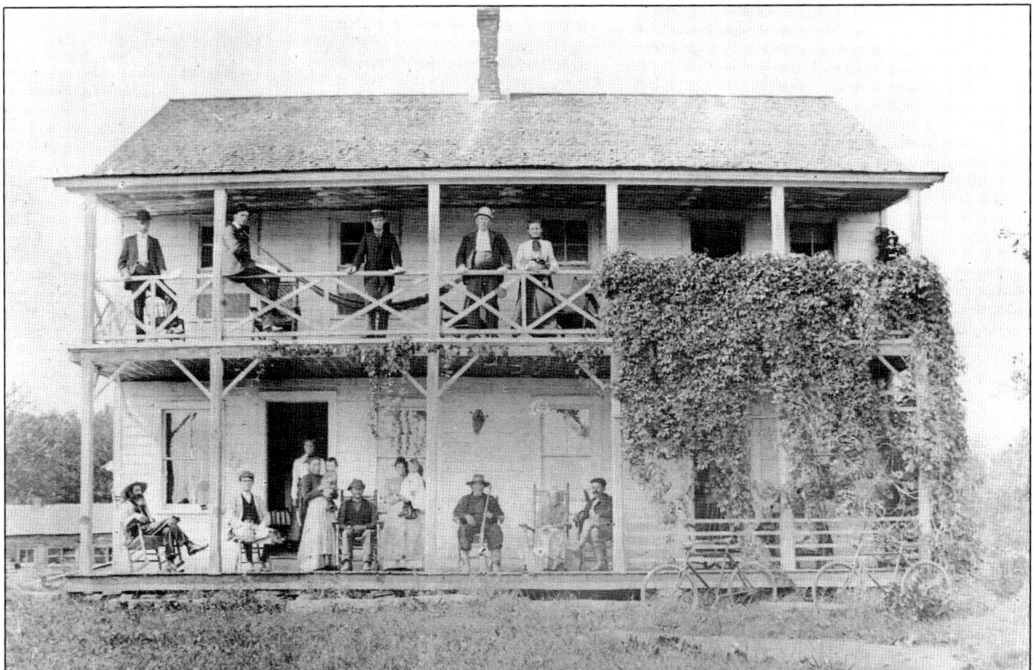

The Letson House was a mid-1880s boardinghouse run by two generations of Letsons. First it was run by Charles Sr. and his wife, Margaret, and then by Charles Jr. and his wife, Dora. It stood on the corner of Route 8 and Page Street.

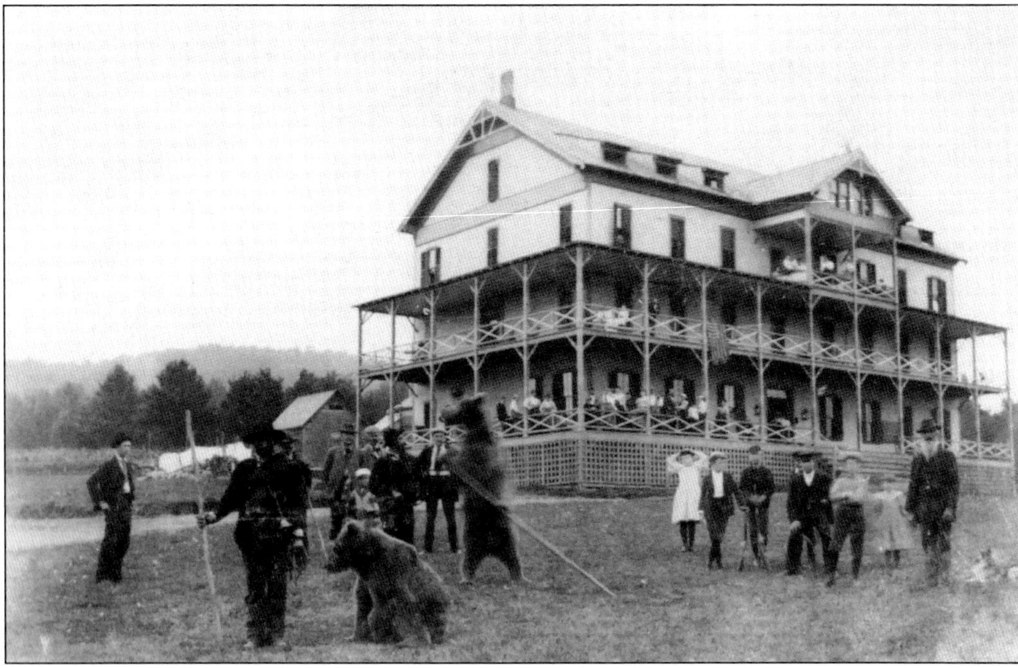

Silas Call's hotel was built in 1880 on the hilltop behind the county courthouse. Hotel rates were $10 to $15 a week, and guides were available for $3 a day. It boasted broad piazzas and magnificent views. The hotel had a capacity of 75. Unfortunately it burned in 1904.

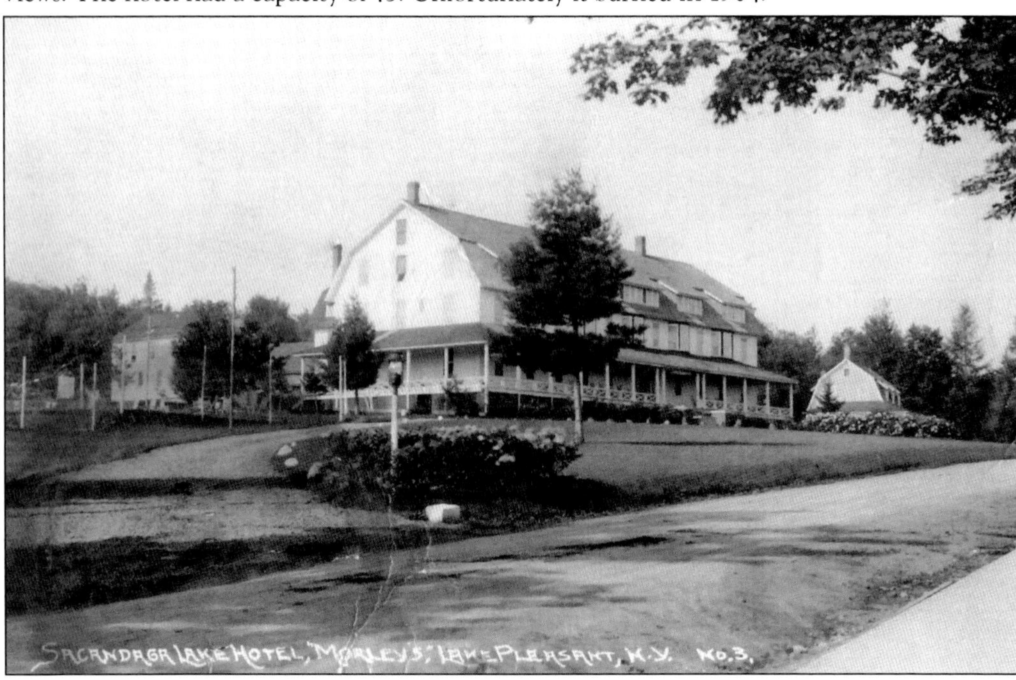

J. D. Morley, then owner of the Lake Pleasant Inn across the road, purchased the site of the former Call's Hotel. By 1907, he reopened with the Sacandaga Lake Hotel with a capacity of 250 guests. Morley sold it in 1909, and by 1915 a syndicate bought it. As preparations were underway to open for the 1916 season, a fire started in the kitchen, and the hotel was completely destroyed.

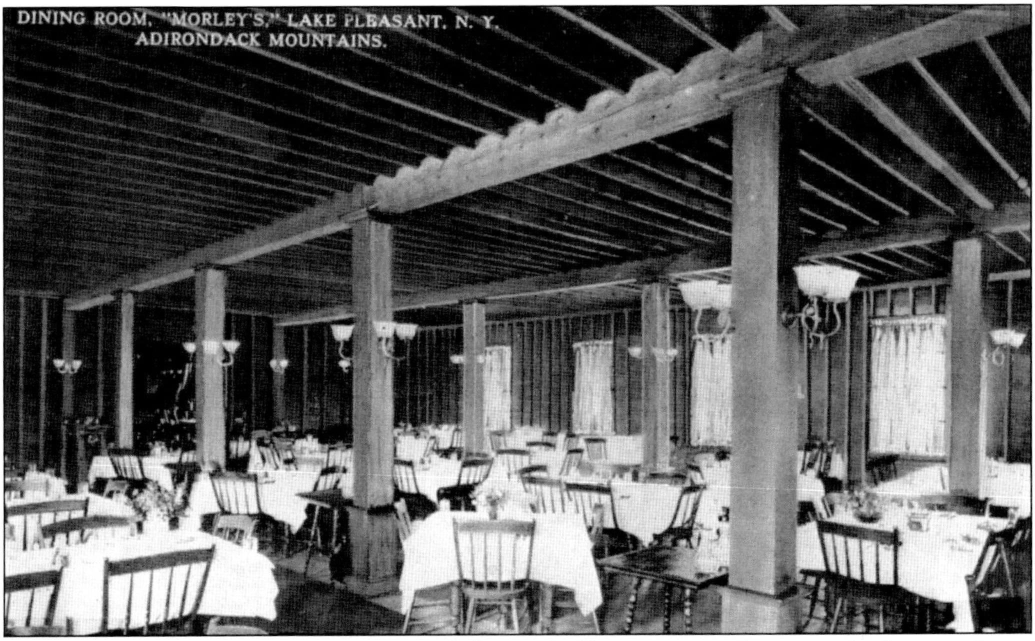

At J. D. Morley's Sacandaga Lake Hotel dining hall, venison and trout were frequently on the menu.

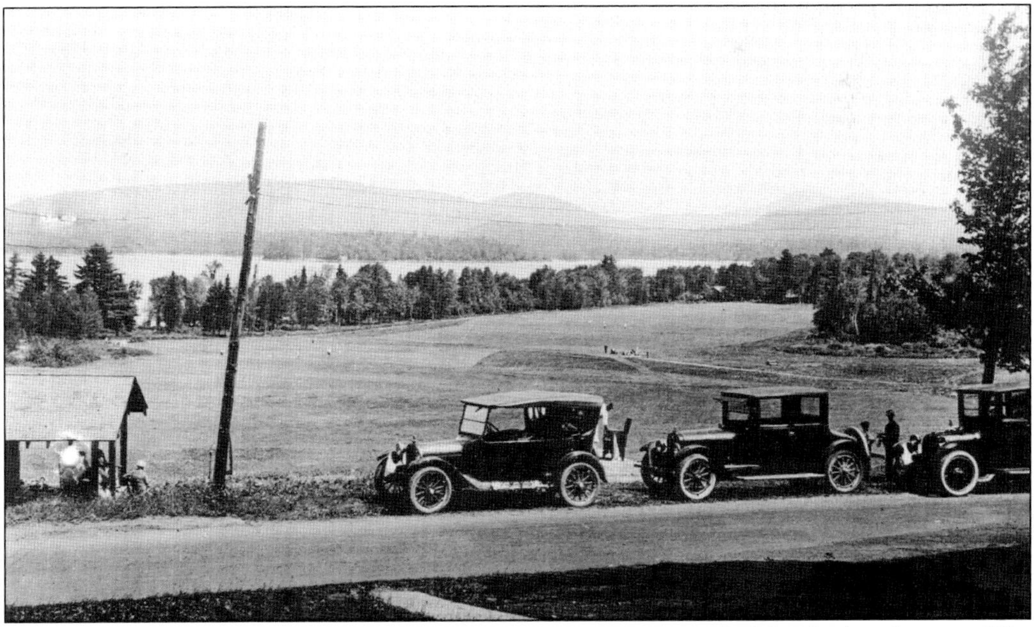

Golf, bowling, tennis, and a variety of entertainments were provided for the hotel guests. The golf course is still in use today as the Lake Pleasant Golf Club.

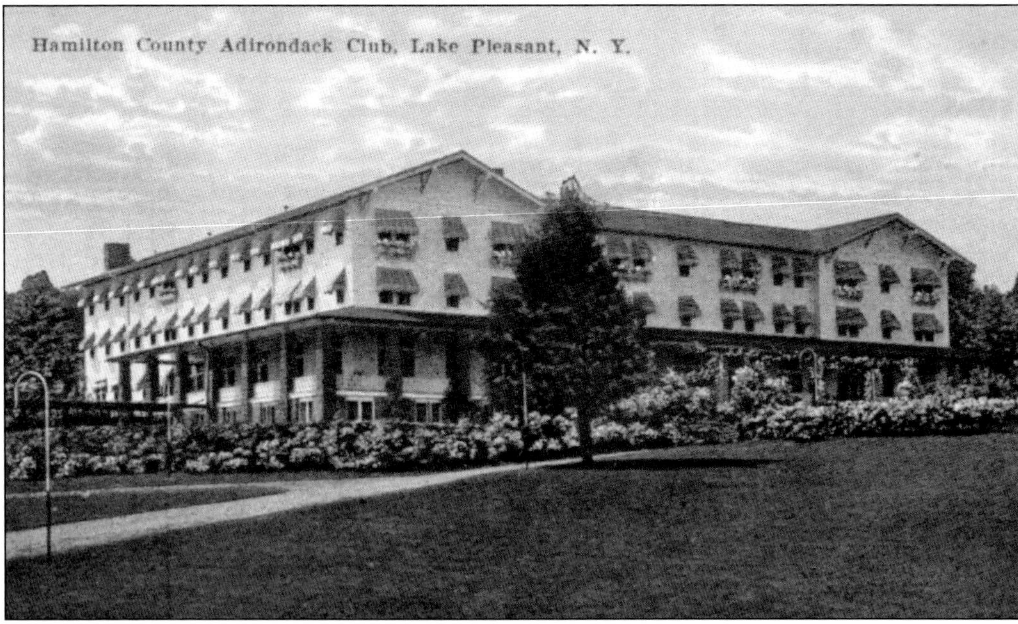

The Hamilton Inn was soon constructed on the same site as J. D. Morley's Sacandaga Lake Hotel and ready for occupancy in the summer of 1917. In the 1930s, a group, including Malcolm Atterbury, builder of the Tamarack Playhouse and later of Hollywood fame, purchased the hotel and it was again a very popular place to vacation.

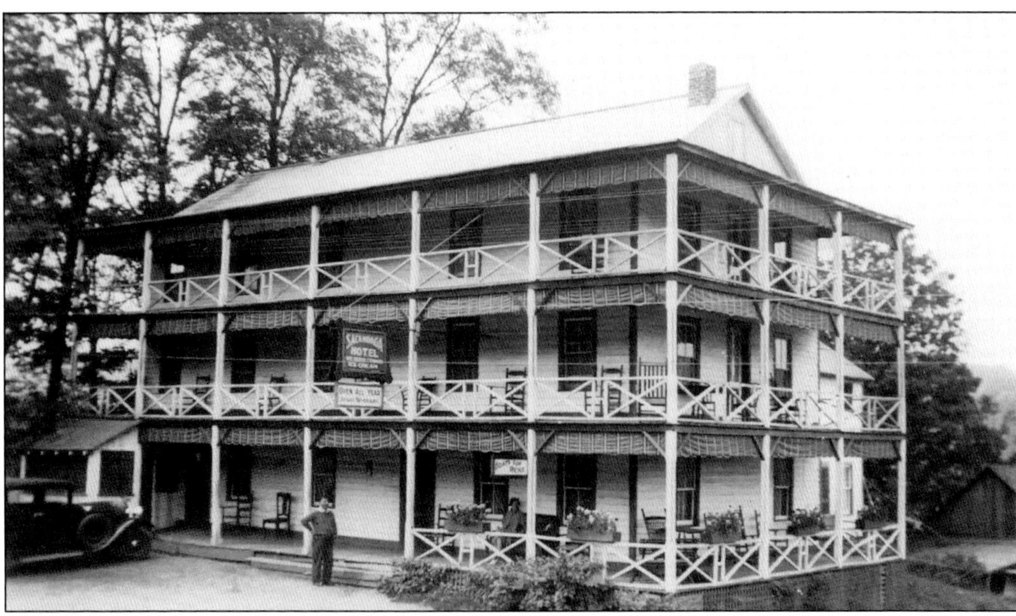

The Sacandaga Hotel was a large, three-story building operated for many years by the George White family on Route 8, just west of the Lake Pleasant village proper. It was later converted to a two-story hotel and at some point nicknamed the "mousetrap."

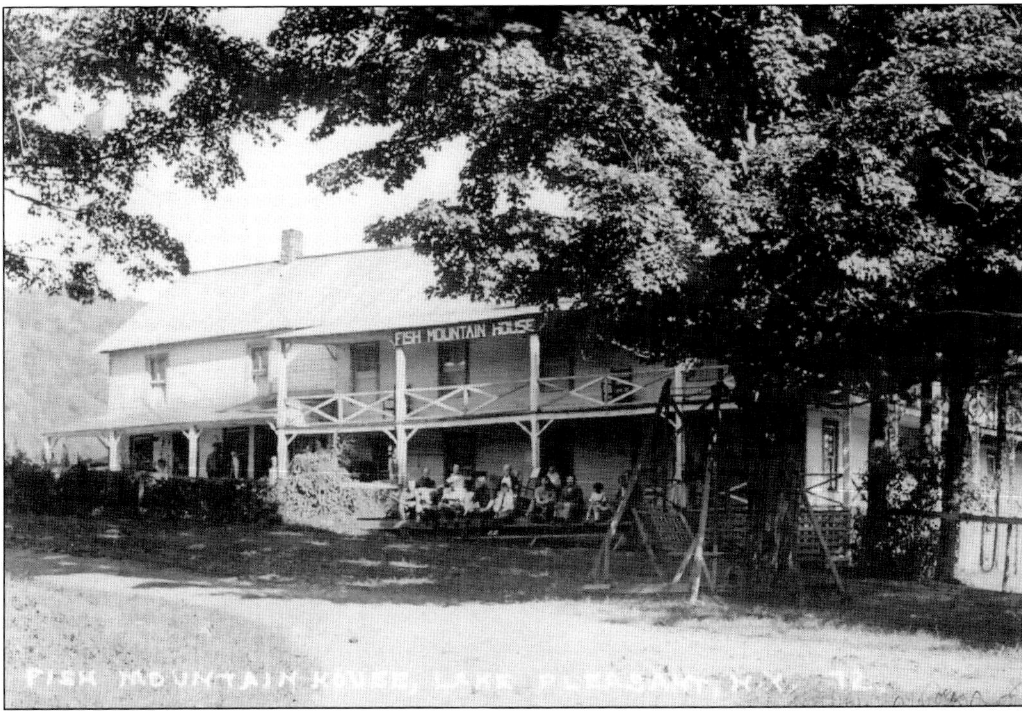

Another large hotel, Fish Mountain House, was down Fish Mountain Road toward the shore of Sacandaga Lake. It was run by David Aird, son of James Aird.

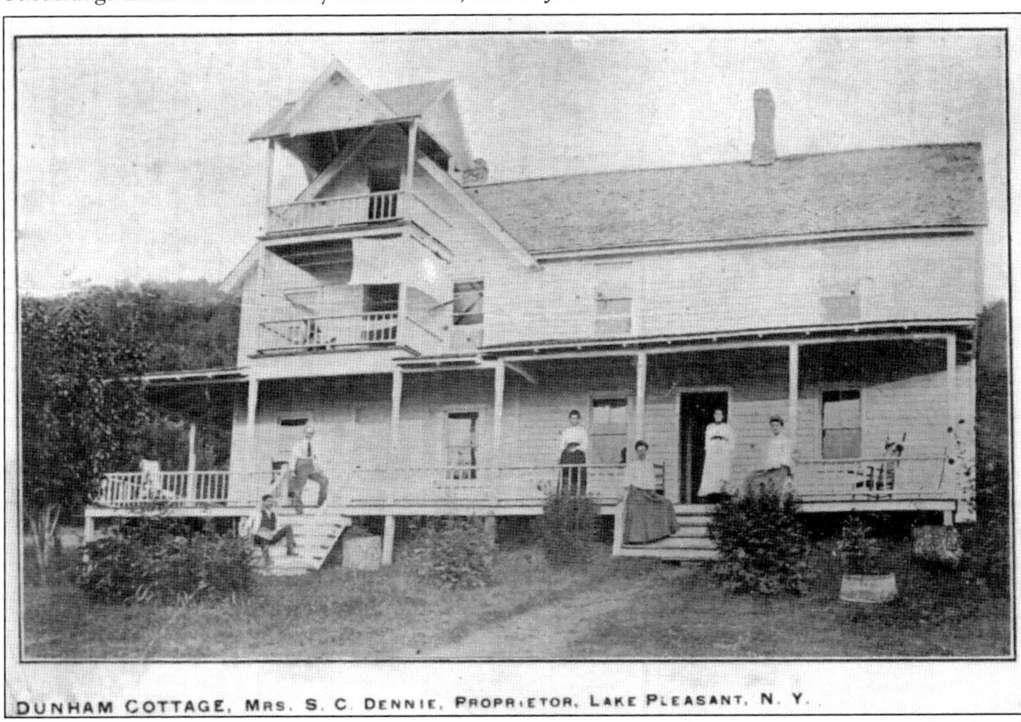

The Dunham Cottage was a boardinghouse on the south side of Lake Pleasant. Susan C. Morrill Dennie was the proprietor in the late 1800s and early 1900s.

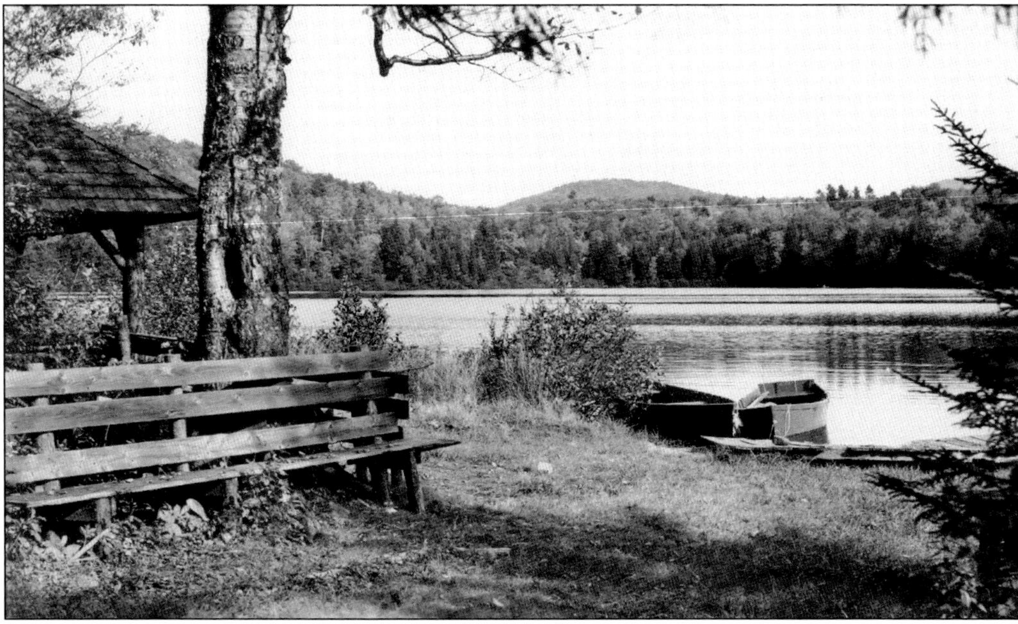

The inviting lake that was part of the Airdwood Hotel was one time called Lily Lake. The original Airdwood Hotel was called the Lily Lake House.

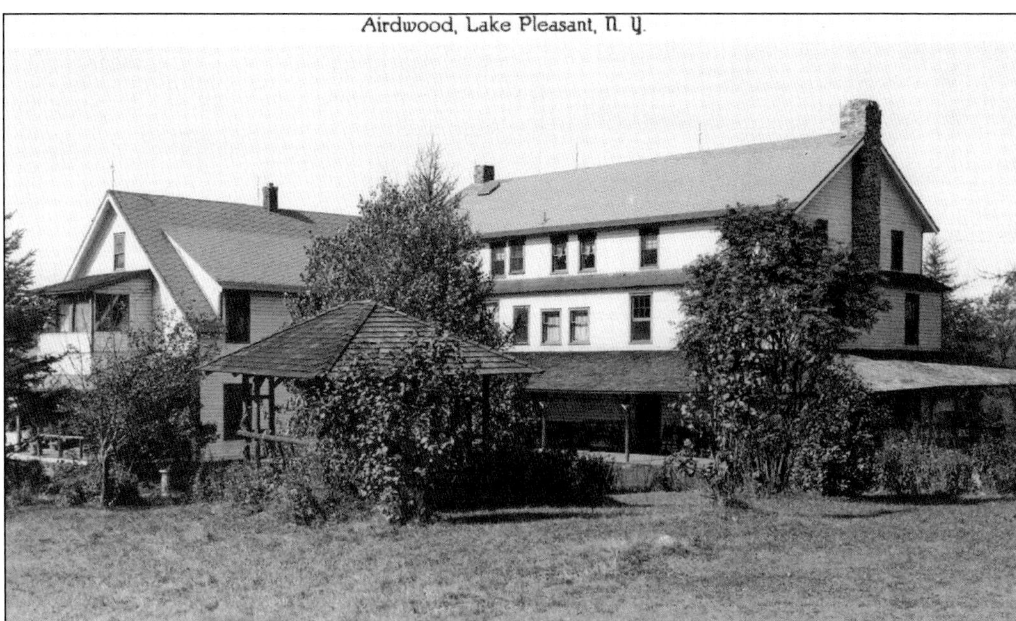

When the first Airdwood burned, David Aird, the son of James, replaced it with a large, three-story hotel. Clarence and Dorthea Pelcher ran it for many years. Clarence was the grandson of David Aird.

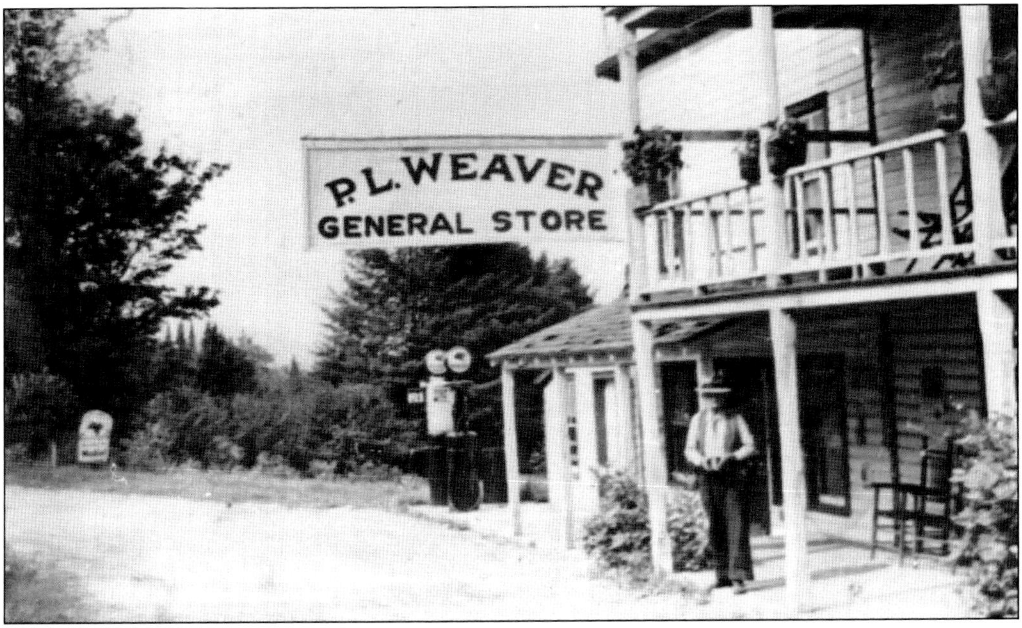

Peter L. Weaver came to Airdville in the 1880s. He built a large, three-story house that he named Mountain View House. At different times, there was a store, barroom, and antique store on the bottom floor. The Mountain View House was about halfway between Lake Pleasant and Piseco. Peter also owned camps across the road and ran a sugarhouse. The house and property are still in the Weaver family.

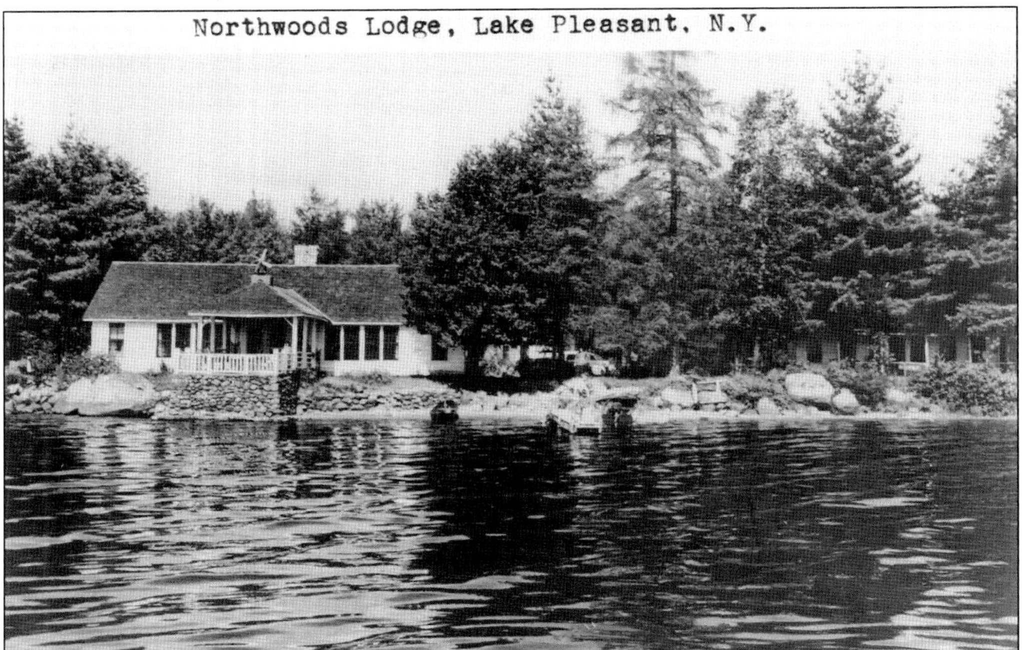

L. Milton Buyce married Ethel McVeigh, whose family had a boardinghouse near the western shore of Lake Pleasant. They added buildings and rented spaces for camping trailers to meet vacationer's needs. Today it is called Northwood's Lodge.

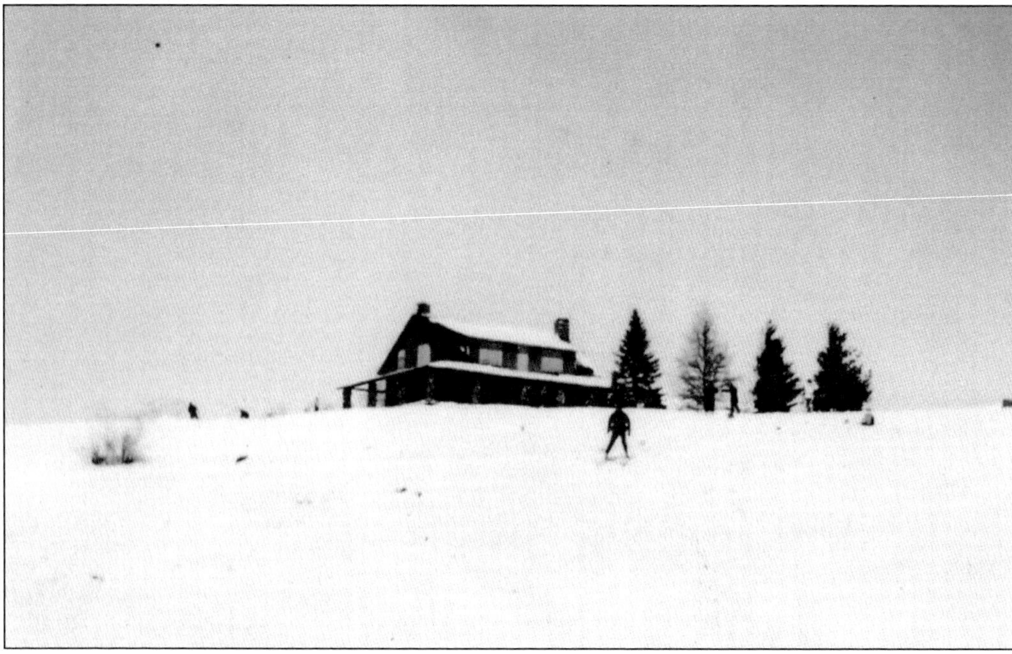

In 1912, Allison Van Hoose, a gifted musician, bought 6 acres of land from Nathan Page on top of Page Hill. Van Hoose built a music conservatory for girls that continued until 1917 when it was sold as a summer home. In 1937, Hamilton and Francis Dunham Chequer purchased the home and opened it as Melody Lodge for dining and lodging. It still stands today.

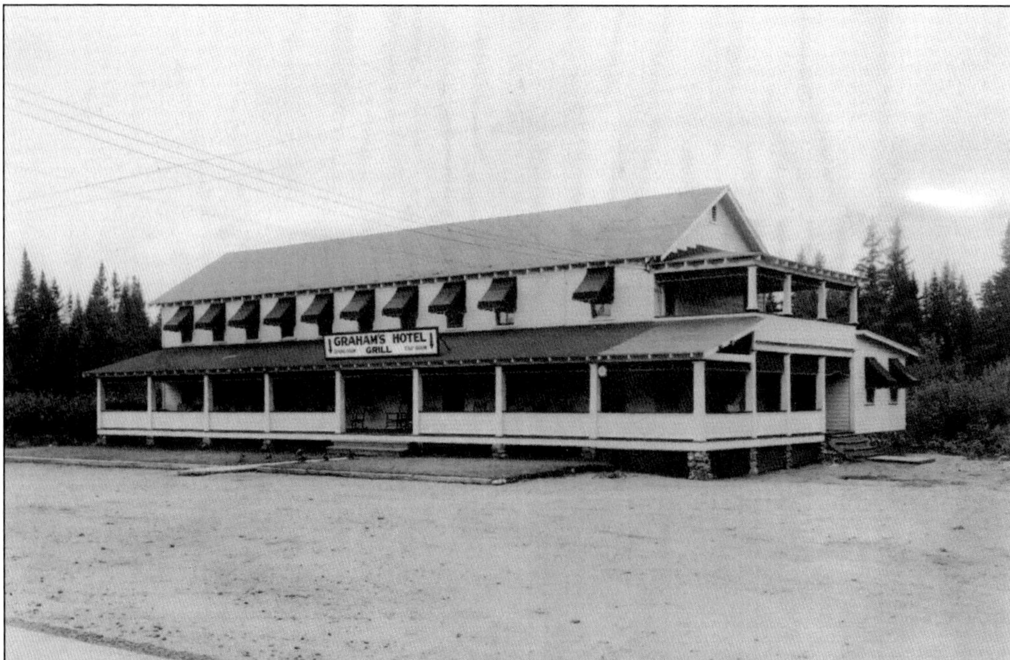

Graham's Hotel was first known as Dewitt Graham's Dancehall. The building was purchased from Earnest Brooks in 1925 and later moved from the Brook's property to its present site on Route 8/30. Dewitt also had a barbershop on the second floor.

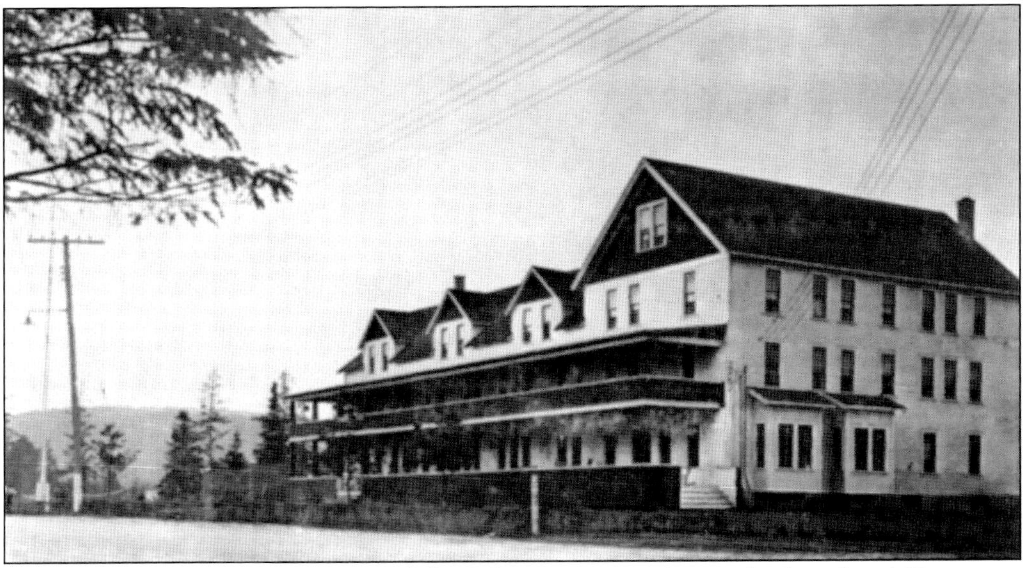

The Osborne family, who also operated the Osborne's Inn nearby, ran this large hotel. For a time, it was rented to the Lawlors and was usually called Lawlor's Hotel. A raging fire in the fireplace led to its demise in 1935.

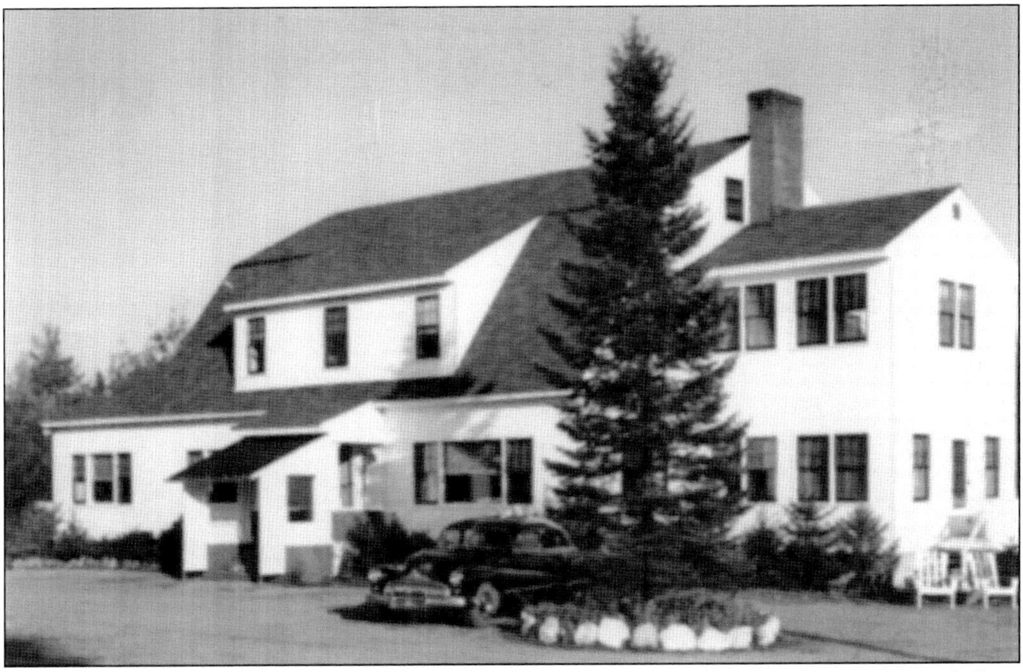

The Bucks restaurant was a fine dining establishment run by Joe and Lena Buck until their retirement. The Bucks is now called The Inn at Speculator and located on Route 8.

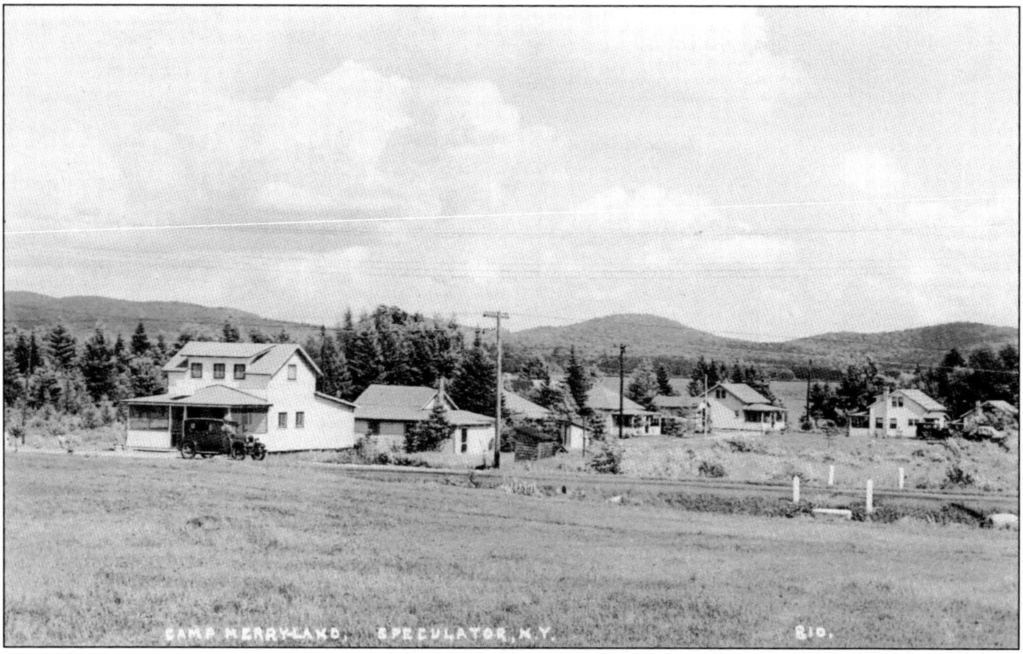

Charlie Brown bought 50 acres, including lakeshore, from his widowed aunt and started building cabins to rent. He bulldozed rocks and trucked in sand for a beach. He added a boardinghouse and a store before he was finished. This area is now called Camp Merryland and Charlie Brown Lane.

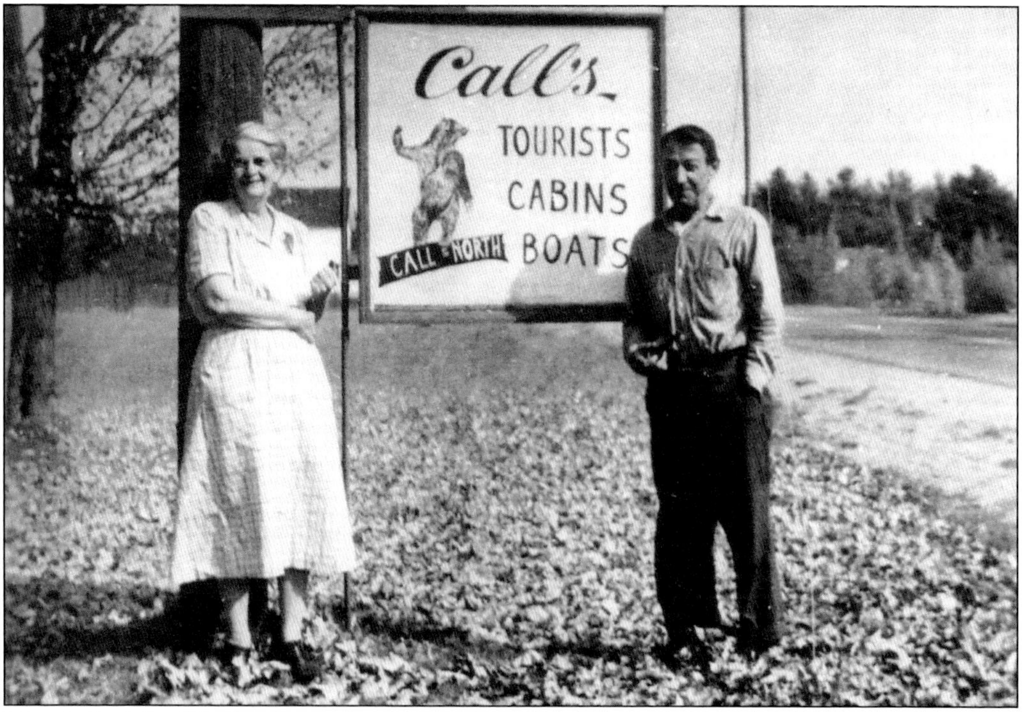

The Call of the North tourist cabins were rented by Burr and Agnes Call. Like generations of the Call family, their service to the tourists came naturally.

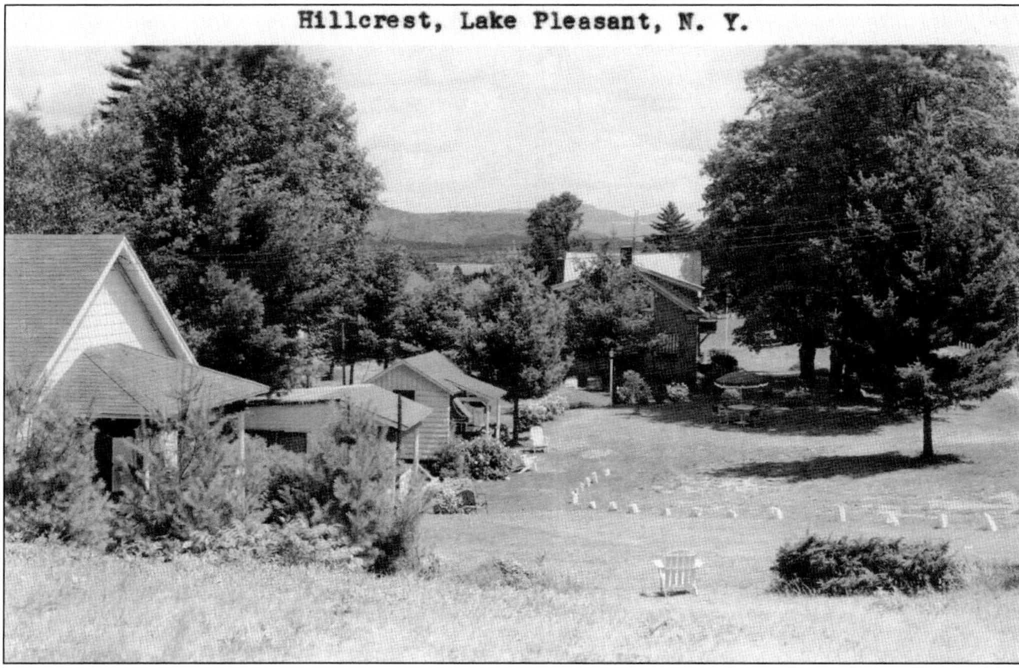

Ann Telfer's Hillcrest cabins were located west of Lake Pleasant and the county courthouse on Route 8. Ann was a great promoter of the area and also guided hunting parties with the best of them. She once owned the Mammoth Garage in Speculator.

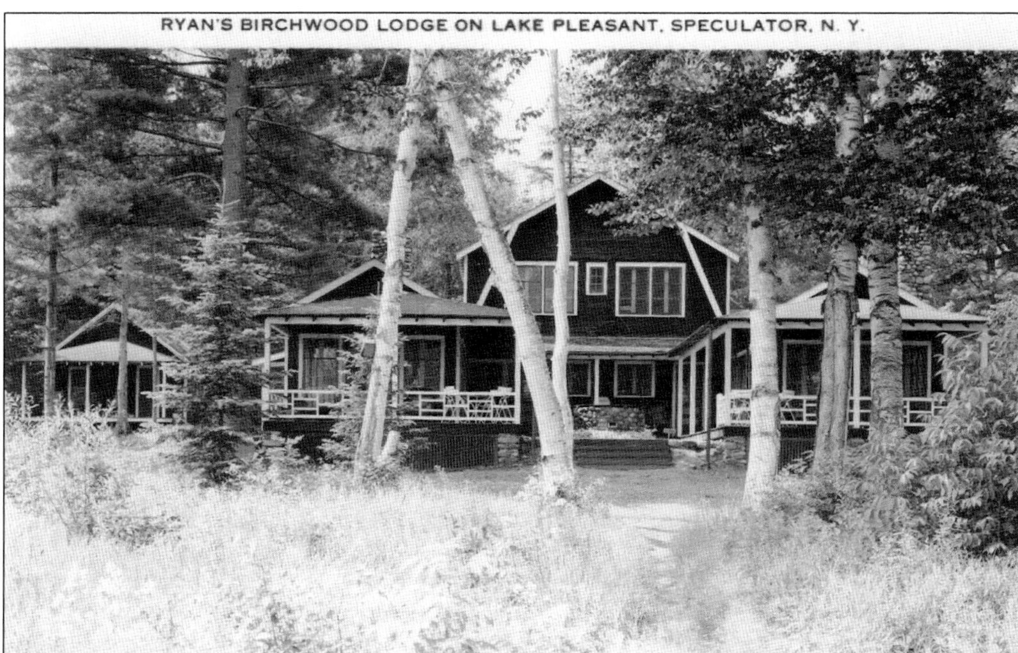

Little is known about Ryan's Birchwood Lodge other than it was a beautiful little place on the shore of Lake Pleasant where guests could find respite.

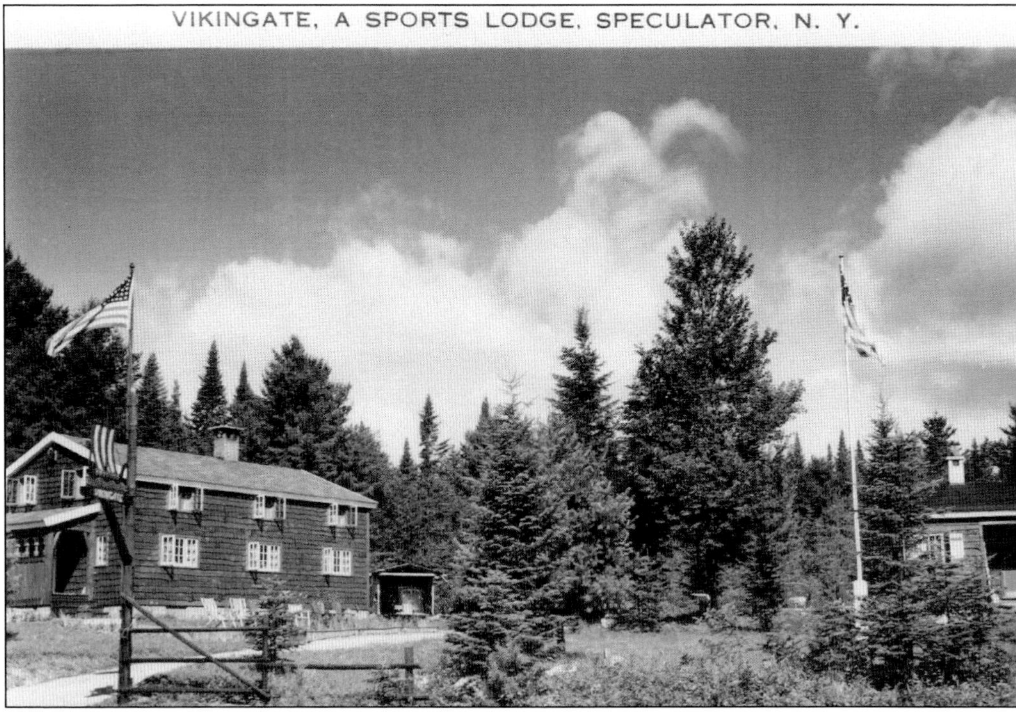

Vikingate was the home of the Winter Sports Club. It was located near the foot of Sturges Mountain where the toboggan run and ski jump were located. Some of the King brothers had a ski shop there.

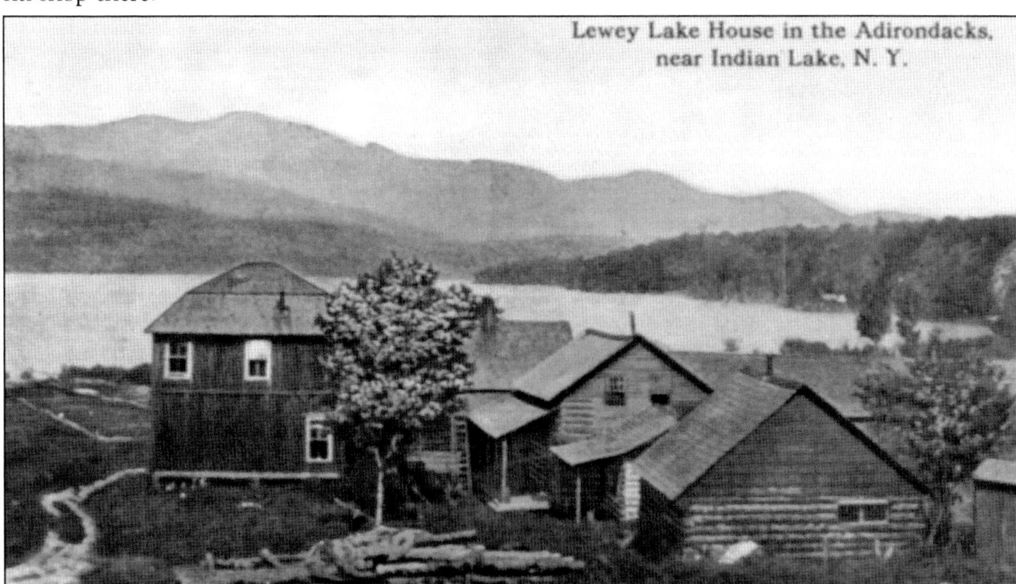

About 10 miles north of the four corners, on a peaceful, little lake, was the cabin of Alvah Dunning, the renowned hermit guide. Later occupants and additions turned it into the Lewey Lake House. Halsey Galusha and John Burgess bought it in 1913 but lost it to a fire the next year. They built a larger hotel, and eventually the ownership was transferred to Halsey's son, Lynn, and his family who named it Snowy Mountain Lodge.

Three

Schools and Churches

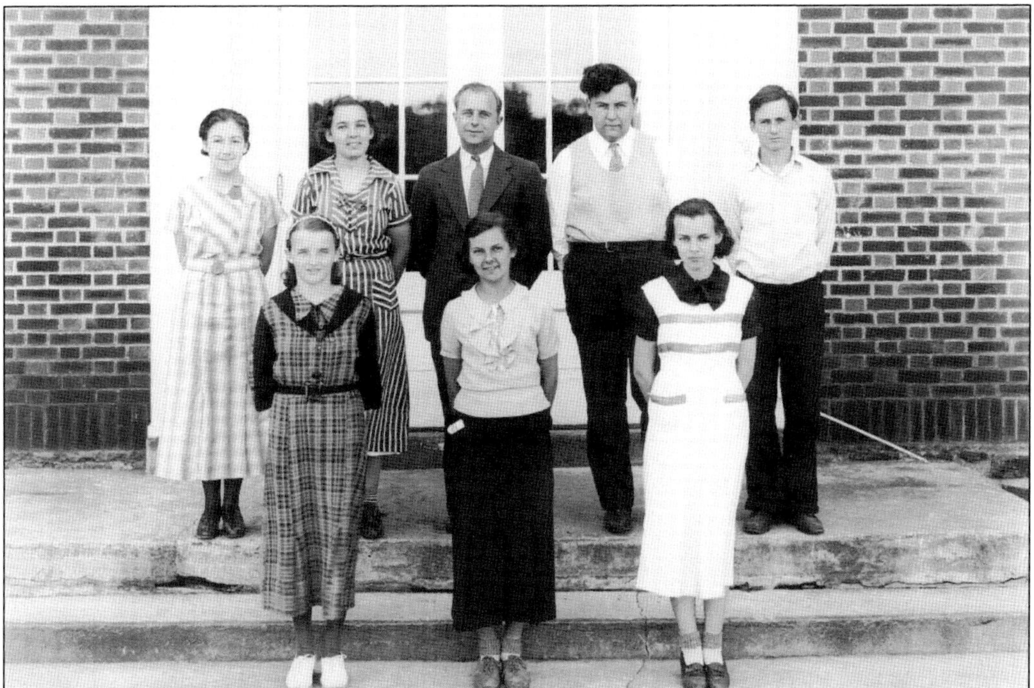

Ninth graders are in front of the Lake Pleasant Central School around the 1930s.

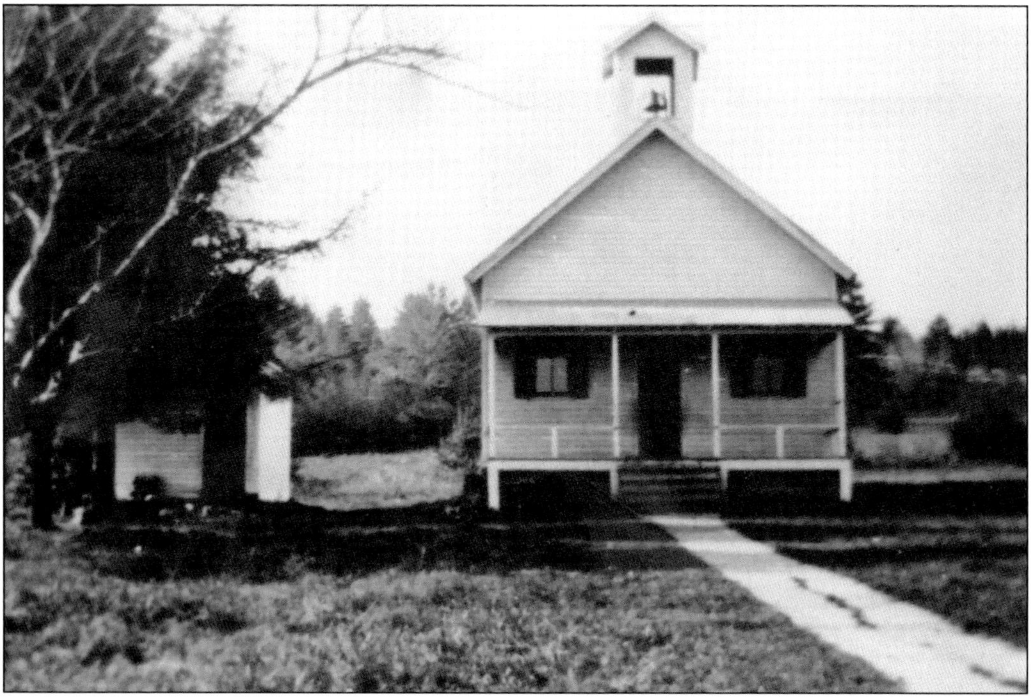

This is one of the one-room schools built in Lake Pleasant. Land was purchased in 1857 for a school in district no. 1; it was located next to the county courthouse lot.

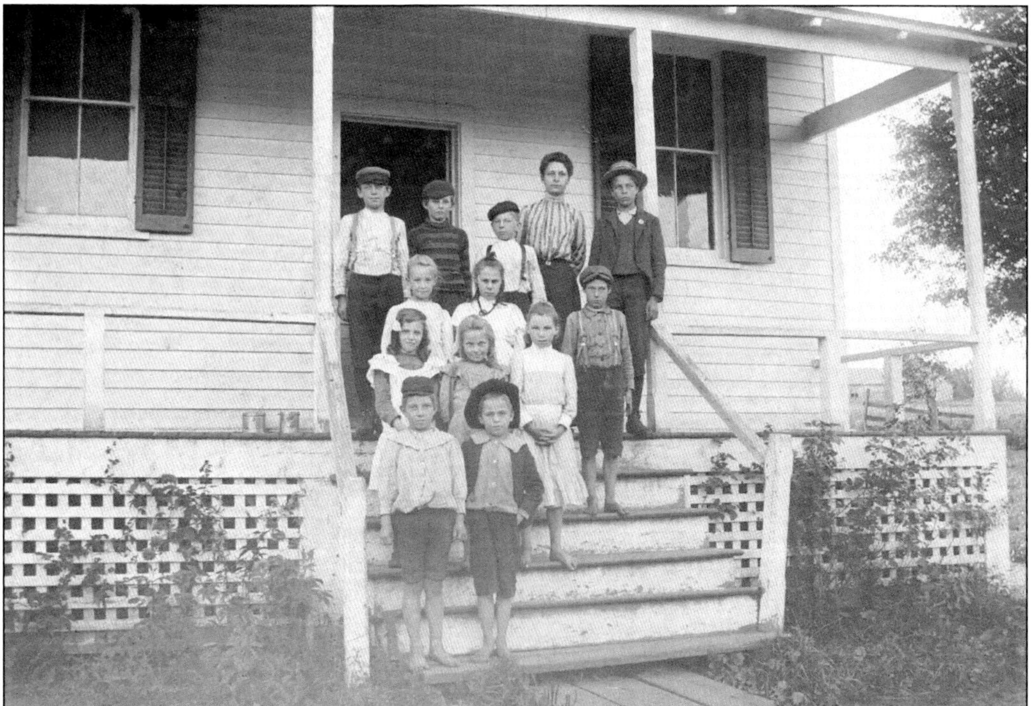

This is a photograph of students at the Lake Pleasant School about 1914. In 1945, the building was converted for the use of the Lake Pleasant Volunteer Fire Department.

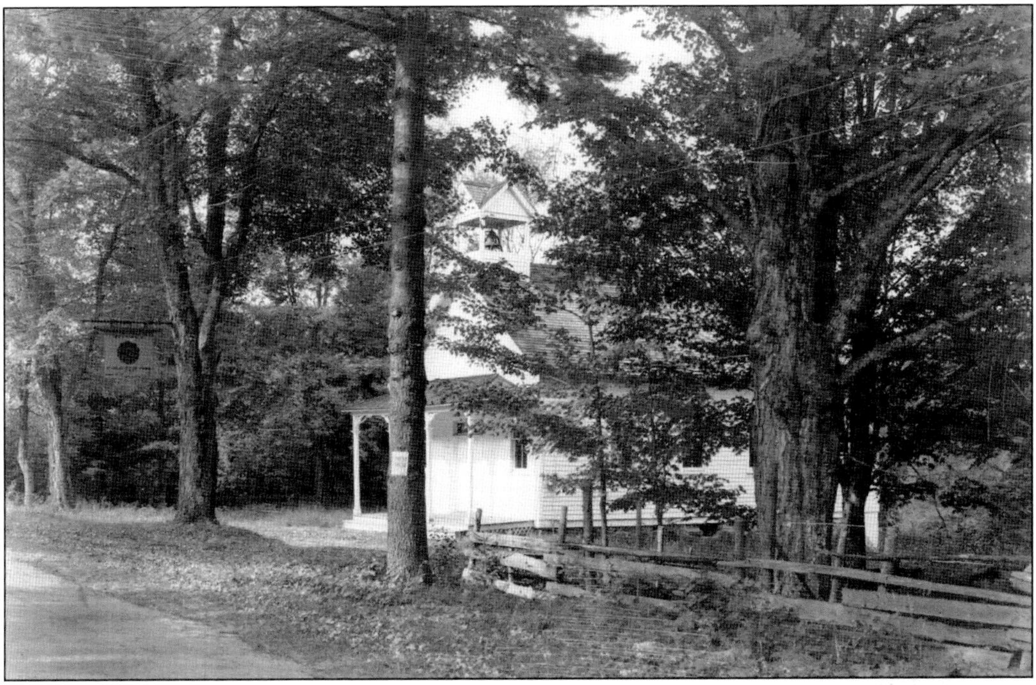

This photograph shows the one-room school by the Airdville Cemetery, located where Route 8 now runs. In 1929, a new Lake Pleasant Central School was built in Speculator that replaced the one-room schools around the area.

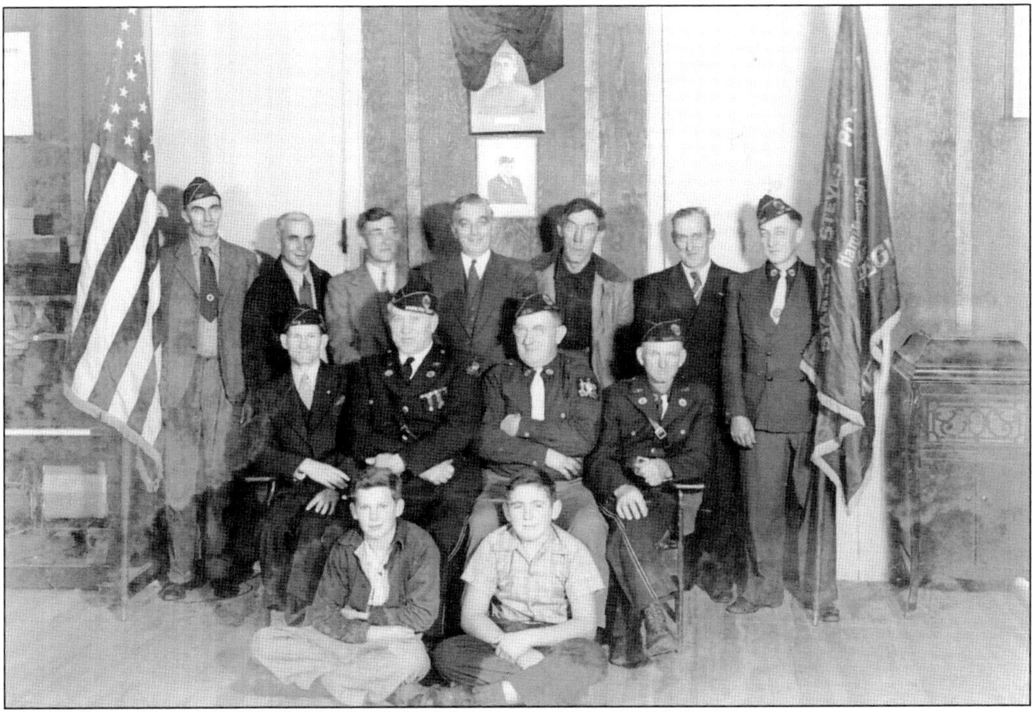

The American Legion used the Airdville School for a time and then the building was moved to make way for a better highway.

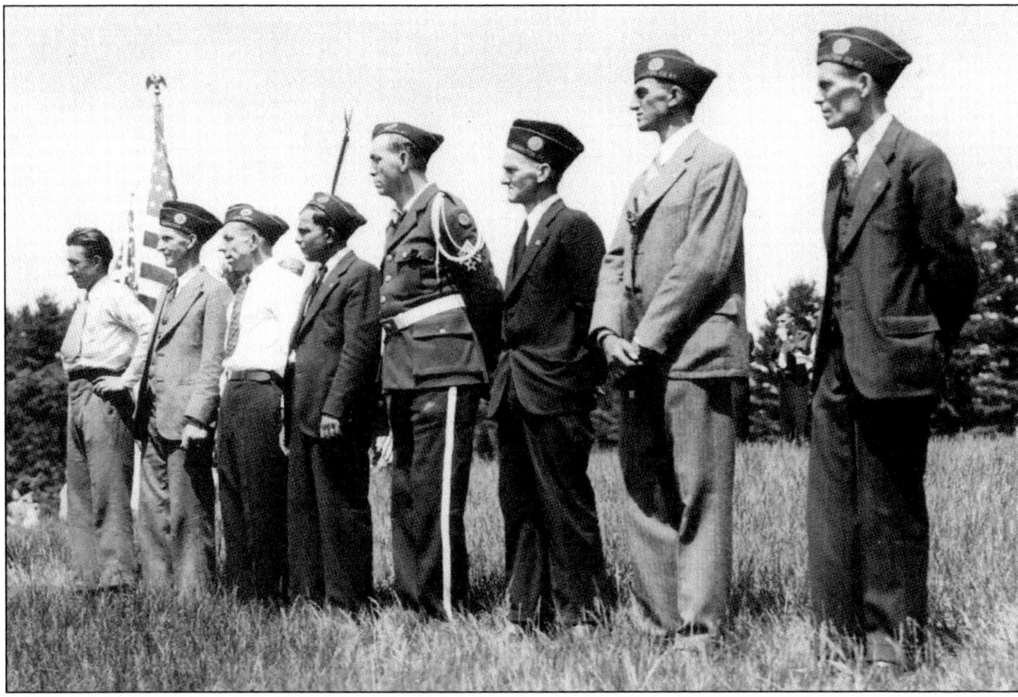

World War I veterans gather for a Memorial Day Parade.

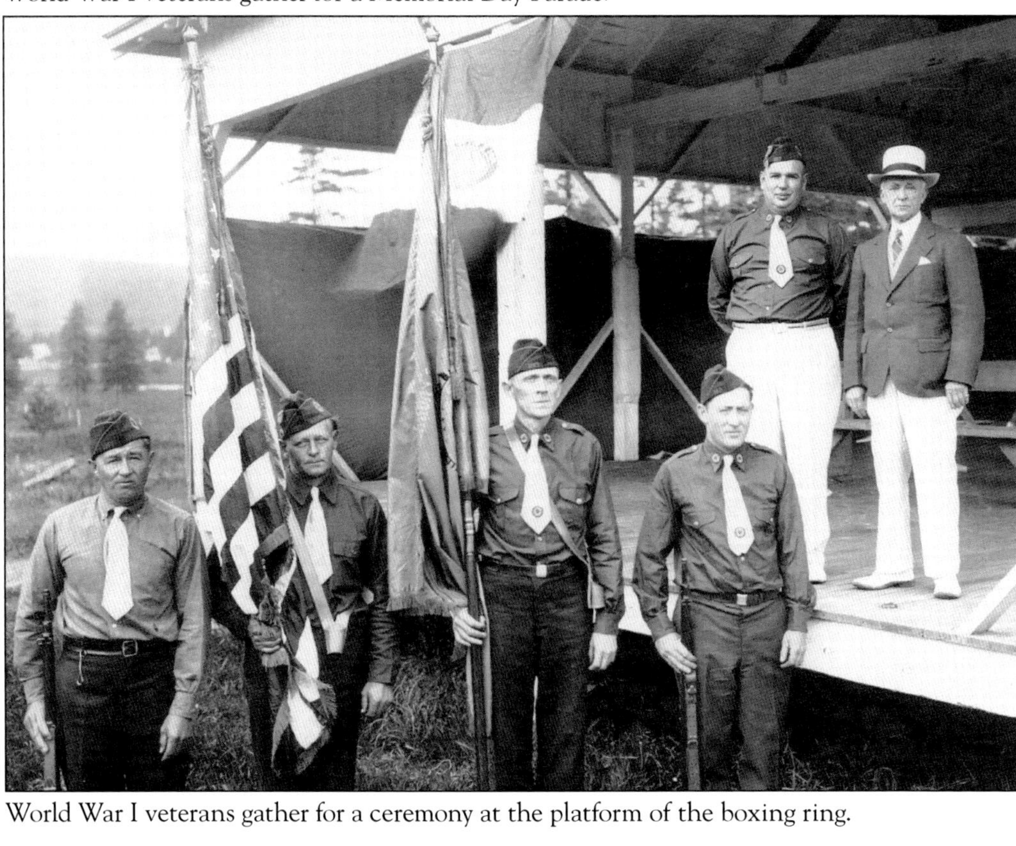

World War I veterans gather for a ceremony at the platform of the boxing ring.

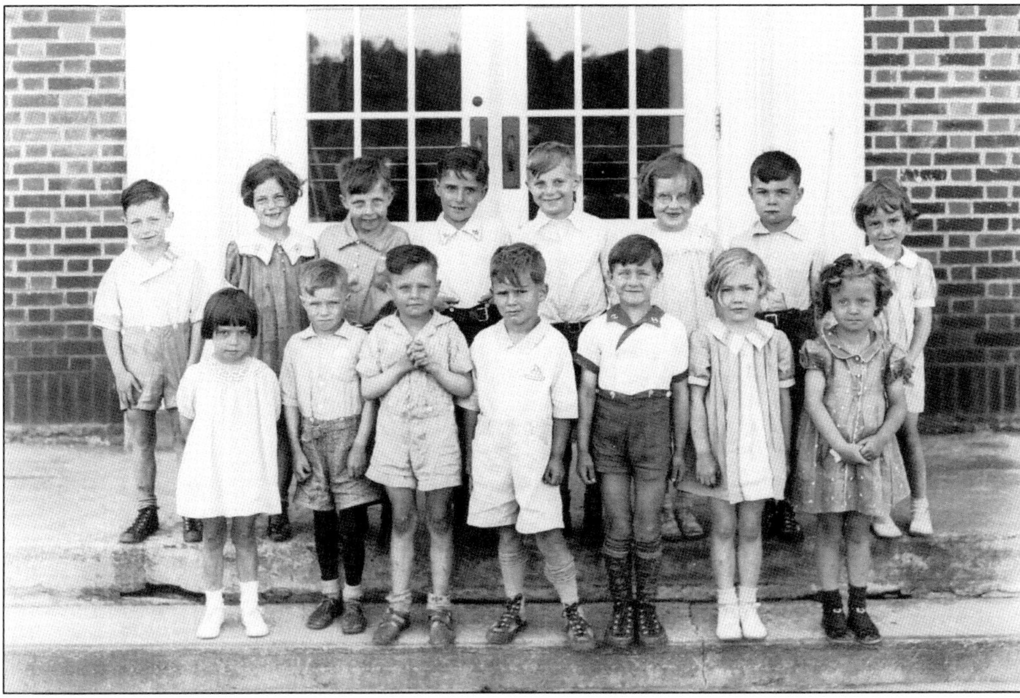

Pictured in front of the Lake Pleasant Central School are the kindergarten and first grade around the 1930s.

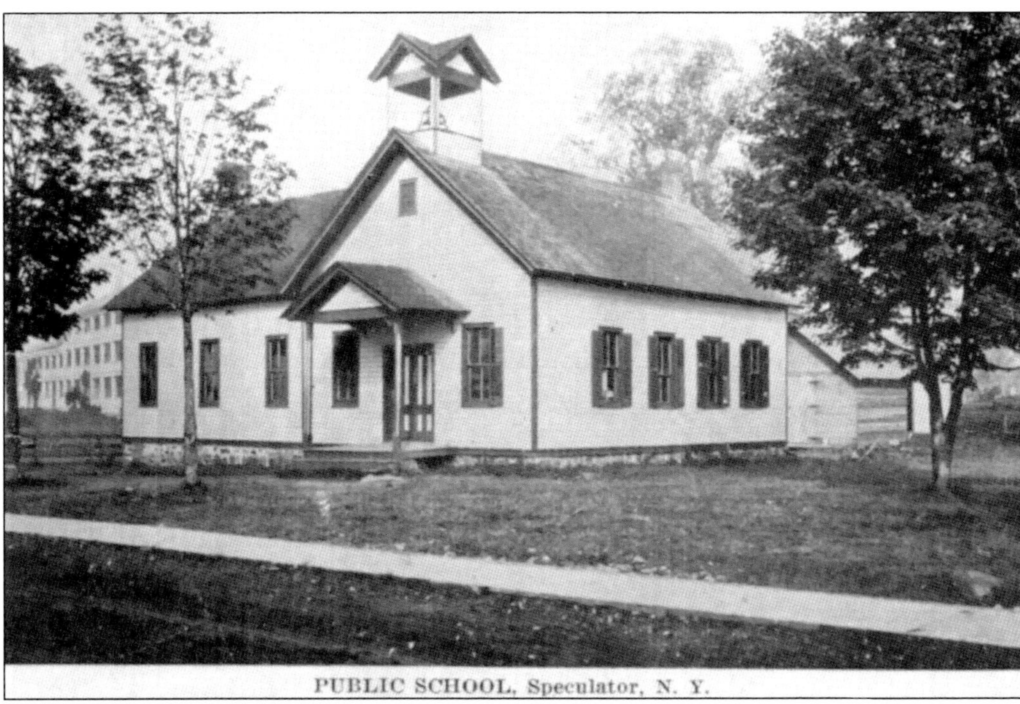

This photograph was taken in the early 1900s of the two-room Speculator school located in front of the cemetery. It was later bought by the Village of Speculator, who moved the building across the street and used it as the Village Hall and village garage where the fire truck was stored.

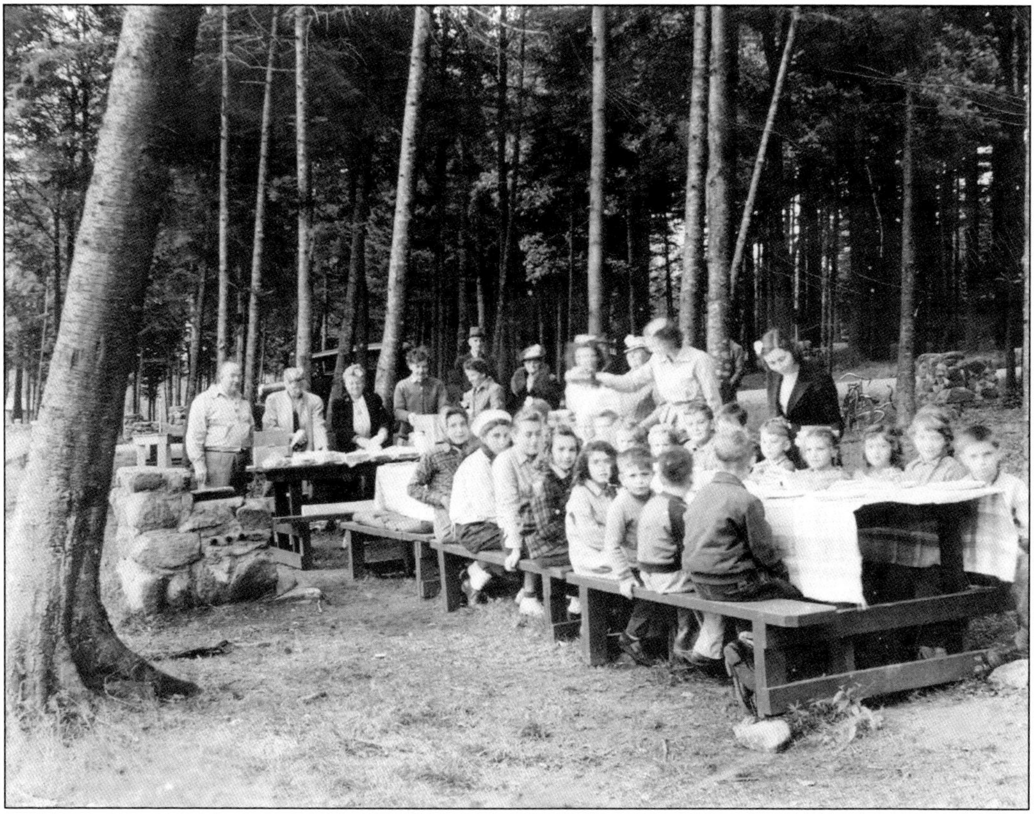

At the end of the school year, a school picnic was held at Moffitt Beach. The children always looked forward to this free time from school.

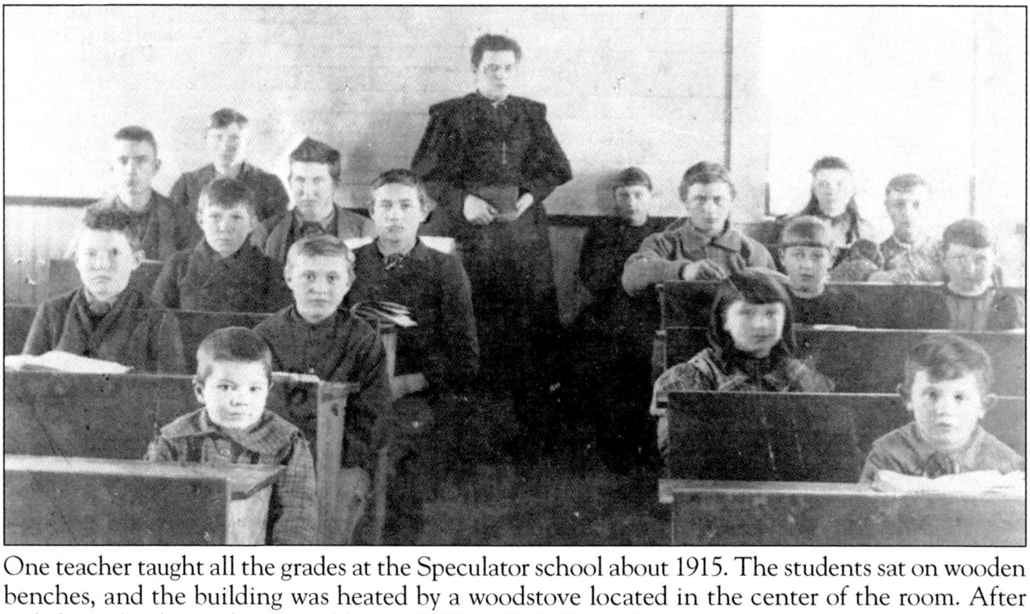

One teacher taught all the grades at the Speculator school about 1915. The students sat on wooden benches, and the building was heated by a woodstove located in the center of the room. After eighth grade, the students would attend Wells High School.

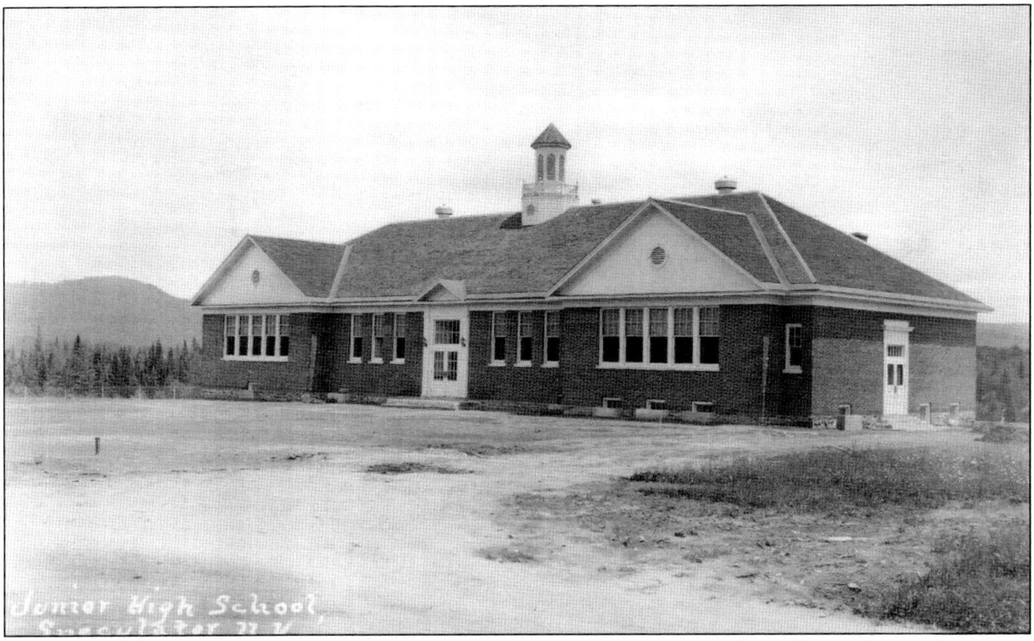

In 1929, a new school was built to replace all of the one-room schools in the area. Kindergarten through sixth grade was taught with two grades per room and one teacher in each room. Seventh through 10th grade was taught with a team of teachers.

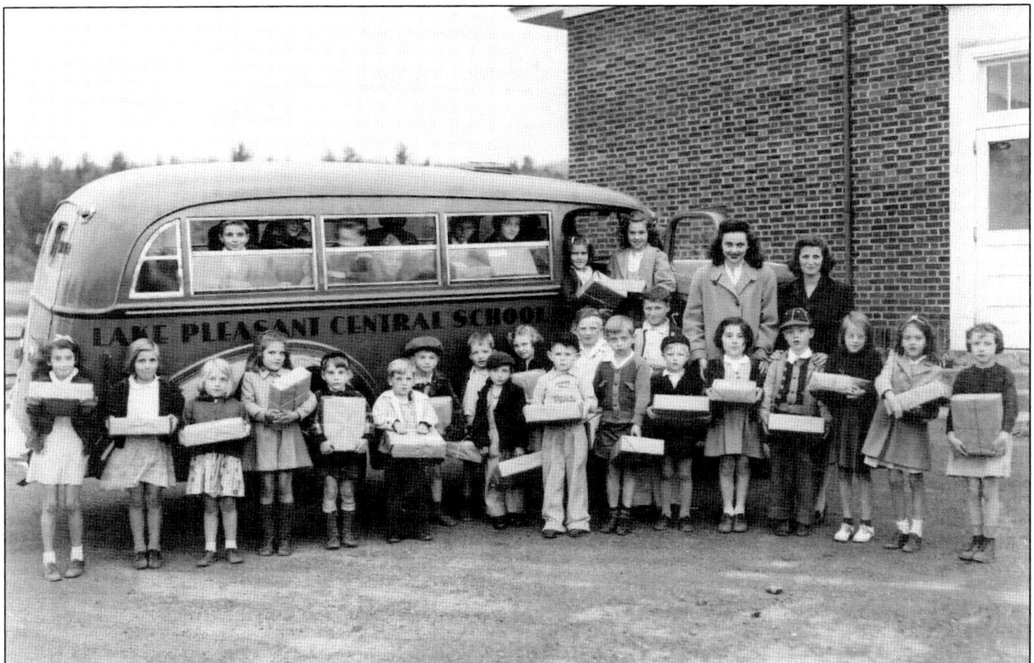

School buses were now necessary to transport students over the longer distances. Lynn Galusha's children were brought in each day from the Lewey Lake area.

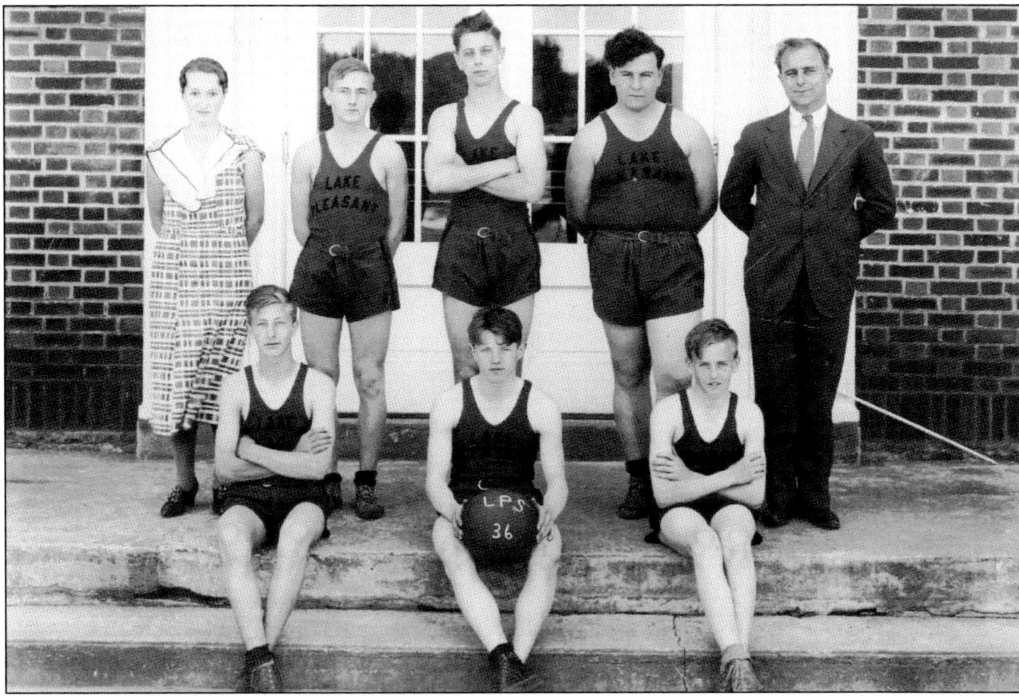

This boy's basketball team photograph was taken sometime in the 1930s. The new central school had a gymnasium, and now the boys and girls could have sports teams.

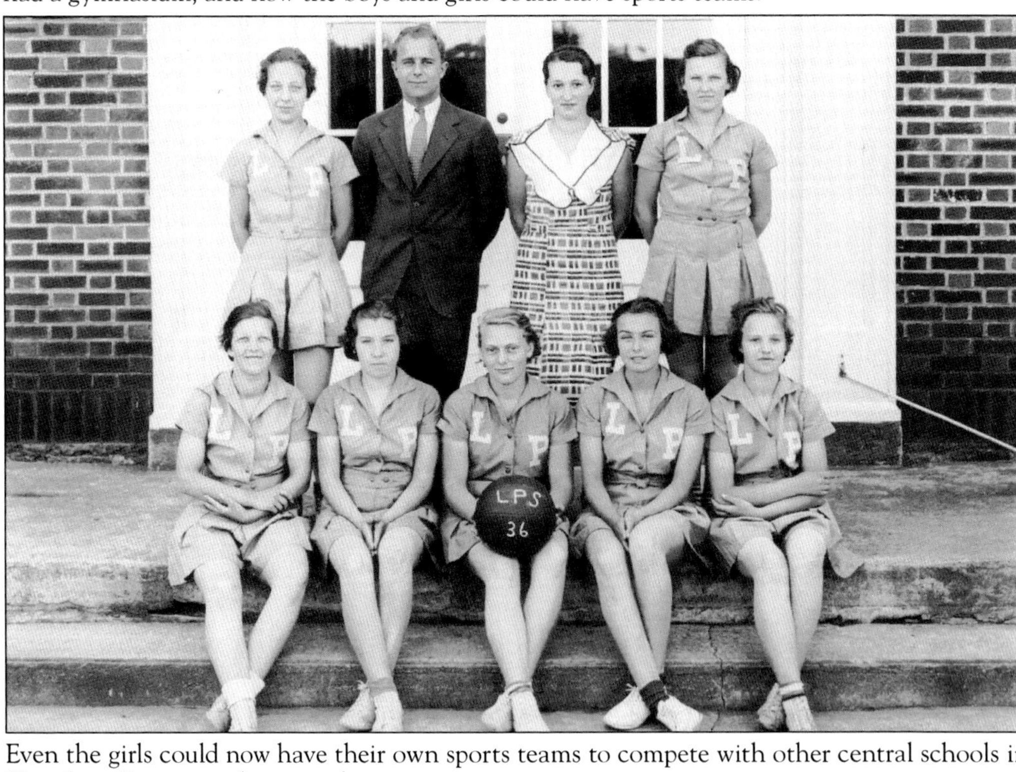

Even the girls could now have their own sports teams to compete with other central schools in Hamilton County and surrounding counties.

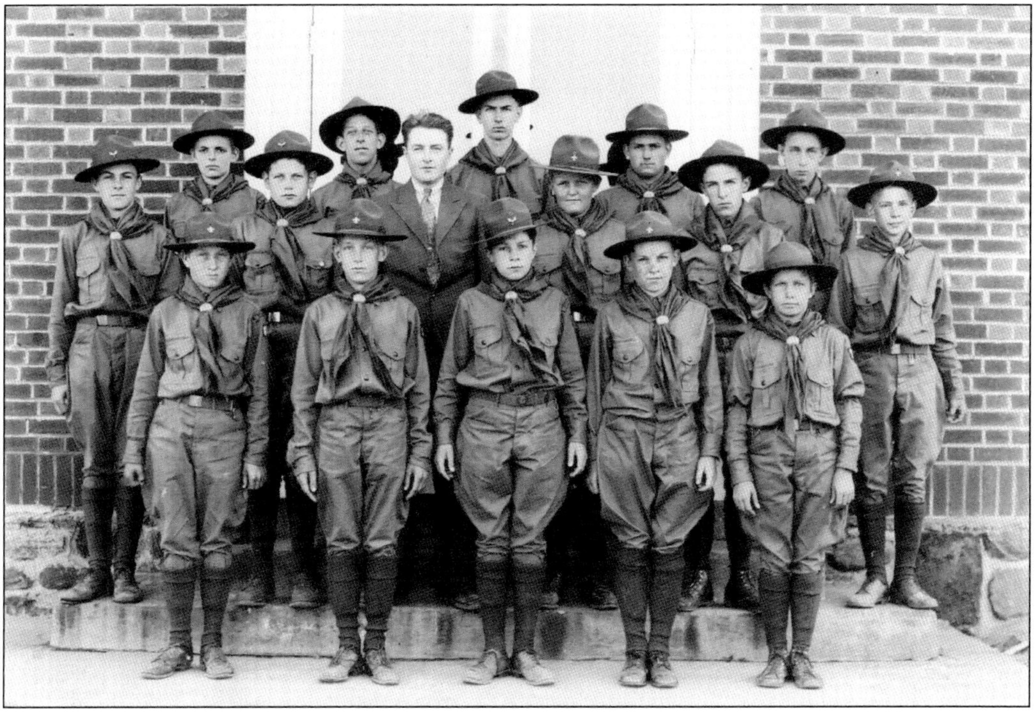

This photograph was taken in 1938 of the Boy Scouts in front of the Lake Pleasant Central School.

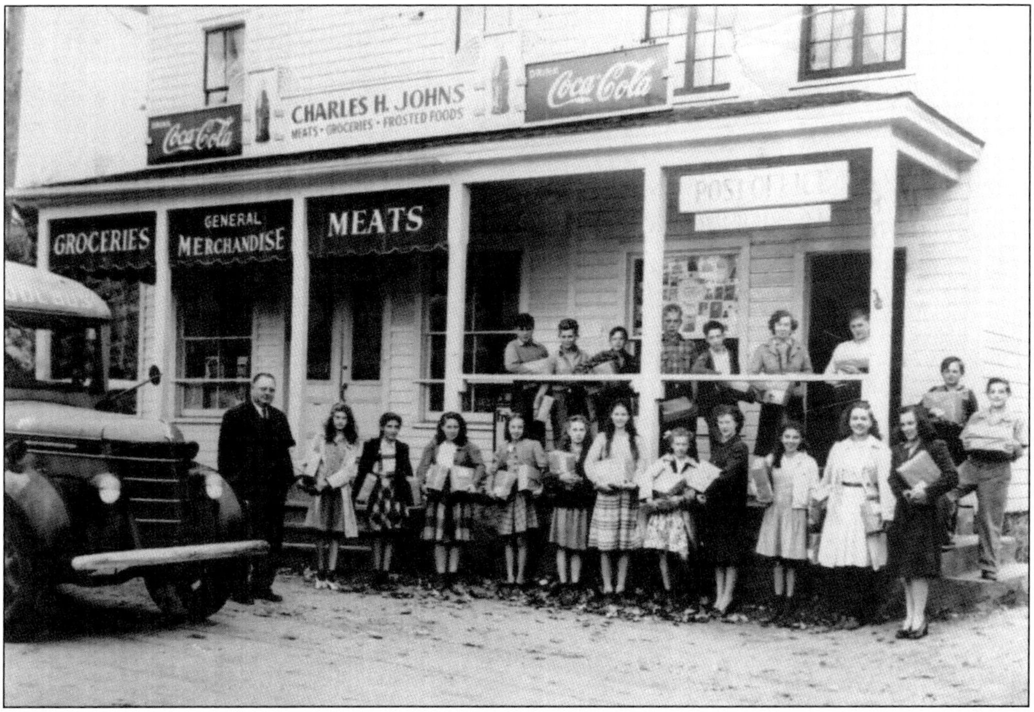

Schoolchildren brought packages to be mailed at the Speculator Post Office. Postmistress Amy Brooks Slack Early is in front of the post office door.

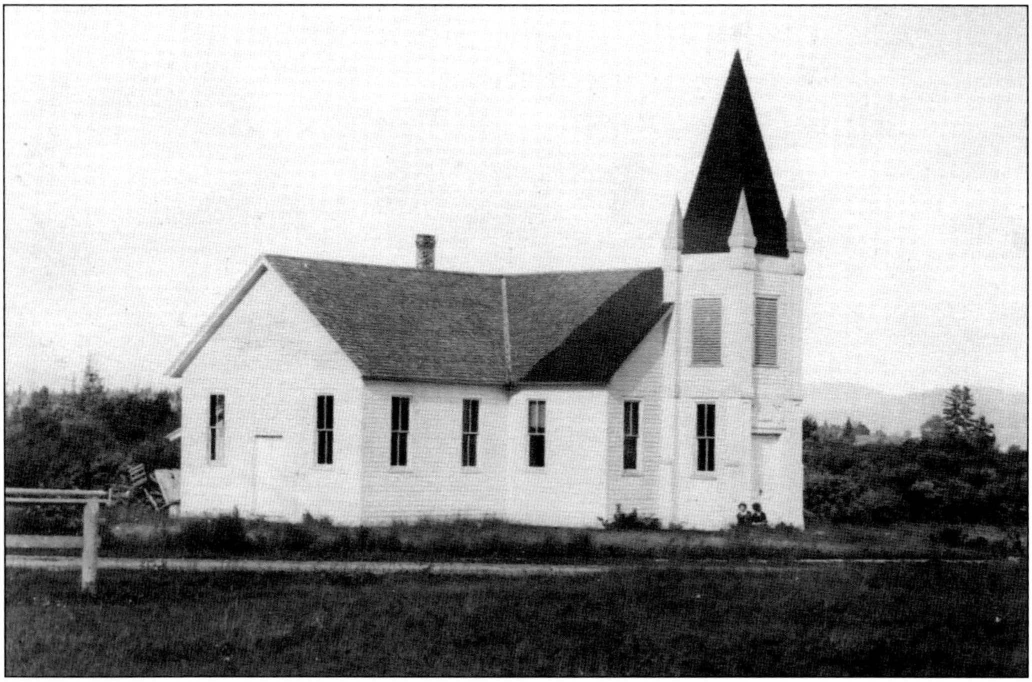

The Lake Pleasant Methodist Church was built in 1891 near the site of the former meetinghouse that was constructed around 1835. Before the churches were built, circuit riders from the Northampton circuit would come to hold services when they could.

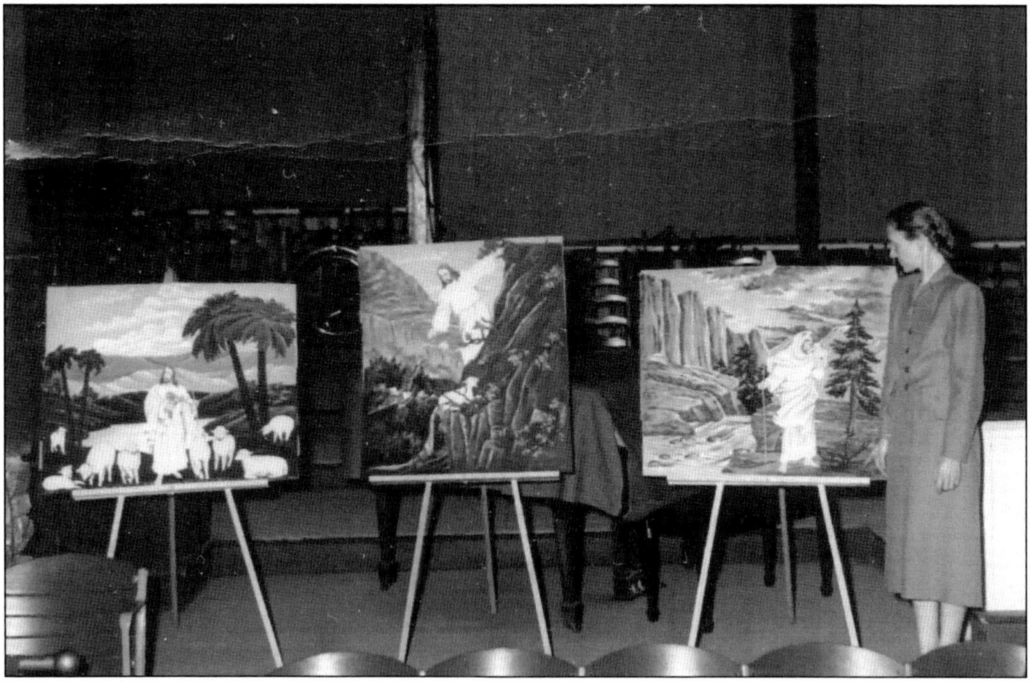

Clara Autilio told Bible stories using flannel graphs. Not only did she use flannel graphs in this area but also in the Gloversville area during the 1940s through the 1970s. She was a Sunday school superintendent at Grace Methodist Church.

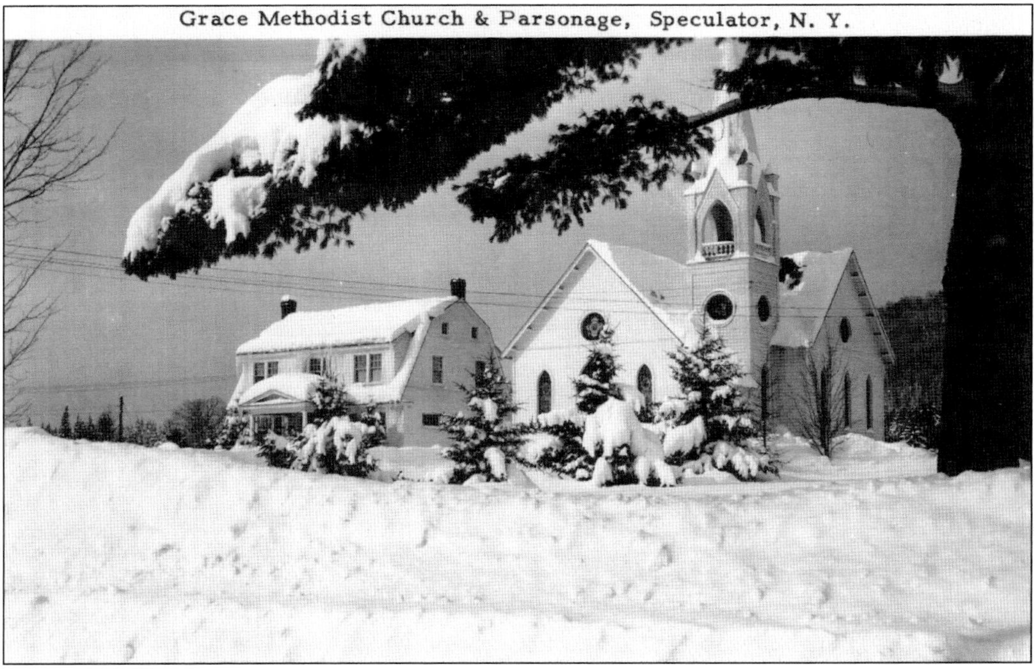

From the efforts of five women who started Sunday school classes and held worship meetings in their homes, a church group was formed. Land was purchased for the Grace United Methodist Church in 1896, and the cornerstone was laid in 1908. The building was completed in 1909 with the help and gifts from summer visitors and local folks alike. The parsonage was completed in 1928 and the church addition in 1957.

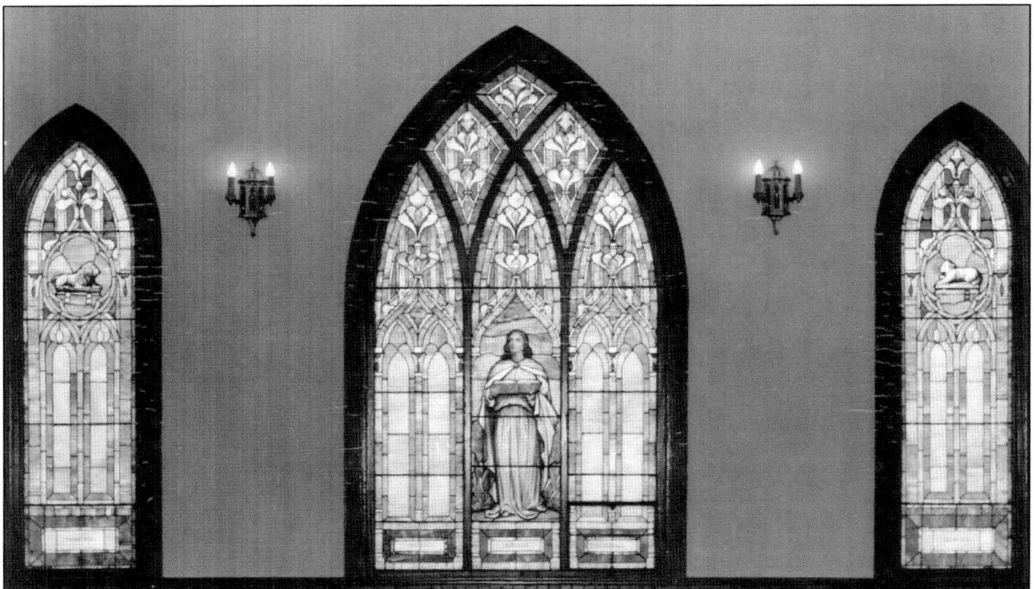

In memory of his beloved daughters Grace and Christine, John Hill donated this beautiful triple stained-glass window to the Grace United Methodist Church. Other equally beautiful stained-glass windows, a heating system, lights, and various other donations completed the church. It was dedicated in November 1909.

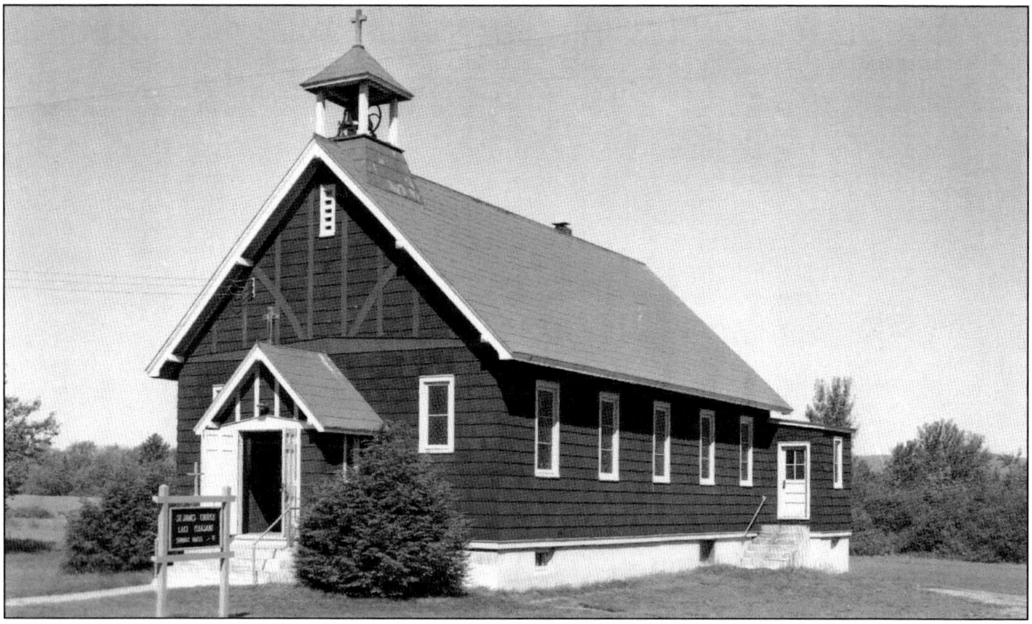

In 1925, the Saint James Roman Catholic Church was built in Lake Pleasant next door to the Lake Pleasant Methodist Church. Priests served the church from the St. Ann's Church in Wells until 1959 when it became a separate charge.

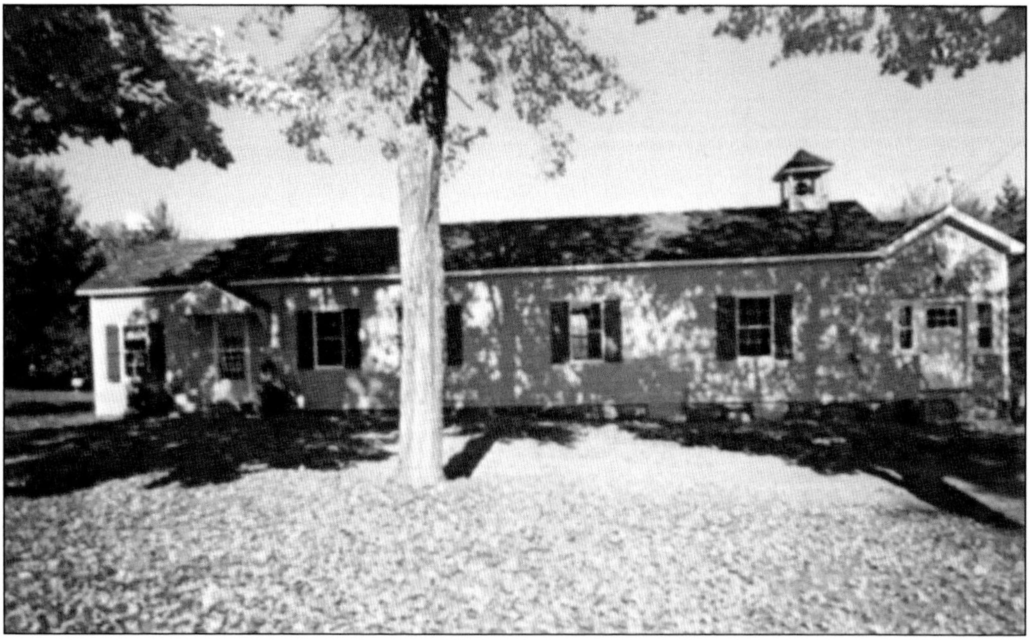

Episcopal services were conducted by the Reverend Harold Kaulfuss, the rector of Trinity Parish in Gloversville, each summer in Lake Pleasant. The first services were at the American Legion Hall, then the Tamarack Theatre, and then at the Hamilton Inn Annex. Dorothy Kaulfuss, in 1957, bought the old Lake Pleasant Inn and remodeled it into a church.

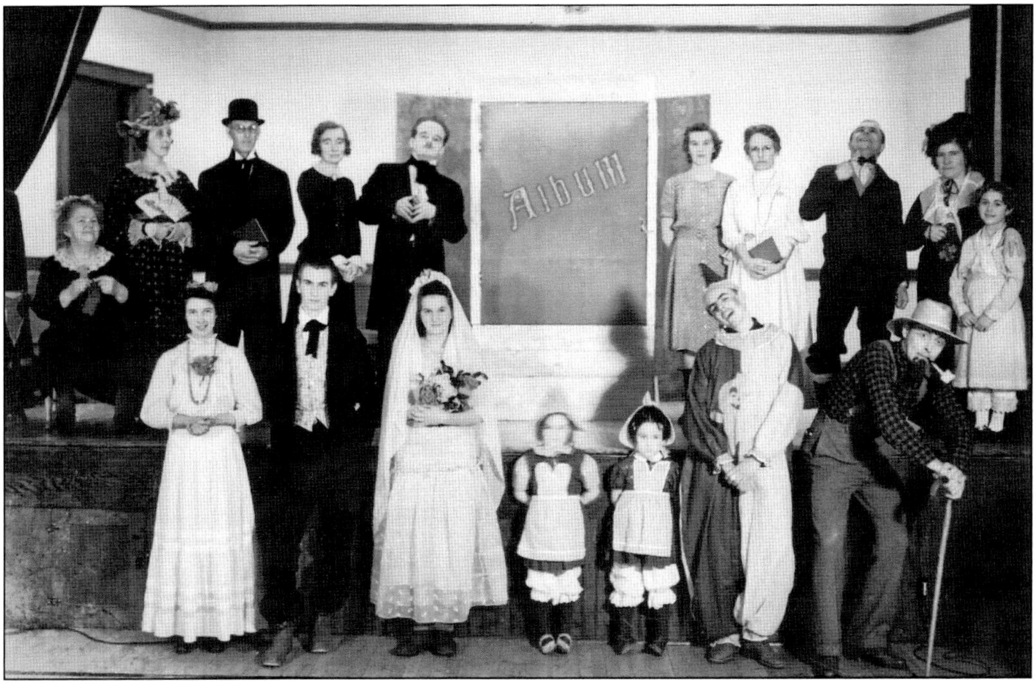

Local people, for entertainment but mostly for their own amusement, performed plays. *The Family Album* had Minnie Stanyon turning pages in her family album showing herself as a bride and showing some of her family.

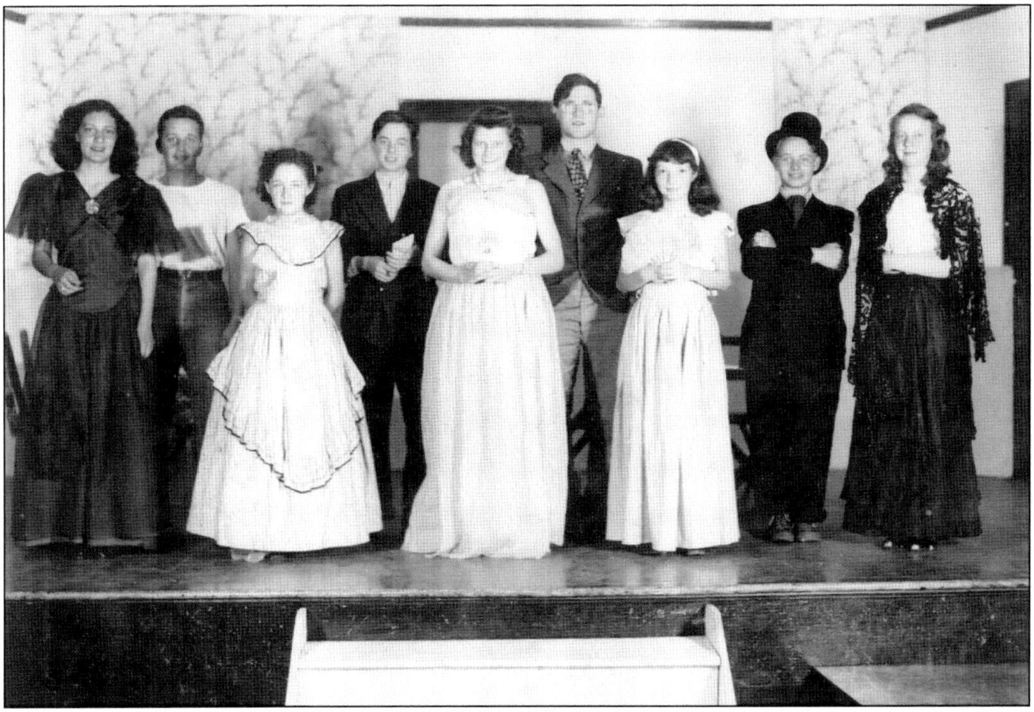

Aaron Slick was a play performed by the young people in the community. Boys from the Civilian Conservation Corps were frequently included.

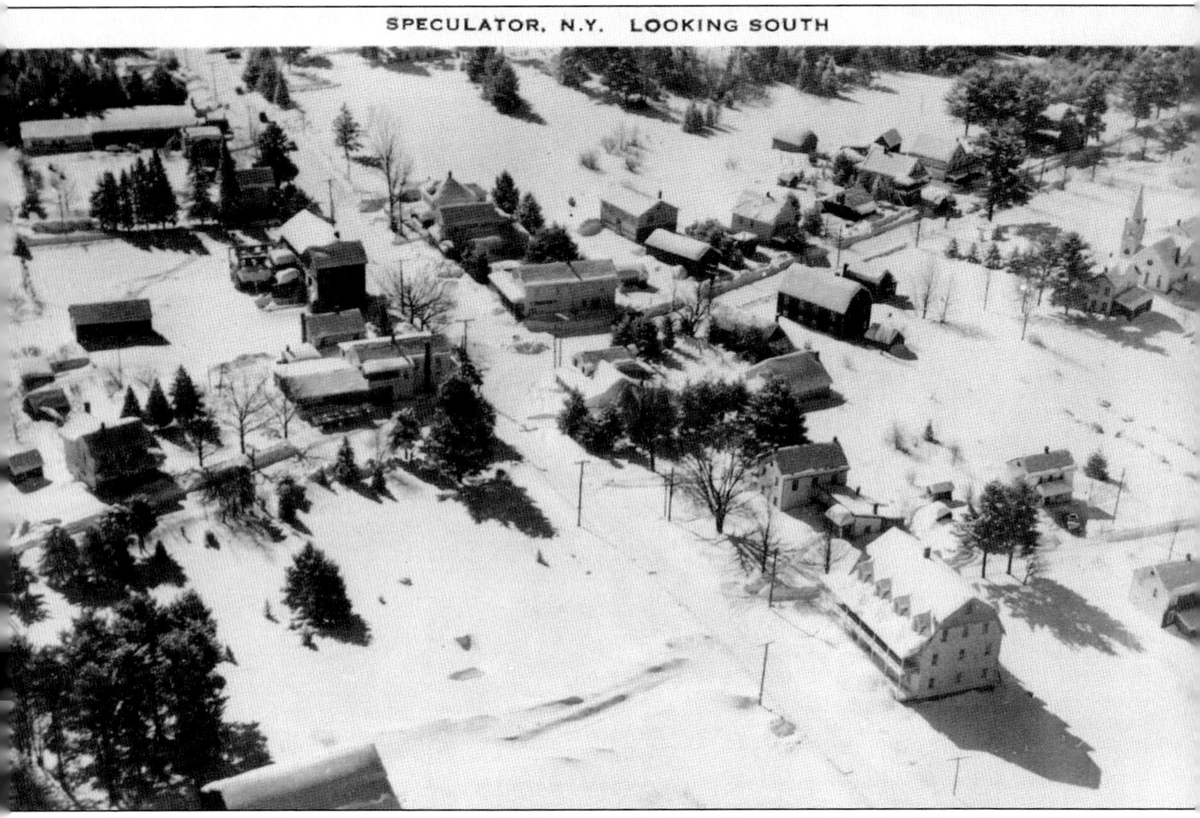

This is an aerial view of Speculator looking south. The Grace Methodist Church can be seen in the right background and has served the community since 1909. In 2009, Grace Methodist Church celebrated its centennial anniversary with many activities.

Four

BUSINESSES

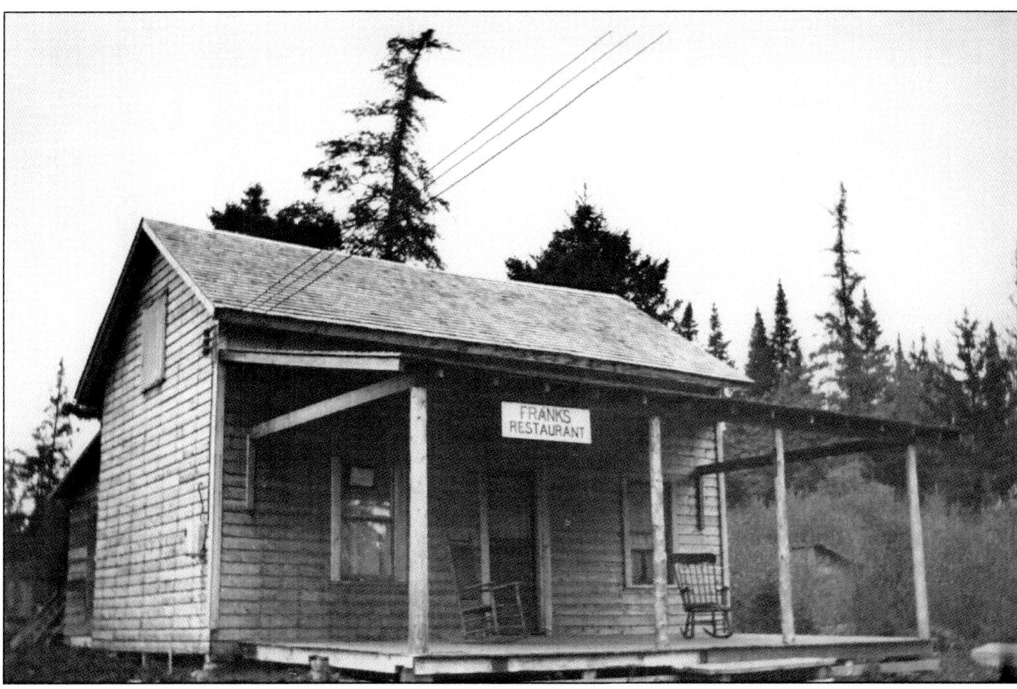

Few remember this restaurant, but Frank and Alice Weaver also had an ice shop where ice buried under sawdust could be bought in the middle of summer, when there was no electric refrigeration. They also sold bait for fishermen.

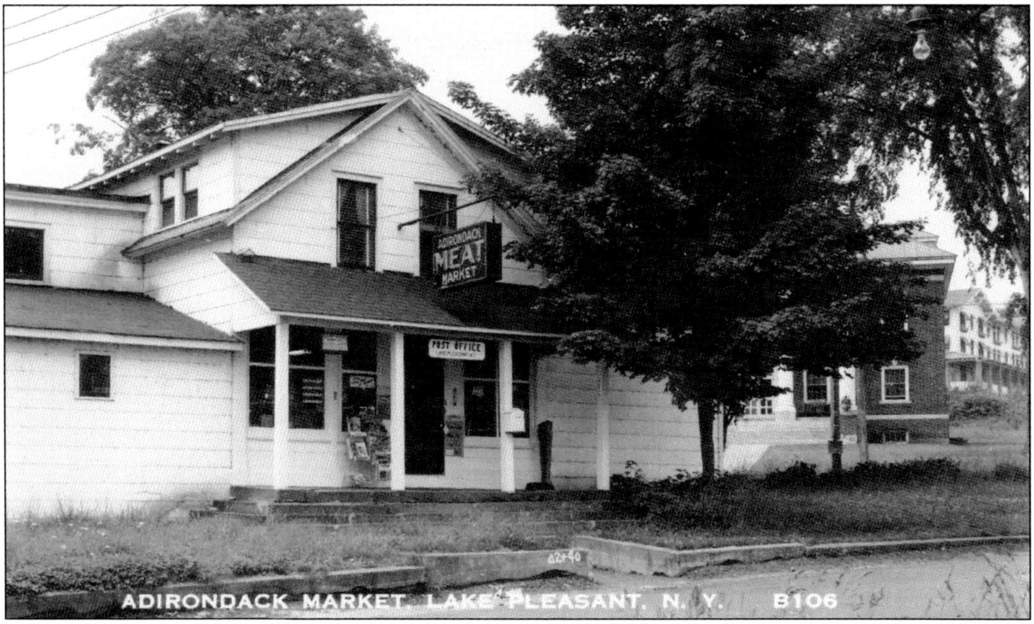

Call's Store was built about 1860 near the inlet of Lake Pleasant when it was first owned by Hannah Pratt. Samuel Call and his sons, Lysander and David, ran the store for over 80 years. At some point, they moved the store to the corner across from the county courthouse.

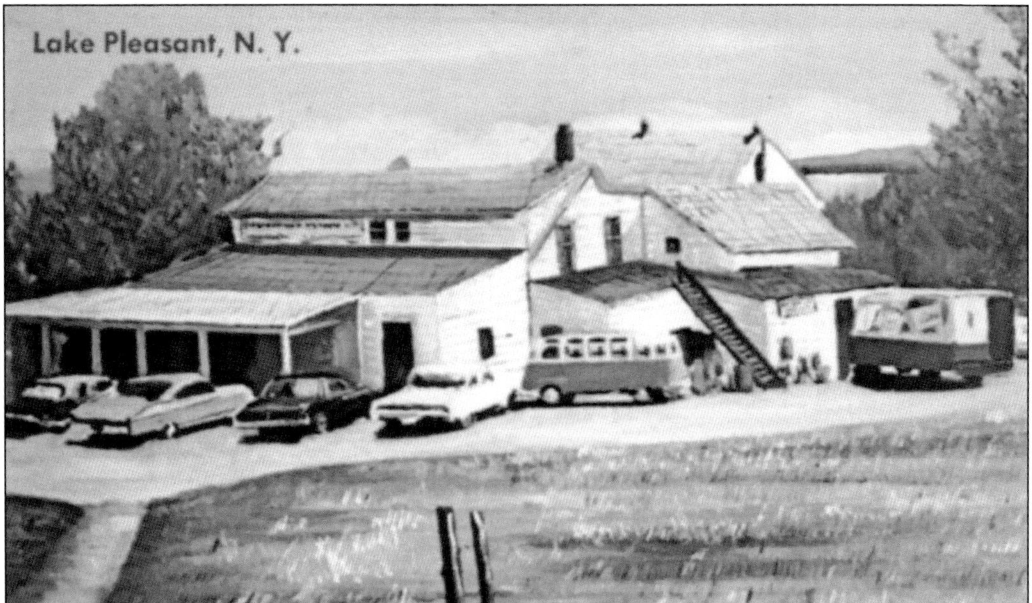

The Adirondack Market was formerly called Call's Store in Lake Pleasant. The store was enlarged, a post office added, and the main entrance changed to the South Shore Road side. It burned down in the 1980s.

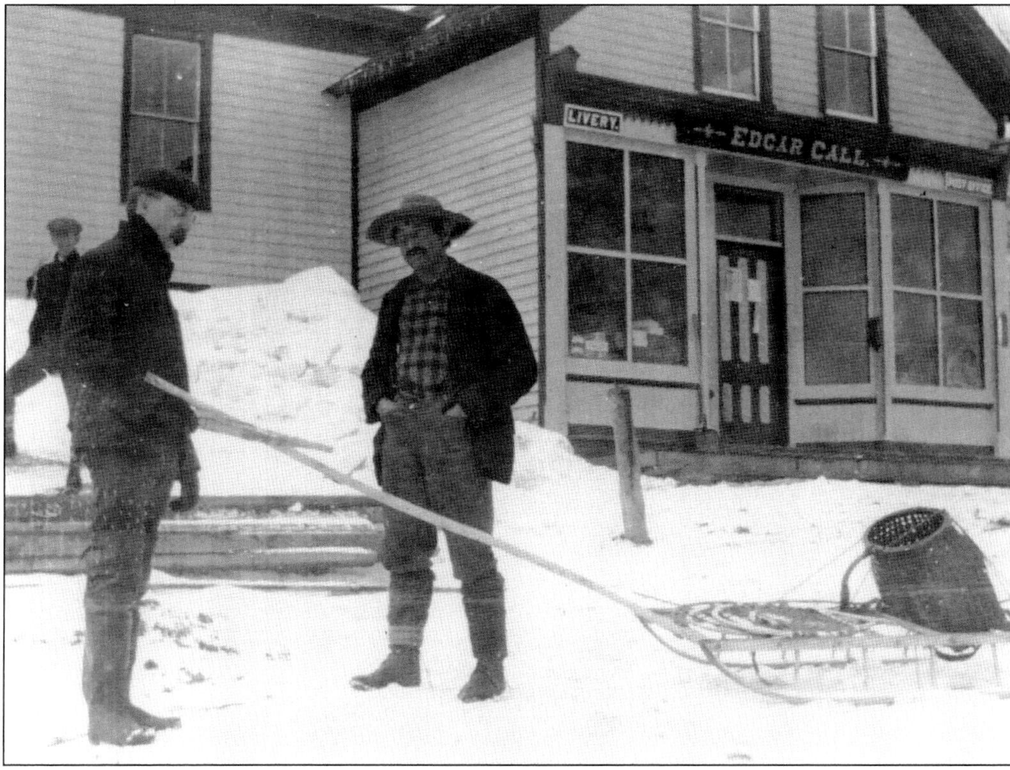

Store patrons are seen at Call's Store coming for provisions with homemade sleds and pack baskets.

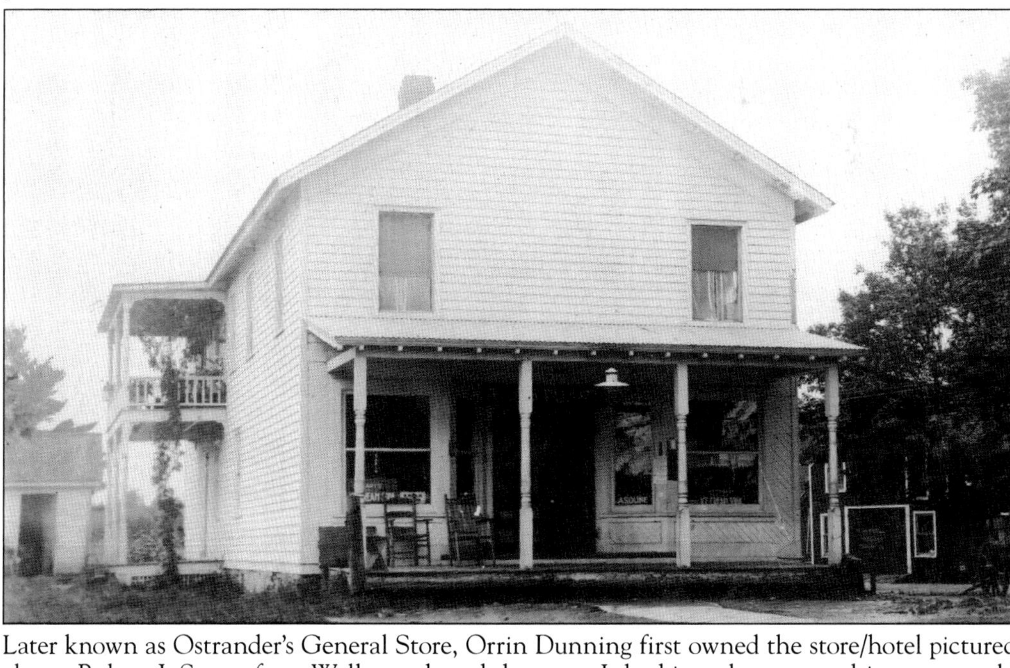

Later known as Ostrander's General Store, Orrin Dunning first owned the store/hotel pictured above. Robert J. Stuart from Wells purchased the store. It had just about everything one would need, including gasoline and oil.

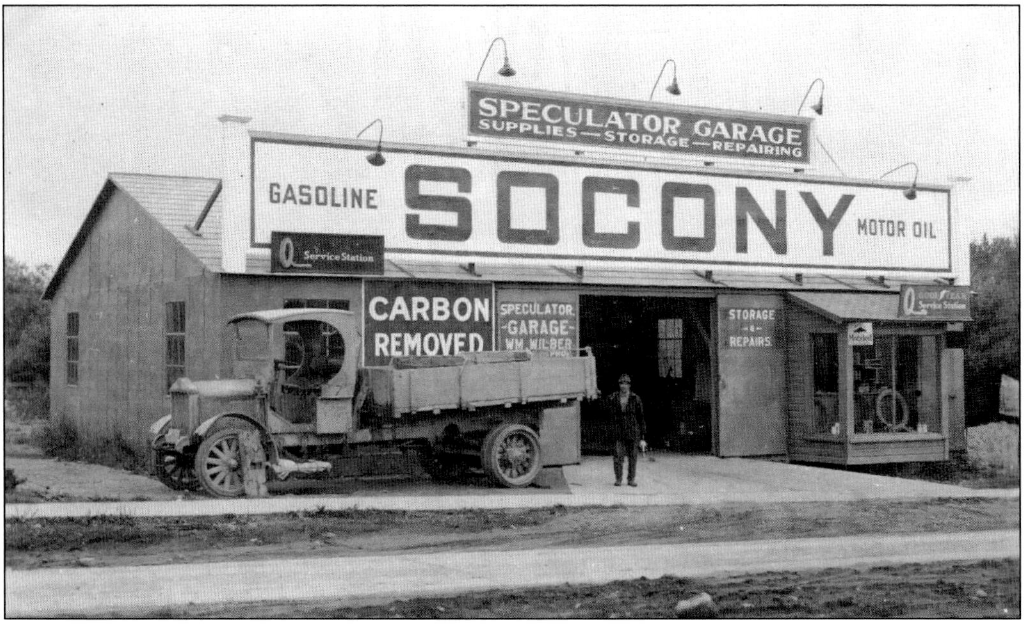

By 1915, automobiles were bringing tourists to the mountains and the need for filling stations and mechanics was soon felt in Speculator and Lake Pleasant. William Wilbur owned this garage. Later Charlie Downey owned the garage and called it Downey's Chevrolet.

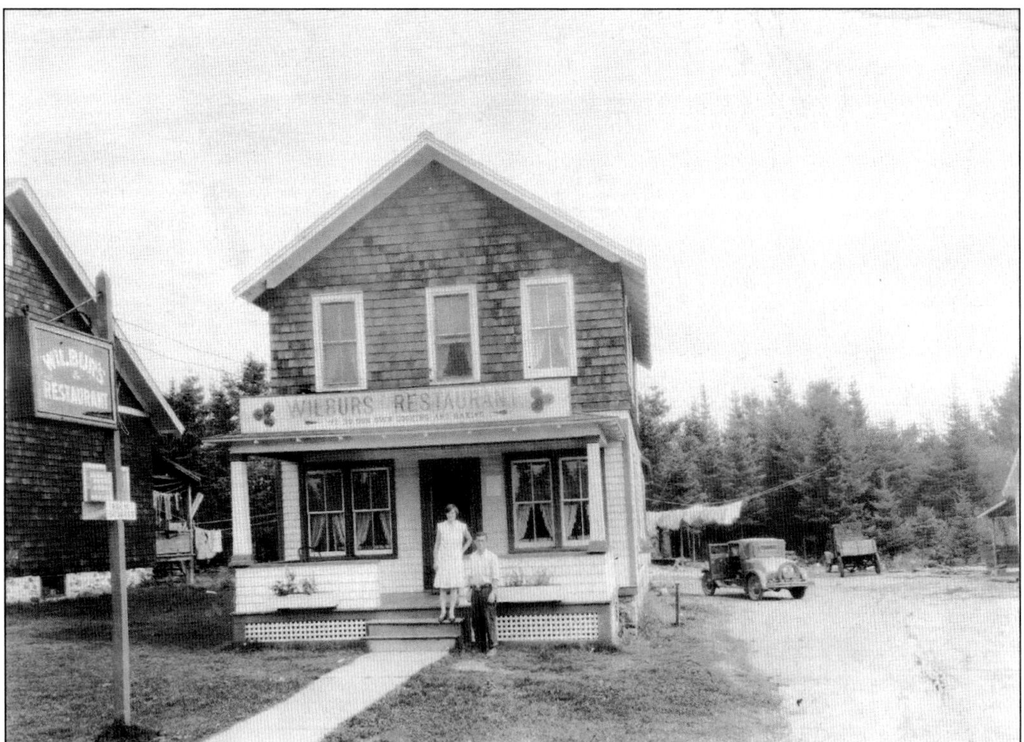

Wilbur's Restaurant was run by Harry Wilbur and his sister, Davida, and located next to their brother Bill's garage sometime in the 1920s.

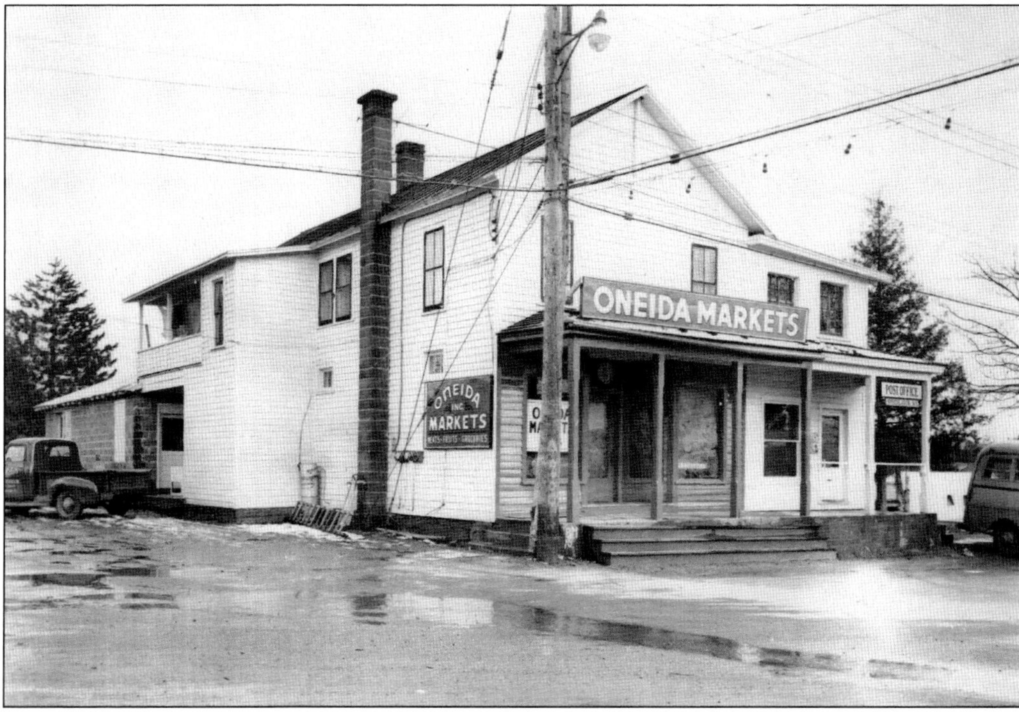

In the 1880s, Henry Slack built his general store just below the four corners. It was well stocked with a large variety of items, but if he did not have an item one wanted, he would order it to be sent by stage or wagon. Sidewalks went right up to his porch steps on two sides. Other proprietors included Charlie Johns and the Oneida Market. The Speculator Post Office was located here for many years.

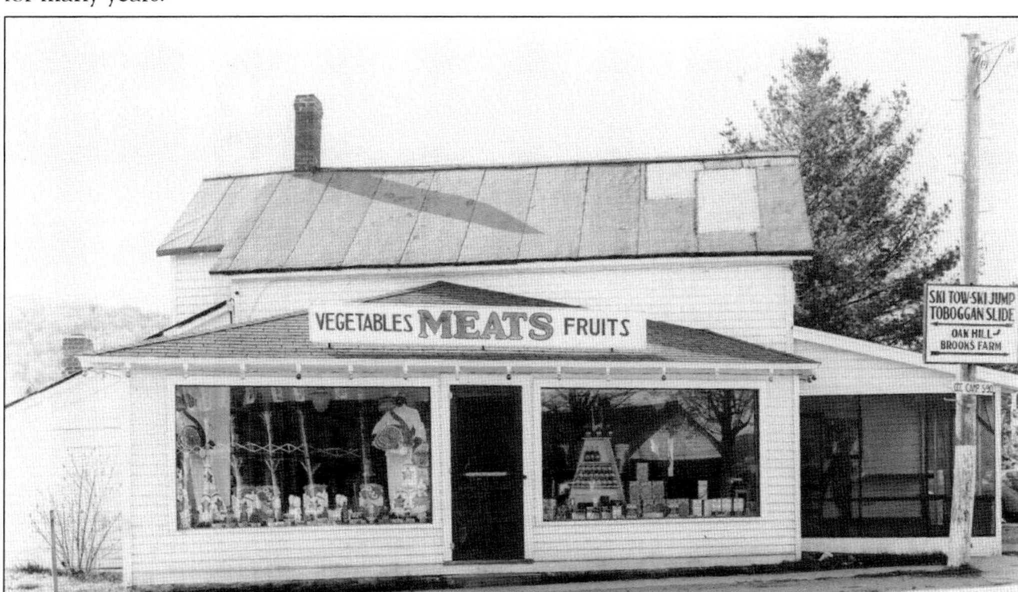

In the 1920s, George Fuller came up from Wells to open a meat market at the busy corner in Speculator.

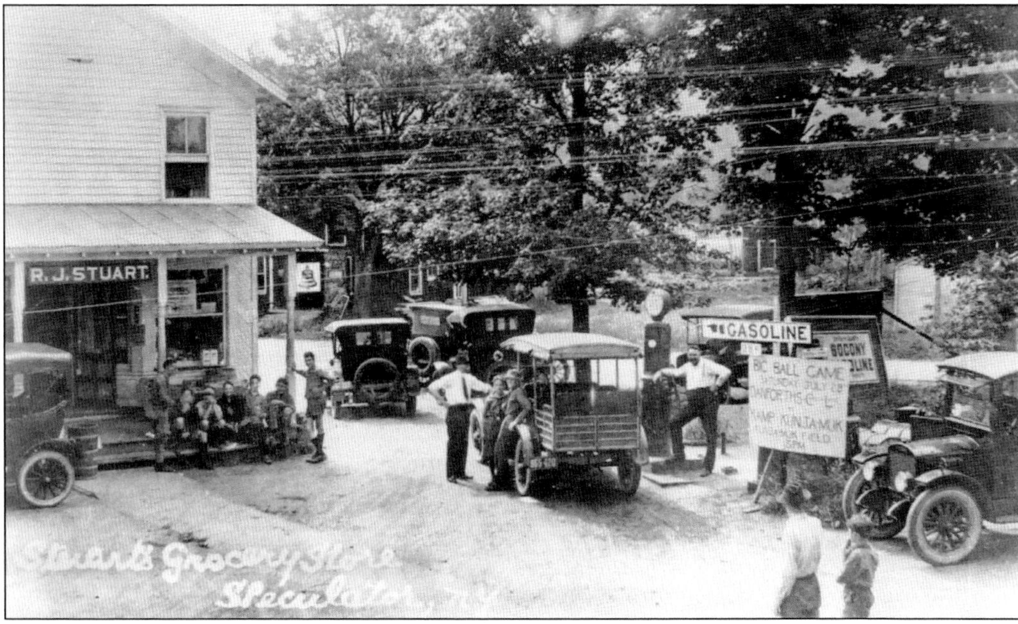

With the popularity of automobiles, traffic flowed into Speculator. When the village was incorporated in 1925, it was deemed necessary to appoint a village policeman to direct the busy traffic at the four corners.

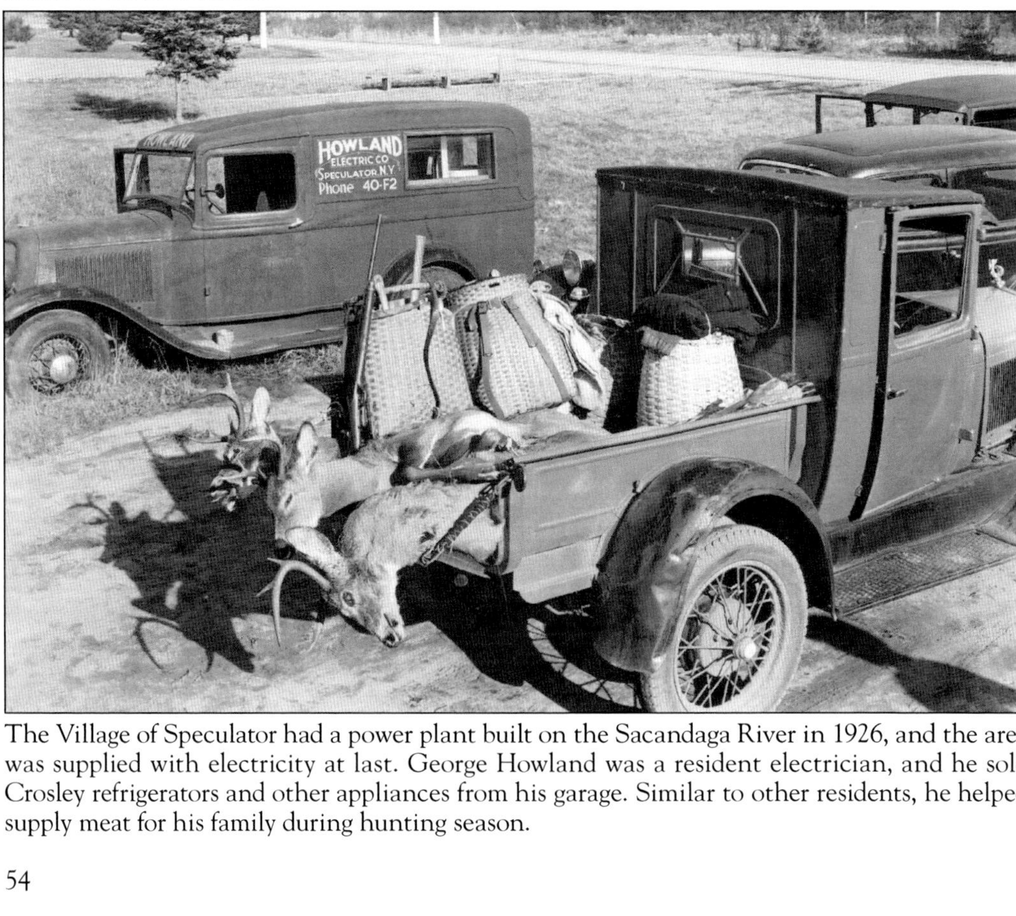

The Village of Speculator had a power plant built on the Sacandaga River in 1926, and the area was supplied with electricity at last. George Howland was a resident electrician, and he sold Crosley refrigerators and other appliances from his garage. Similar to other residents, he helped supply meat for his family during hunting season.

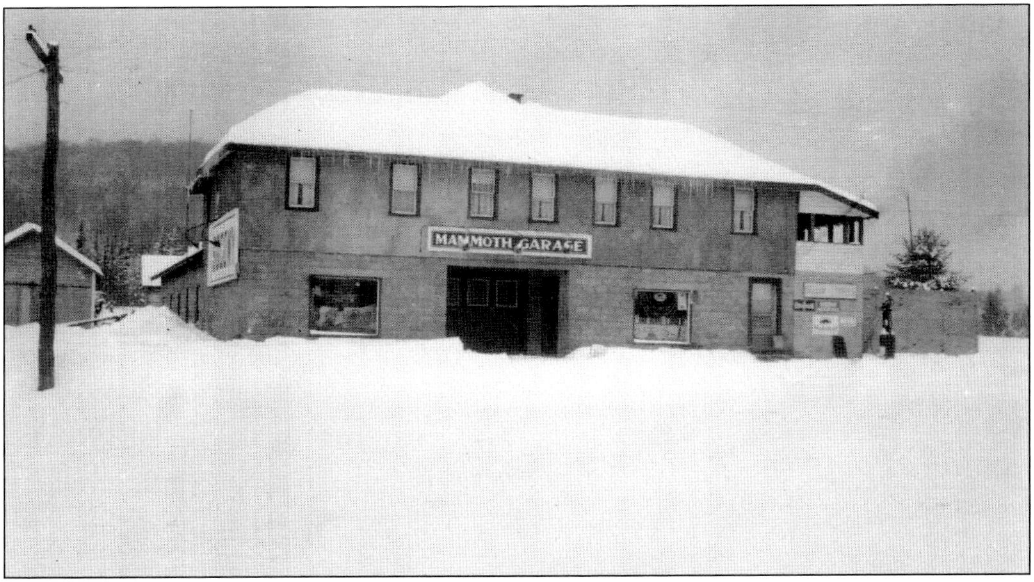

Ann Telfer first owned the Mammoth Garage in the 1920s. The garage was later bought by Eugene Greene, who sold Ford cars and trucks. Many in the town either owned a Ford from Greene's or a Chevy from Downey's.

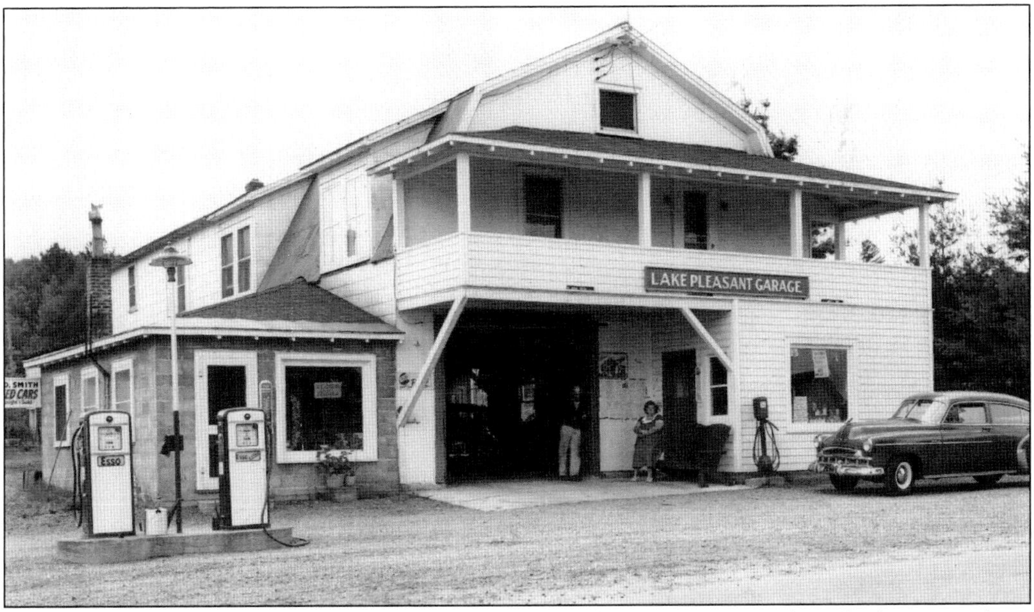

Harry and Lena Slack ran the Lake Pleasant Garage. They sold Esso gasoline, had a repair shop, and in the office area sold snacks and soda. In 2010, the building still stands across Route 8 from the Lake Pleasant Post Office.

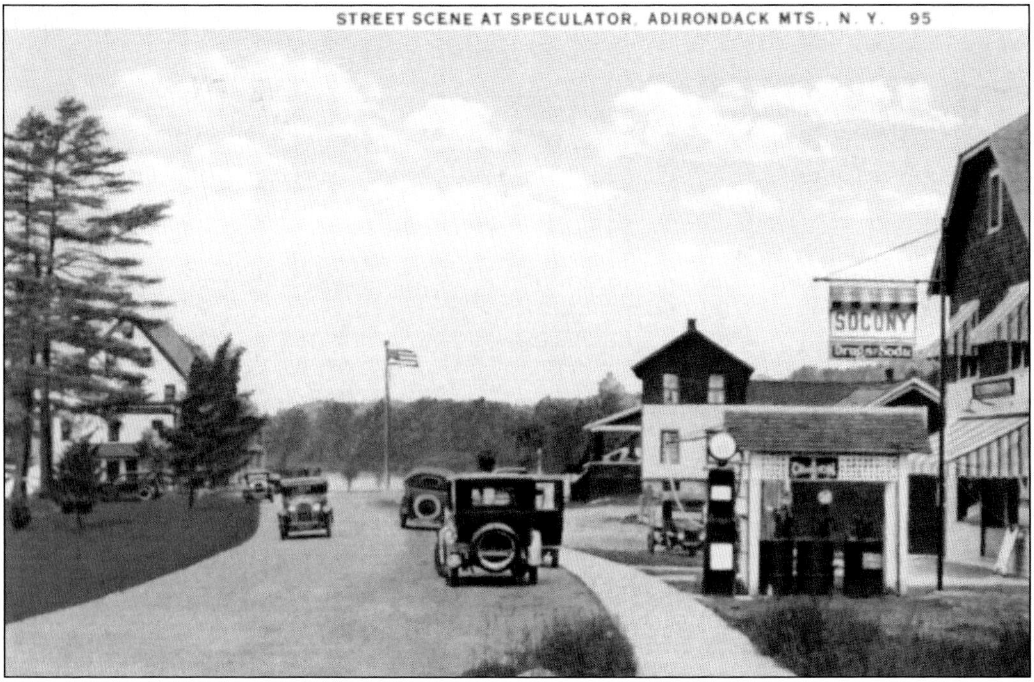

Stanley Schoonmaker from South Bethlehem met and married Pamelia Osborne, the daughter of hotel owners William and Nora Osborne, and had a drugstore below the outlet of Lake Pleasant. His young wife passed away leaving him with a young daughter.

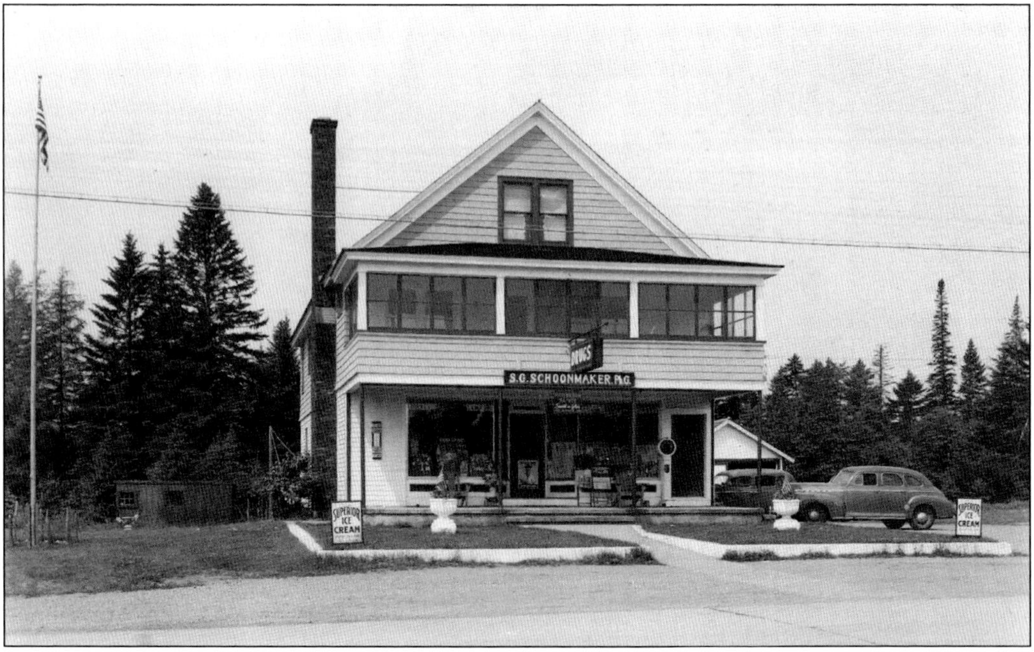

Stanley Schoonmaker, along with his second wife, Edith Abbott, built a new store. They also had a soda fountain and sold souvenirs, greeting cards, and miscellaneous other items. They had a son and daughter who both worked in the store. Stanley Jr. returned to run the Schoonmaker Drugstore when he became a pharmacist.

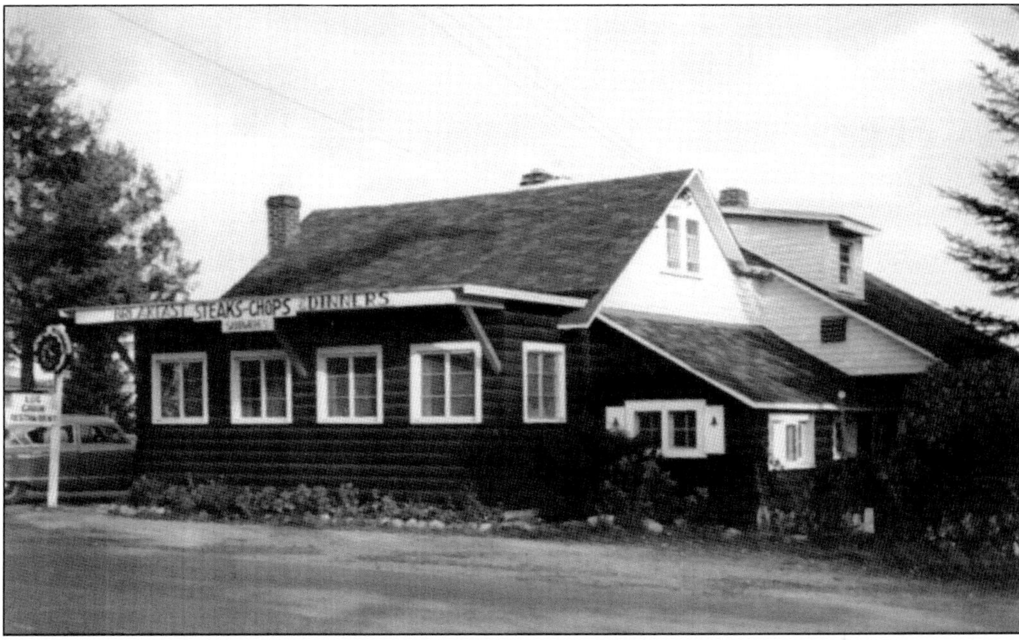

Howard and Toni Romaine came to town with the Tamarack Theatre group and remained in the area. They built the Log Cabin Restaurant with living quarters and raised their family here. Remodeled through the years, it is now Logan's Bar and Grill on Route 8.

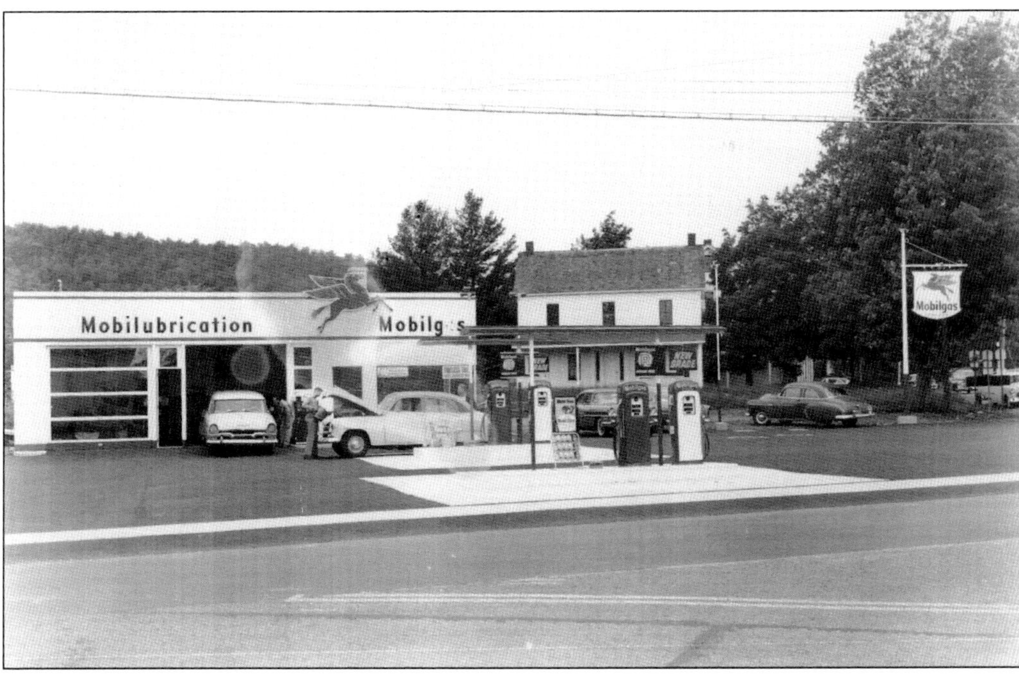

Clyde Elliott owned a taxi service and trucking business in Speculator. About 1957, he built a Mobilgas filling station and garage on the four corners. At one time there were at least seven places for motorists to buy gasoline in the area.

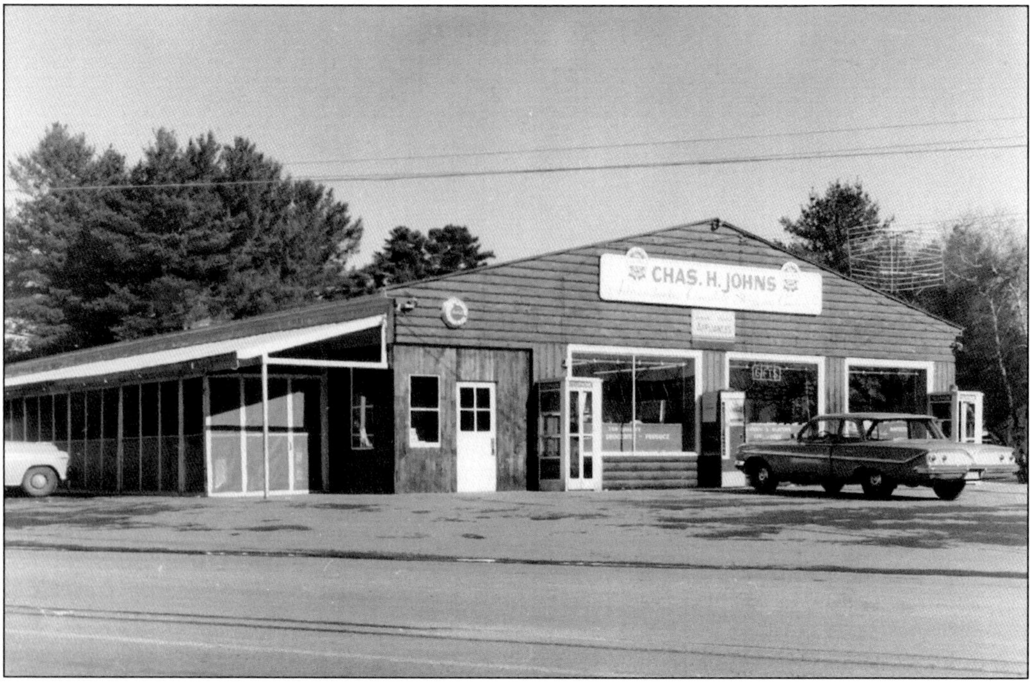

Charlie Johns, owner of the former Slack's Store on the four corners, built a larger store in 1961 on the opposite corner. He also had a new post office and bank building complex constructed during the same time period. The old Slack store was torn down to allow for the widening of the road.

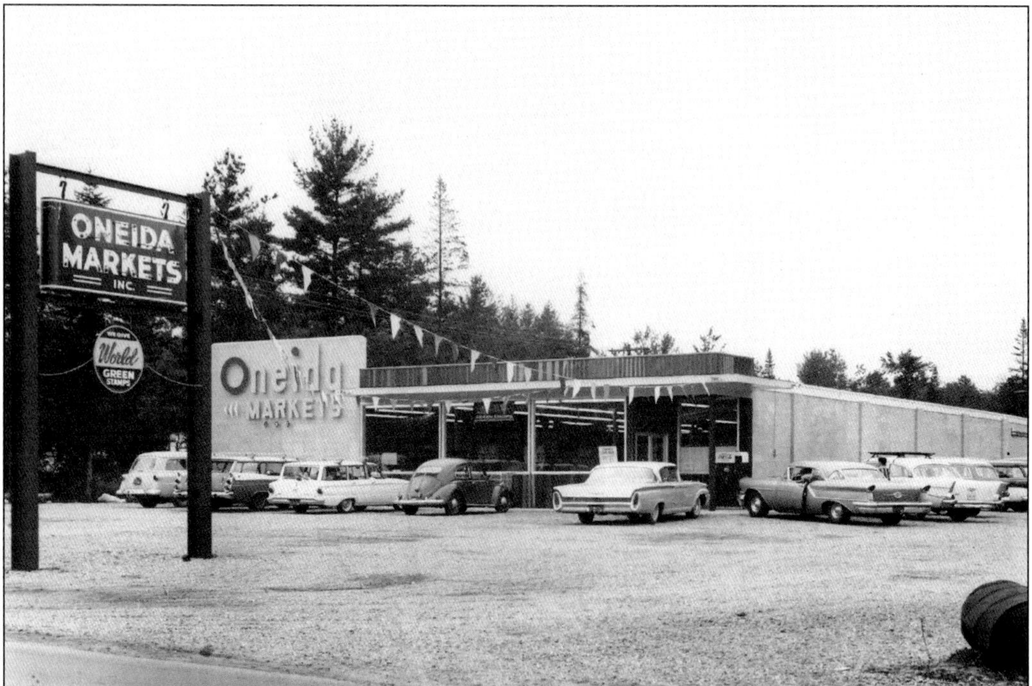

The Oneida Market chain also built a larger, modern store in 1961. Presently the Sunmount Day Treatment Center is located in the remodeled store building.

Five

Camps

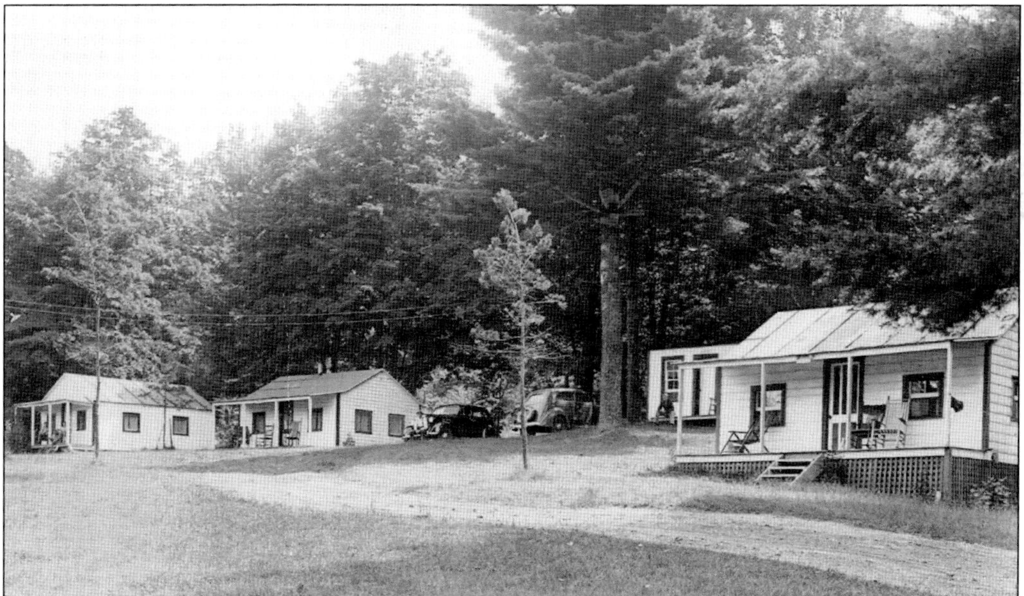

Peter L. Weaver, who lived in Airdville, built cabins for hunters and tourists in the early 1900s. Most of these cabins were two rooms with only the basic necessities. Many of the cabins were used to make a two-story house for one of his sons, but a great-grandson of his is still using one of the cabins.

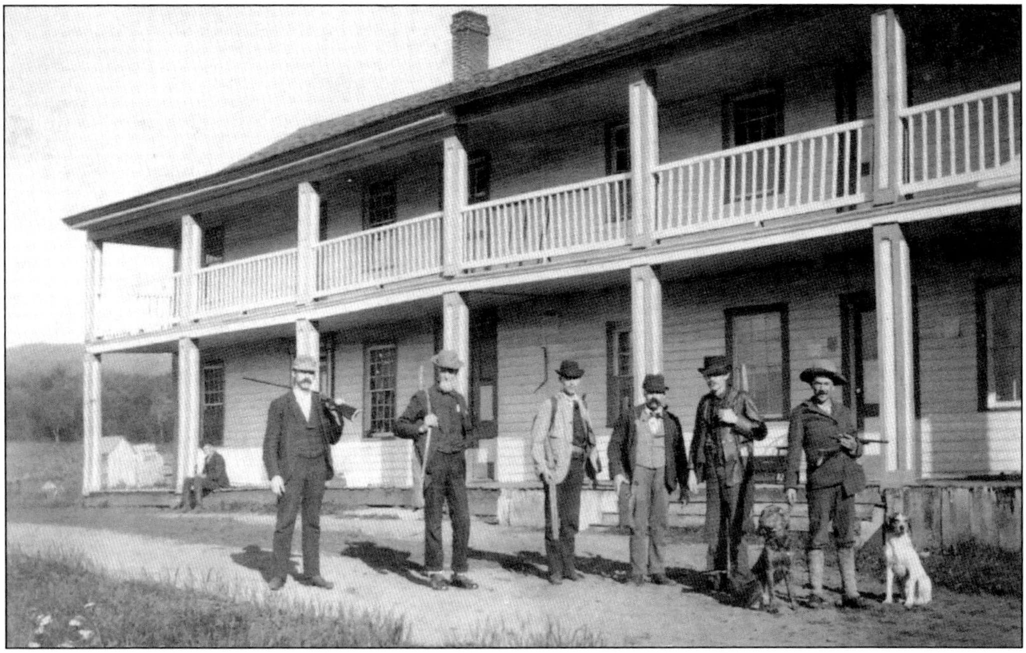

For any Adirondack man in the 1800s, hunting was a necessity to provide his family with meat and fish. It was not hard for an Adirondack man to be hired as a guide for the city sportsman who came to Lake Pleasant or Speculator to hunt and fish. These men are pictured heading out from Sturges House in Speculator.

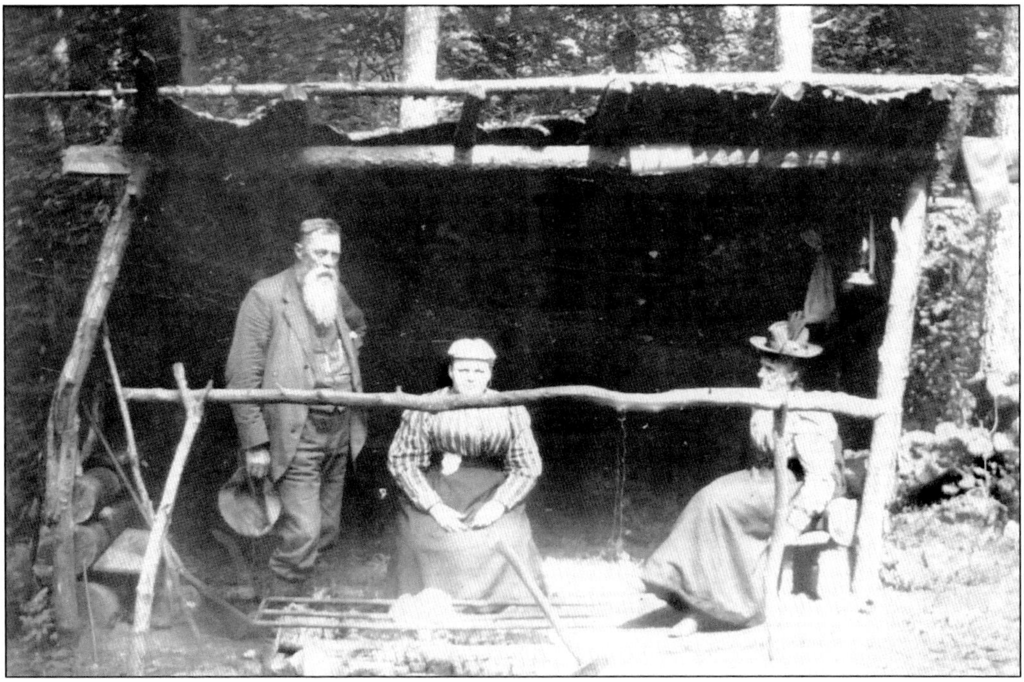

Dave Sturges, who owned Sturges House in Speculator, was taught at a young age to hunt and fish. At age 16, he was guiding city sportsmen to his father's camp at Lewey Lake. This is Dave's camp at Dug Mountain.

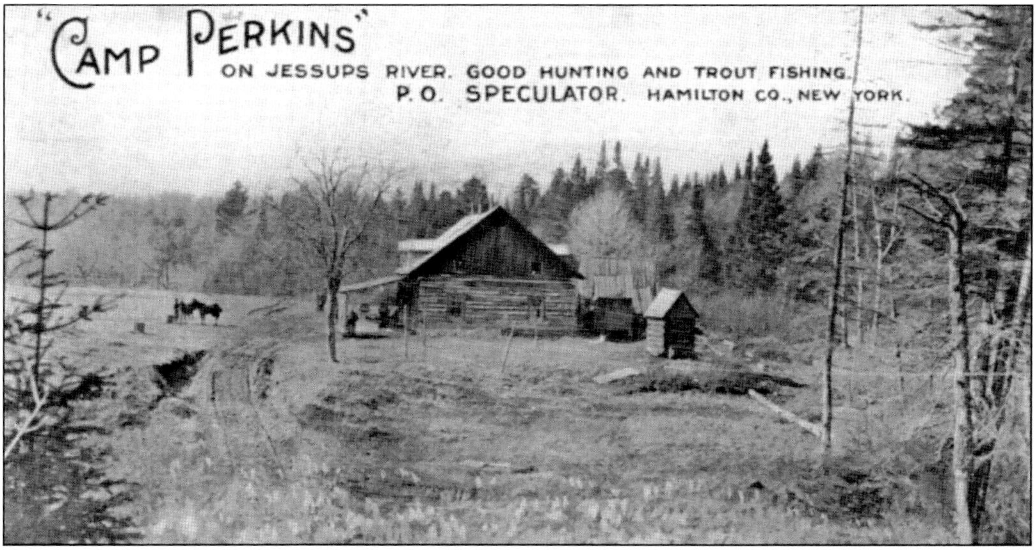

Isaiah Perkins owned Camp Perkins, and many sportsmen would hunt from this camp. City sportsmen started traveling to the Lake Pleasant and Speculator area in the 1850s, and guides were soon needed to take them to the prime hunting areas, and hotels were needed to house them.

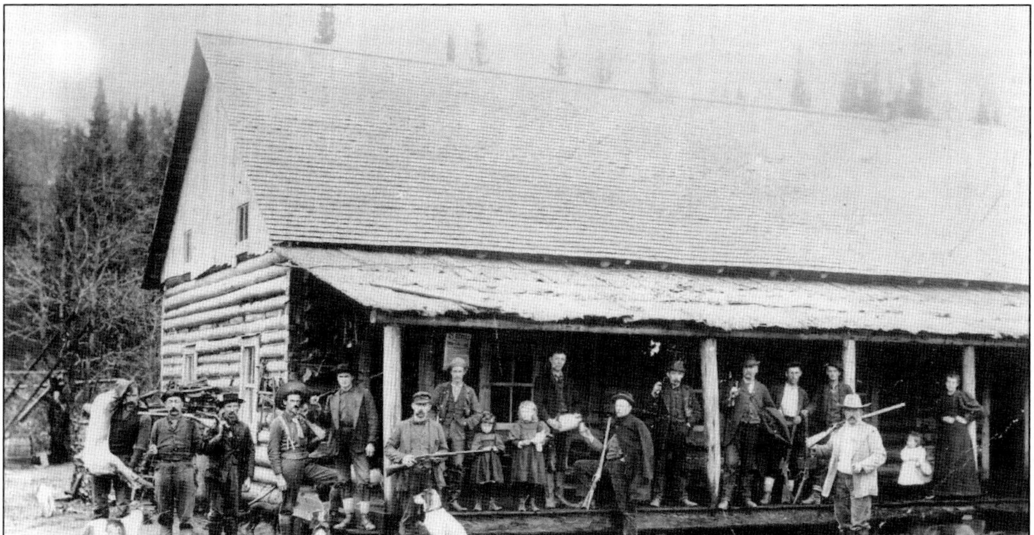

Camp Perkins was the ideal place for any sportsman. Among the local men in this picture are Sam Lawrence, George Perkins, C. H. Wilber, Lee Fountain, and Allie Buyce, names that were well-known in the communities of Lake Pleasant and Speculator. Camp Perkins was located in the area that is now called Perkins Clearing.

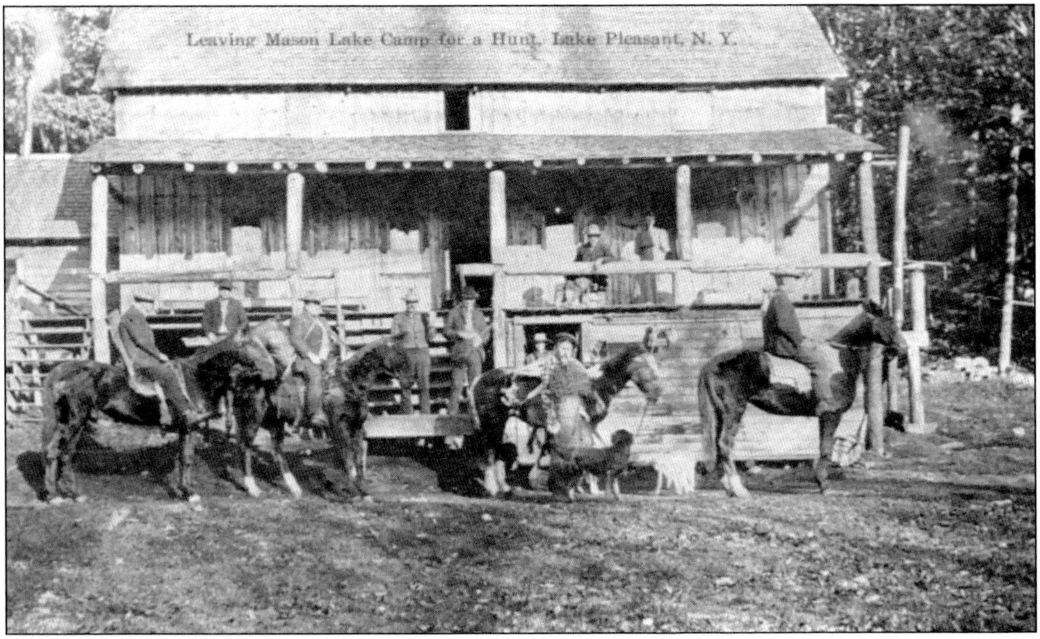

Hunters used dogs and horses, as seen here, at the Mason Lake Camp. Mason Lake was near Perkins Clearing and Camp Perkins.

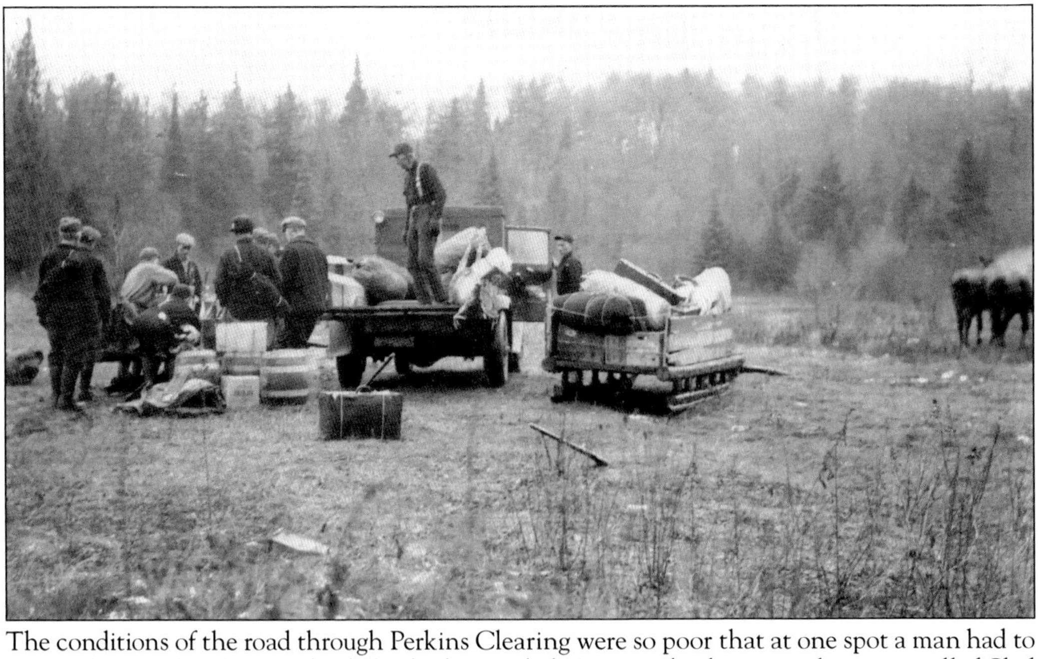

The conditions of the road through Perkins Clearing were so poor that at one spot a man had to change his supplies from a wheeled vehicle to a sled. As a result, there is a place now called Sled Harbor that was one of the spots to change to sleds.

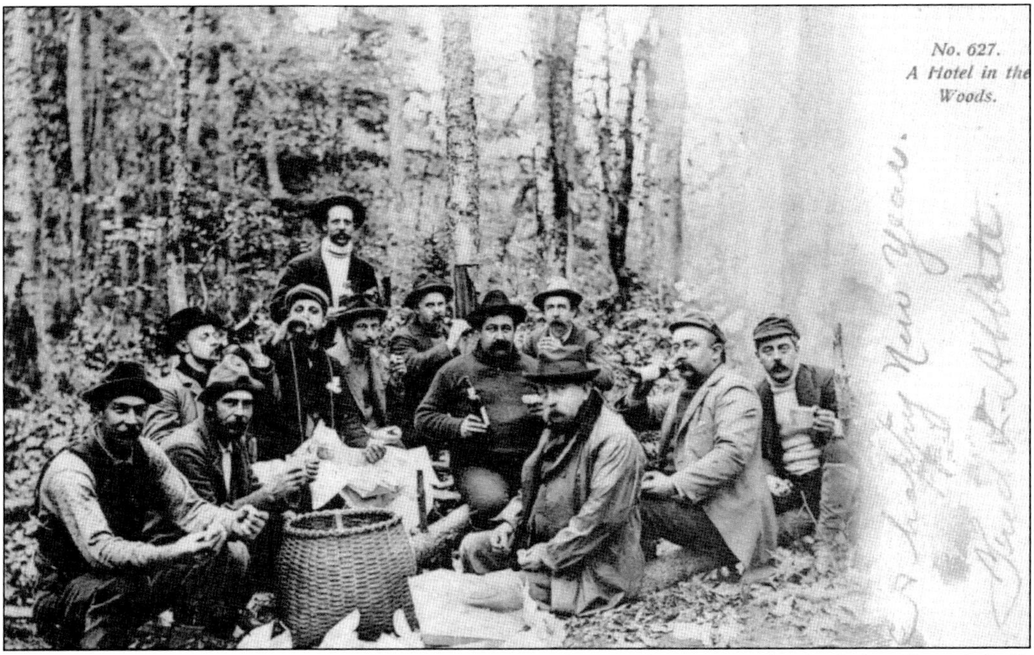

This picture was titled, "A Hotel in the Woods." The gentleman on the far left is David Call, who is listed in the 1905 census as a guide. His wife was Kitty Sturges, who was a niece to Dave Sturges, proprietor of the Sturges House.

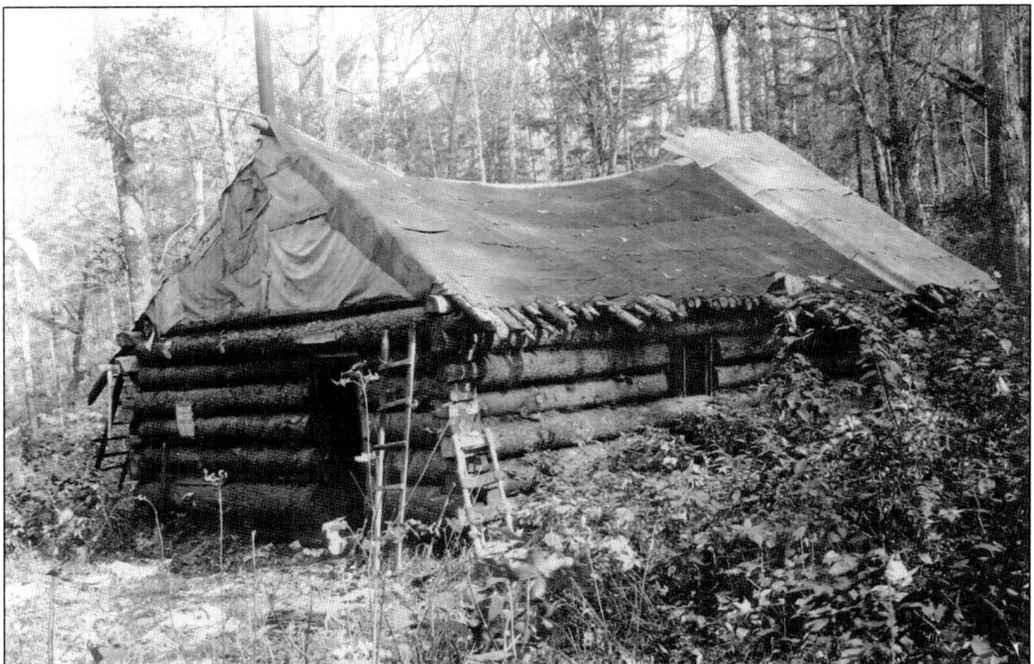
Some hunting camps were built with whatever material they could get their hands on. This camp was at Potash Mountain in 1919 and belonged to the Slack brothers.

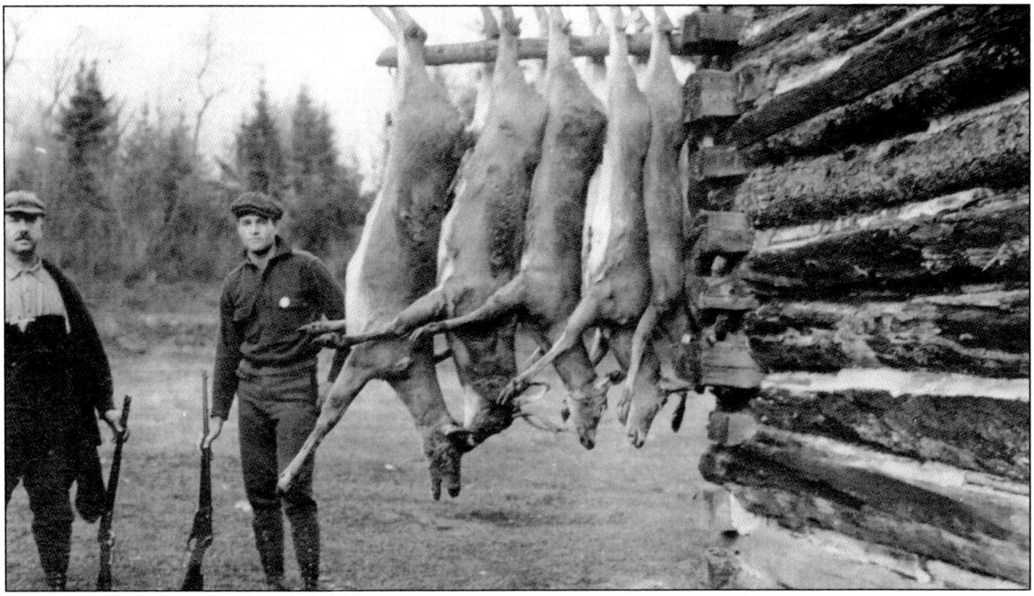

Oregon territory consisted of the area out toward Elm Lake Road and past Rhinelander's Estate, following the Kunjamuk River upstream. In 1918, a large group of men would go out hunting and it would be possible for each one of them to bring back a deer. The deer population was plentiful in those days.

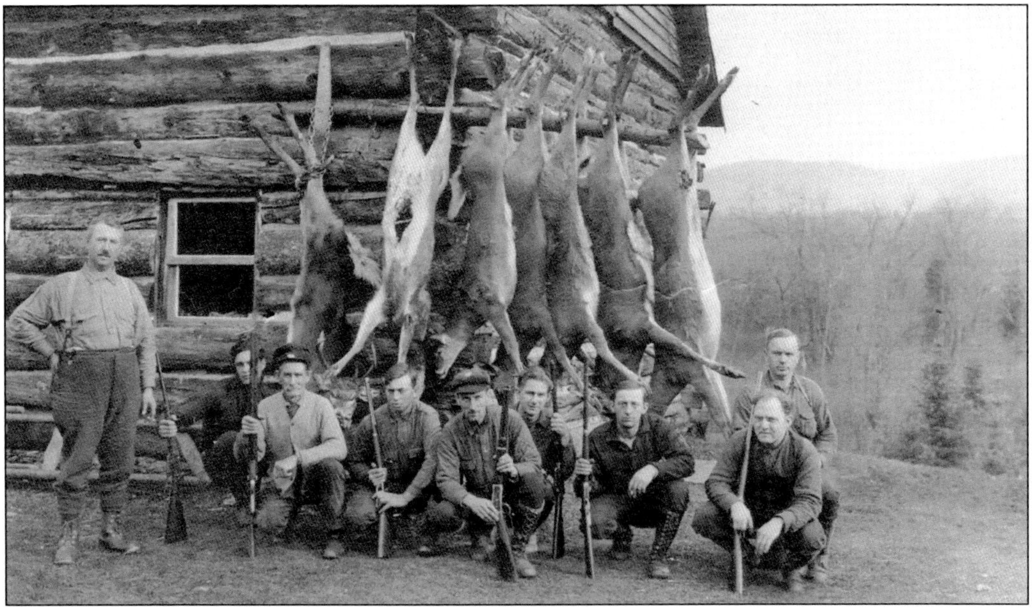

There are seven deer for seven guns. Not a bad day of hunting for these men in the Oregon territory in 1918.

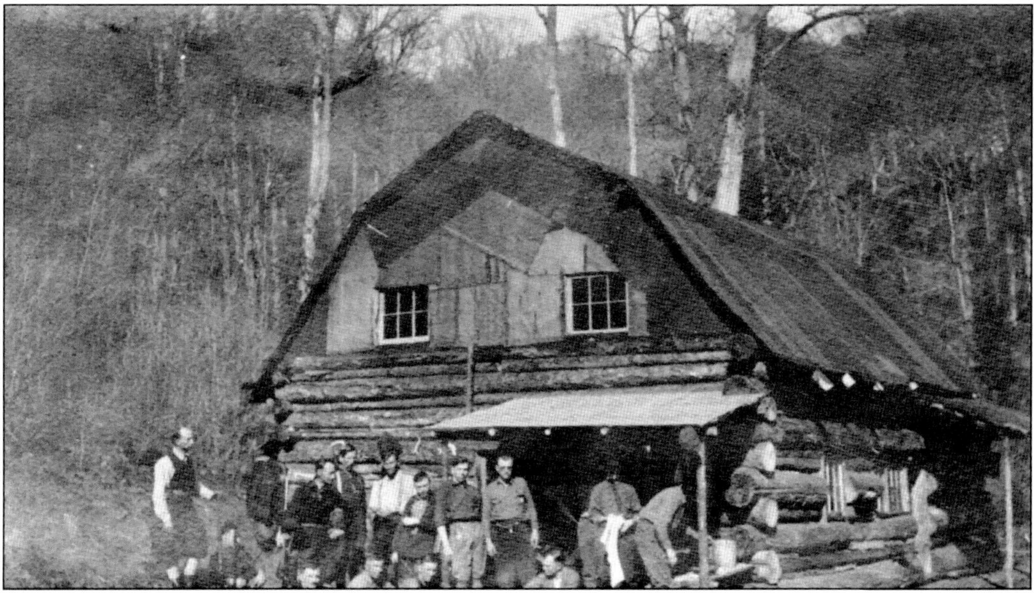

The Slack brothers had a hunting camp at Whitaker Lake. Later in the 1930s, Deerfoot Lodge would take over this area as a Christian boy's camp.

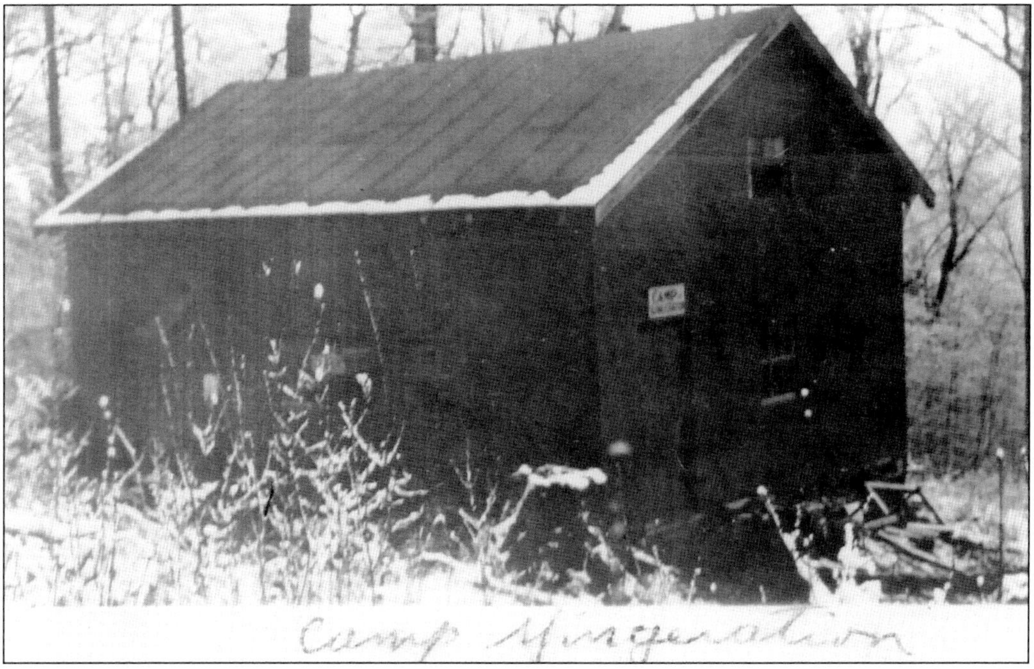

Another Slack brothers' camp was Camp Gingeration. Many hunting parties came from this camp. The Slack brothers included Dave, Thomas, George, and Malcolm, all sons of Benajah and Jennie Aird Slack.

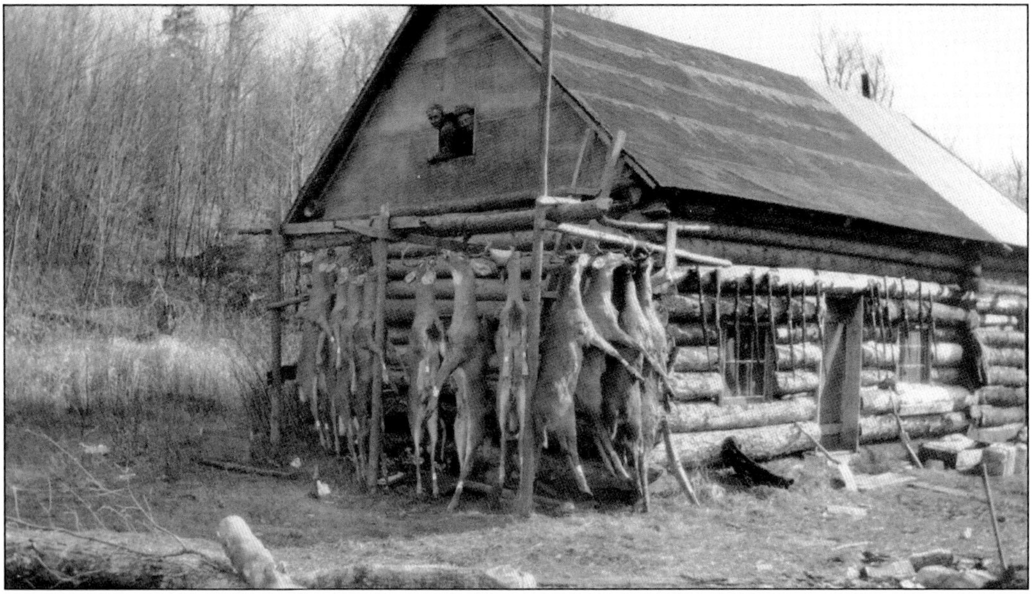

Mossy Fly is north of Fawn Lake and south of Potash Mountain. Mel Slack had a hunting camp there, and the deer were just as numerous there as at the other Slack camps.

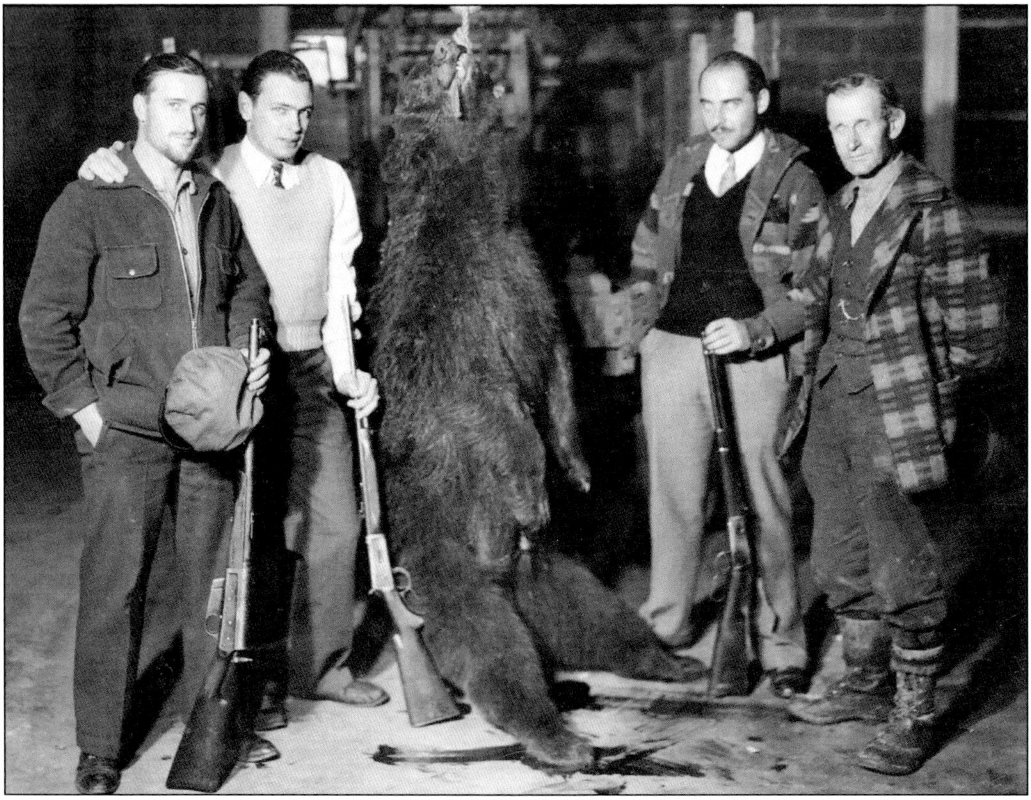

Bear hunting was just as popular as deer hunting. Sometimes the city sportsman would hunt in his business suit, so one could usually tell the difference between the guide and the sportsman just by their clothing.

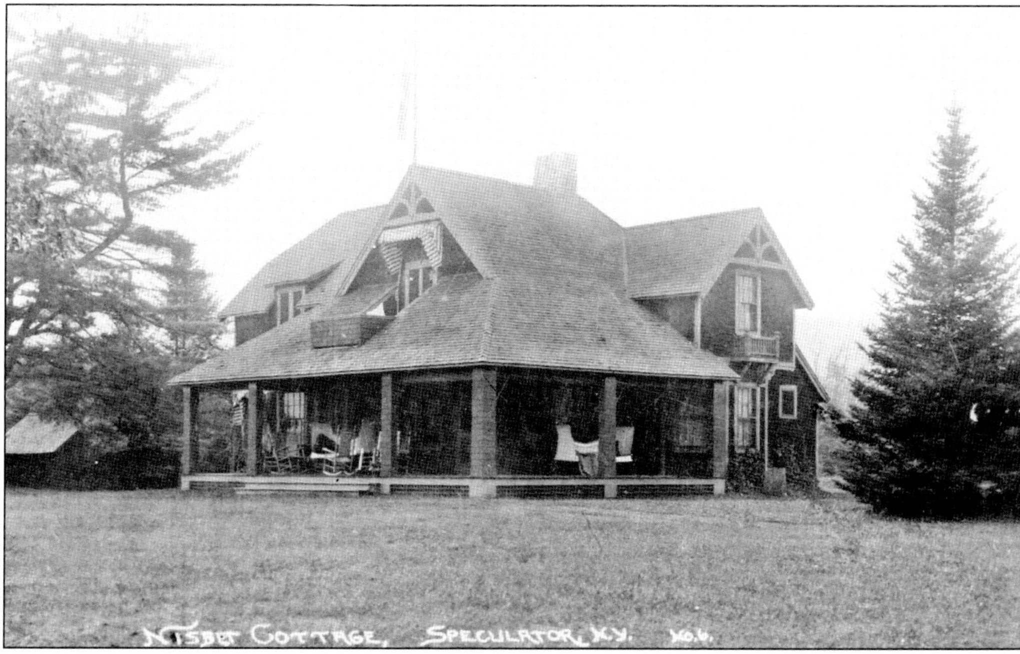

E. Barton Whitney, a lawyer from Gloversville, bought land adjacent to the village beach from Aaron Sturges in 1889, and he built the first summer residence in Speculator. Charles S. Nisbet of Amsterdam bought the residence in 1910 and called it Nisbet. Later it was part of the Gables Motel and then the Lake Pleasant Inn.

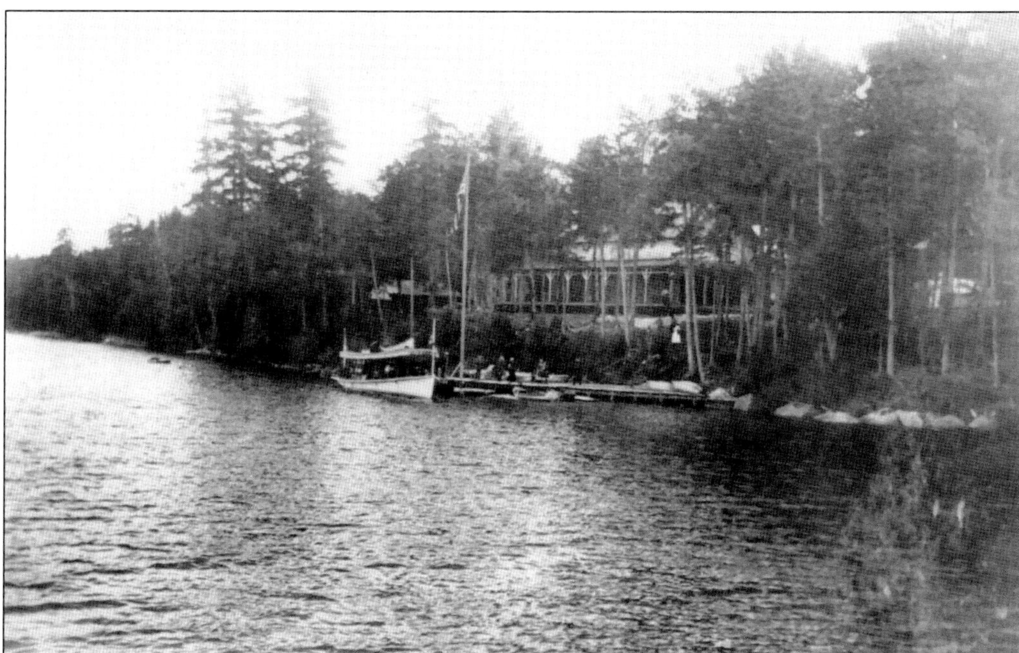

A group of New York businessmen—Emil Meyrowitz, Charles Shay, and Carl Jussen—acquired 100 acres of land near Cherry Brook. In 1895, Meyrowitz bought out the other two and erected Bearhurst, which still stands today.

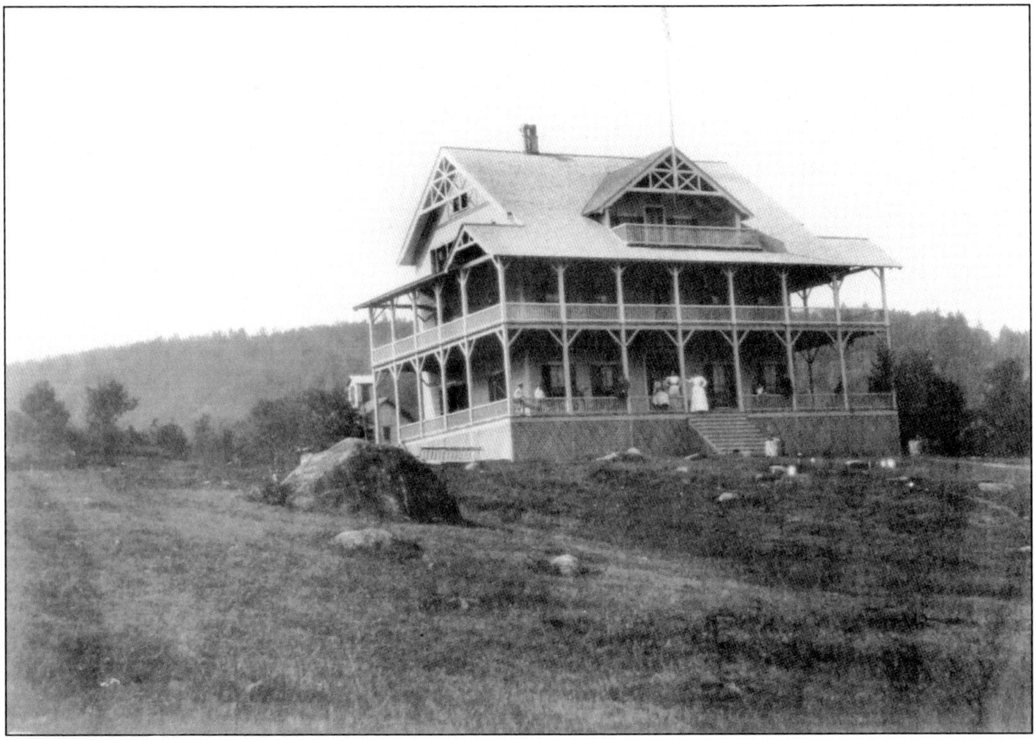

John L. Hill, a prominent Brooklyn attorney, bought land at the head of Lake Pleasant in 1891 and built a three-story summer residence that remains today. He named it Derloch, and in 1910 he willed Derloch to Ada Higgins, who sold it to David Chalmers in 1918.

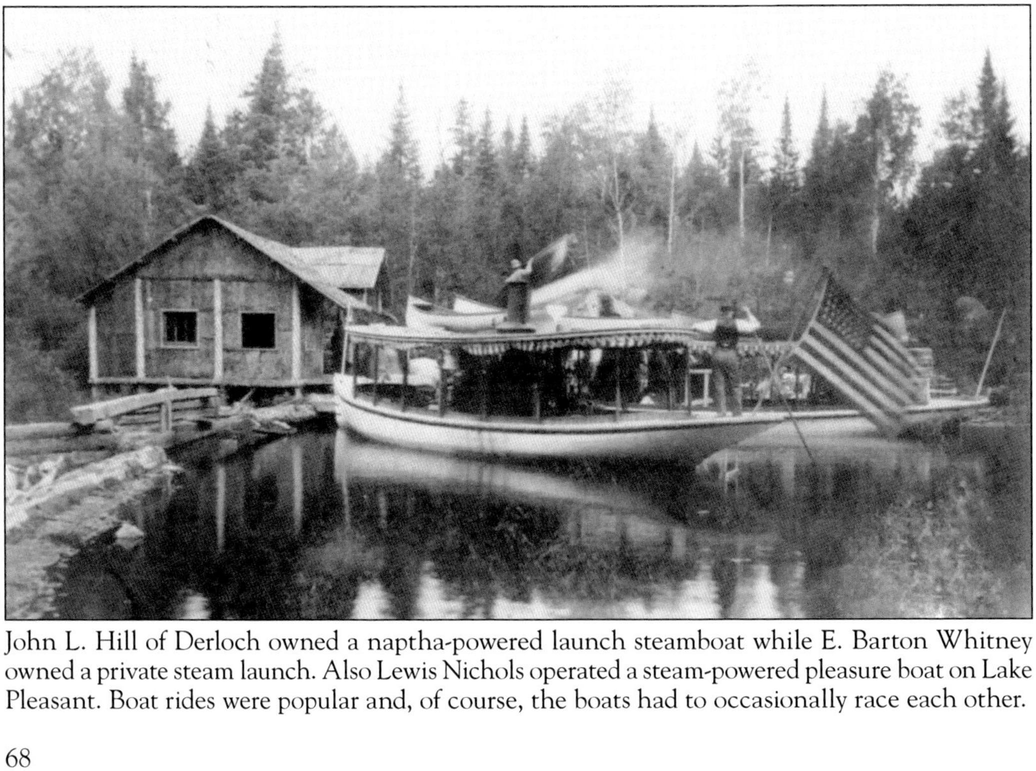

John L. Hill of Derloch owned a naptha-powered launch steamboat while E. Barton Whitney owned a private steam launch. Also Lewis Nichols operated a steam-powered pleasure boat on Lake Pleasant. Boat rides were popular and, of course, the boats had to occasionally race each other.

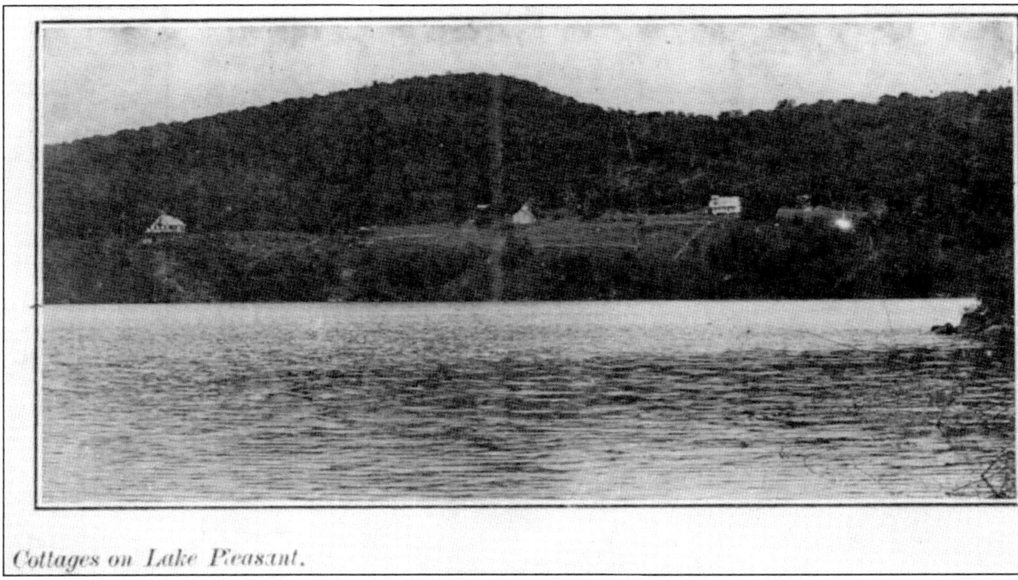

Many cottages were built on the shores of Lake Pleasant, as this picture testifies of the south shore. Cottages could be seen sprouting up in the early 1900s, not only on the shores of Lake Pleasant but also on the shores of Lake Sacandaga, Echo Lake, and Oxbow Lake.

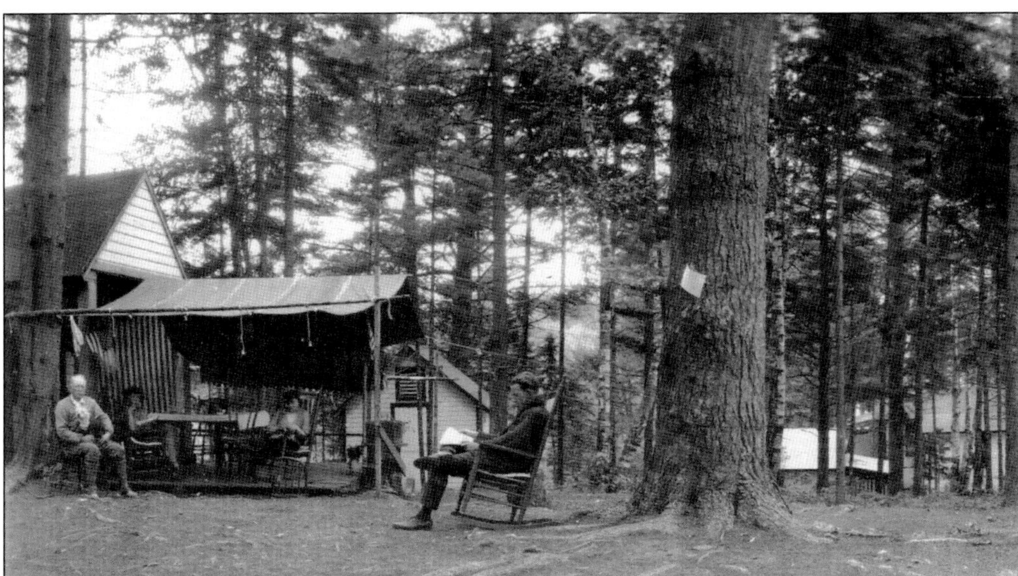

Camp Demarest on Lake Sacandaga was a true example of how the new cottages looked in this area. Wooden buildings as well as tarps and tents were used to camp out in the Adirondacks on a cool summer day.

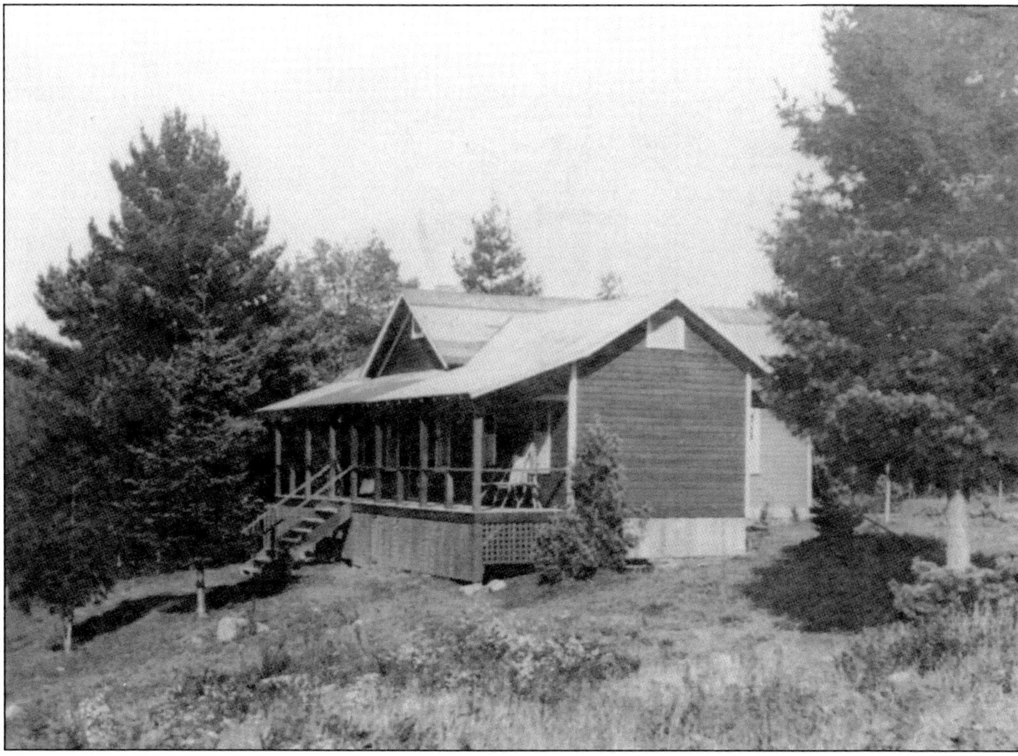

This camp was situated on the shores of Oxbow Lake. About half of Oxbow Lake is in the town of Lake Pleasant. It is a unique, small lake shaped like an oxbow.

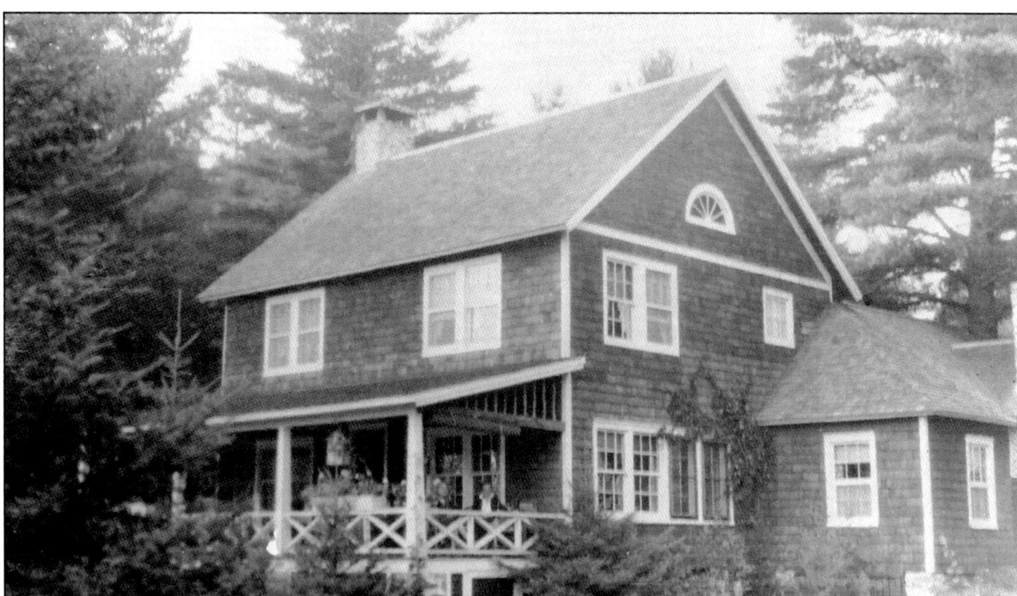

The Kline-LeFavour camp on the shores of Lake Pleasant is a wonderful example of the use of wooden shingles on the side of cottages. Shingle making was an occupation that many local men did to help support their families.

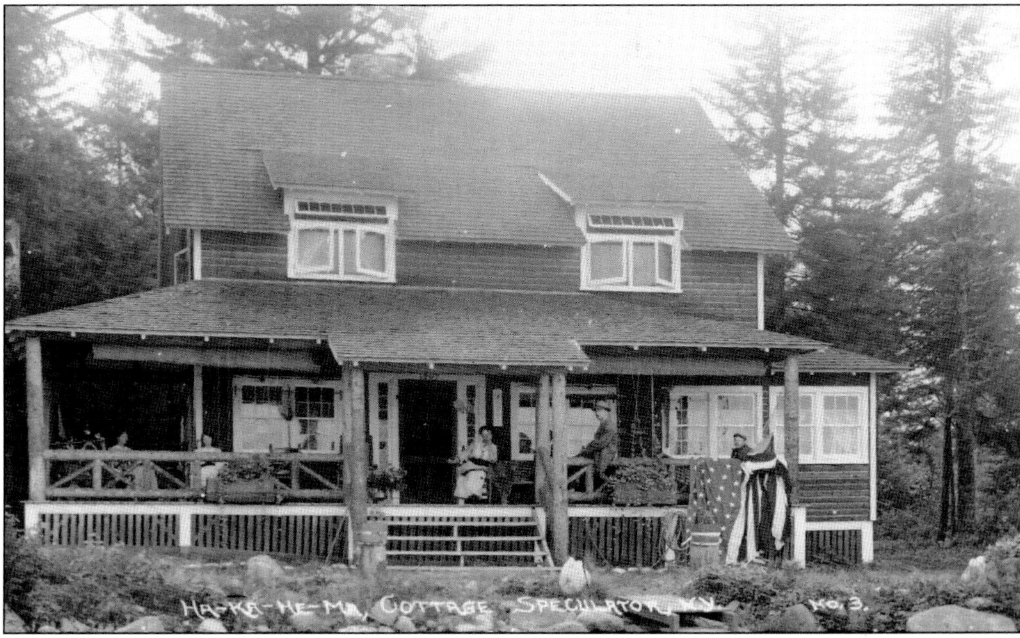

Ha-Ka-He-Ma Cottage was located on the shores of Lake Pleasant and was used as a boardinghouse at times. Many cottage owners named their cottages with unique names and the meanings have been passed from one owner to another or passed down through a family.

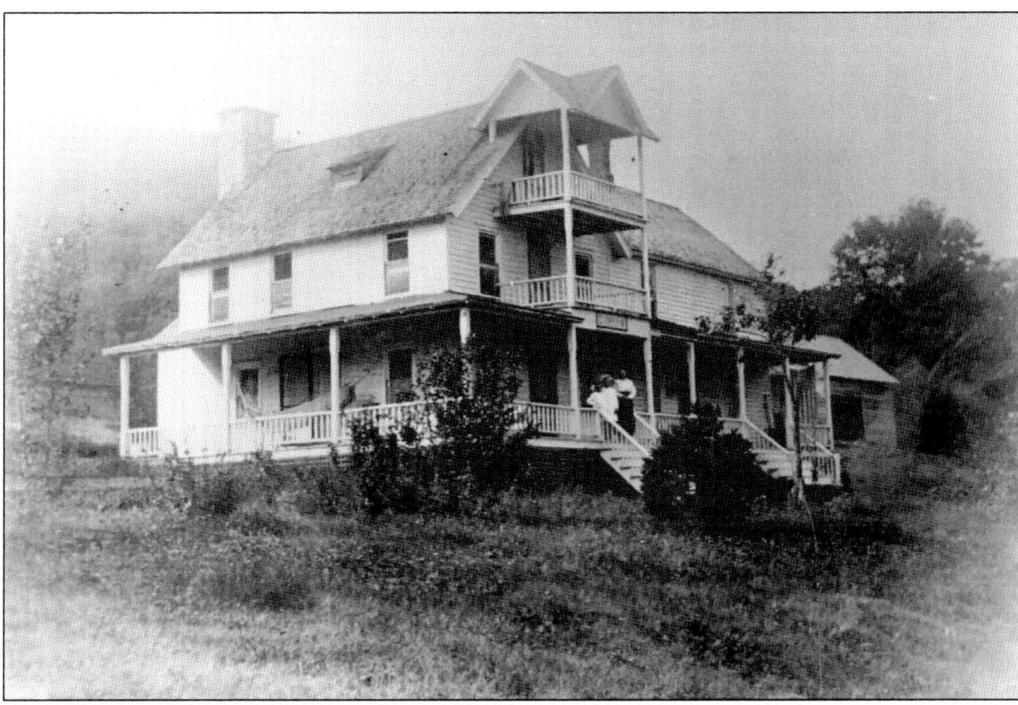

Madam Setag started Camp Setag in 1914 for young girls. Situated on the south shore of Lake Pleasant, it ran for at least six seasons from July to Labor Day weekend. The girls would perform plays from classical works like *Henry VIII* and *Mary Queen of Scots*.

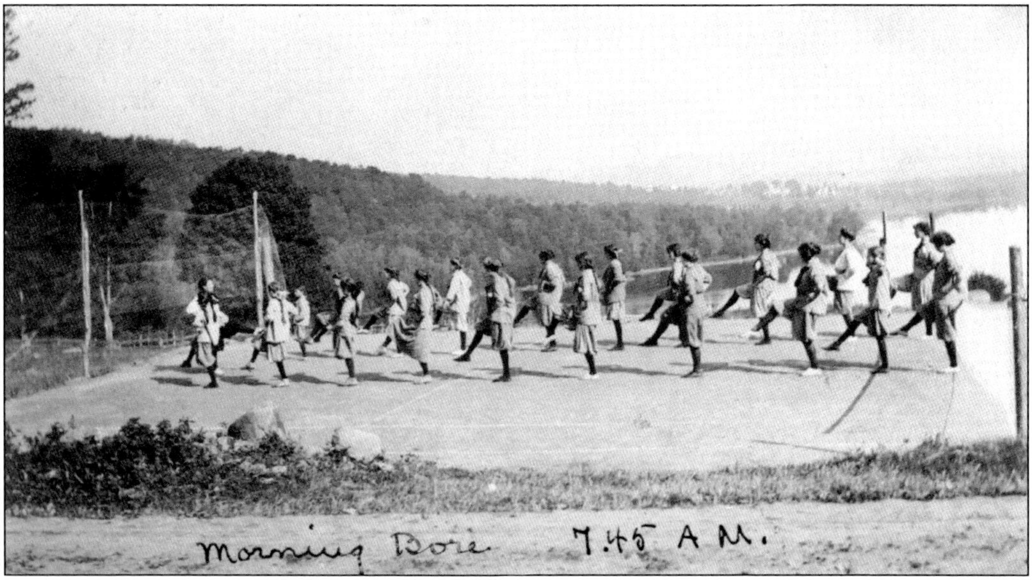

Camp Setag started at 7:45 a.m. with exercises. The girls went on hikes up Hamilton Mountain and Blue Mountain Lake, picnicked at Fly Lake, took excursions to Piseco Lake, canoed and swam on Lake Pleasant, and took hayrides to wherever they went.

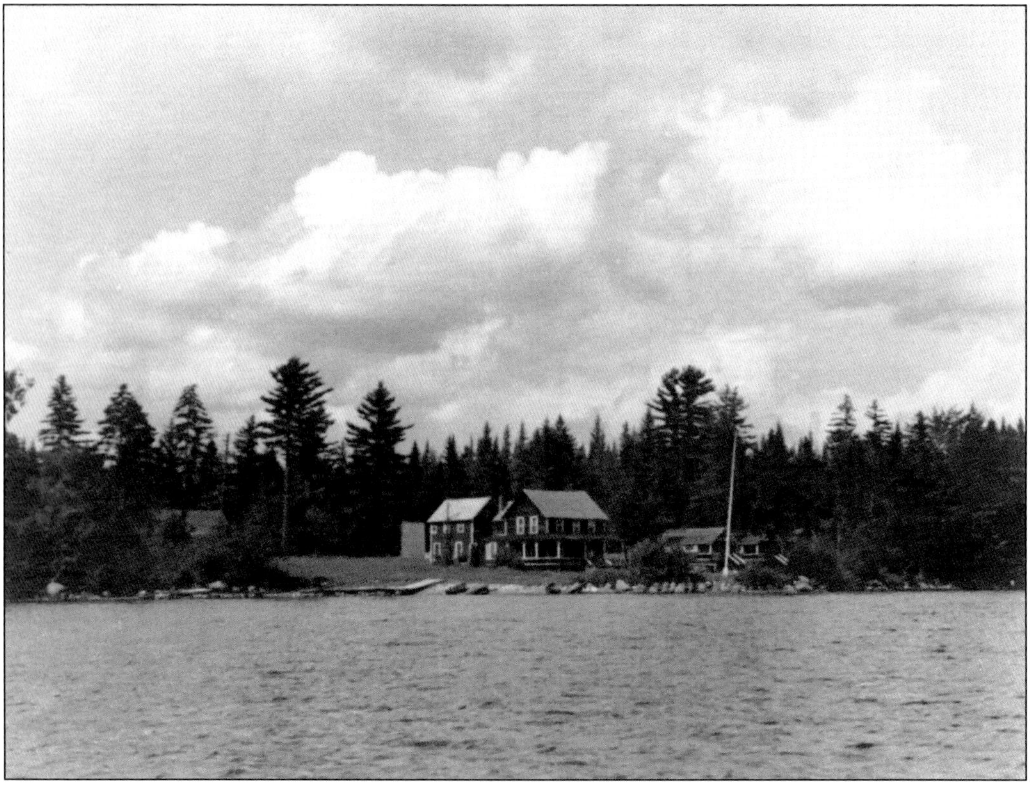

Kamp Kun-ja-muk for boys on the north shore of Lake Pleasant was run by Conrad Saphier. The camp started in 1915 and ended around 1941; some of the camp buildings are still used today by private cottage owners.

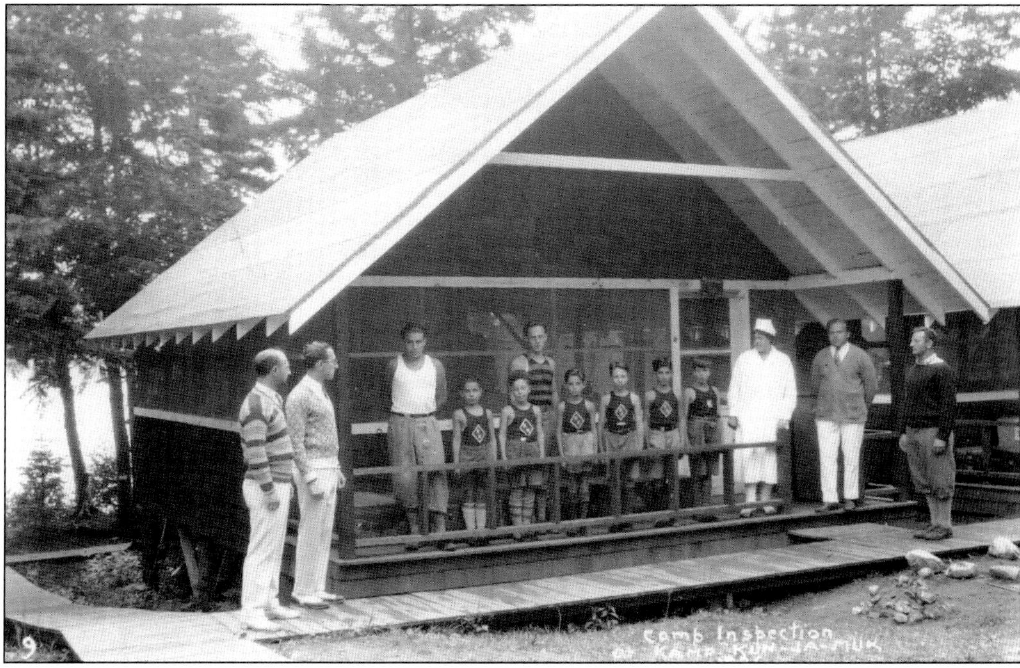

This picture was taken in 1926 and is the camp inspection at Kamp Kun-ja-muk. The boys enjoyed many great activities, including swimming, boating, canoeing, and hiking in the Adirondacks.

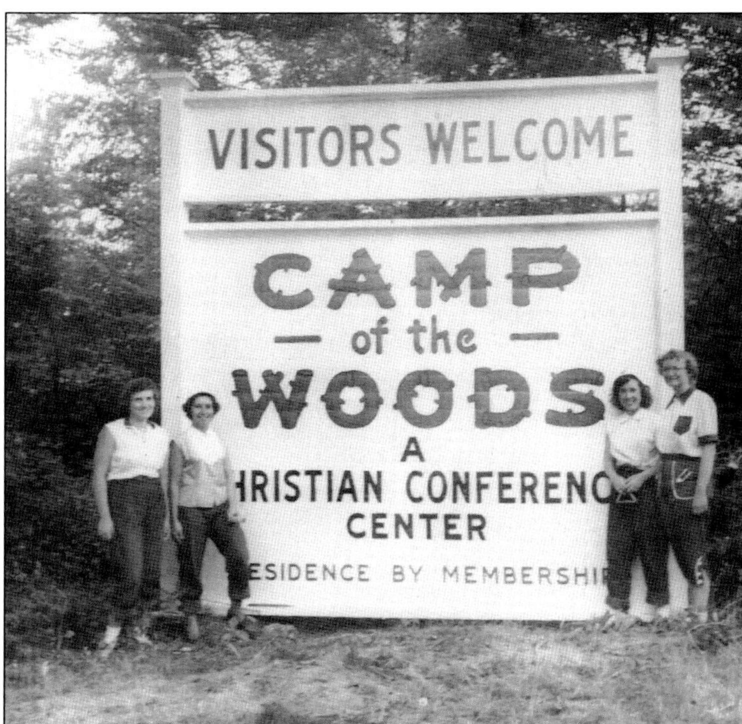

Camp-of-the-Woods is operated on the old Spier and Brown Tract of land at the foot of Lake Pleasant. The camp was developed in 1917 by George F. "Pops" Tibbitts to "build an altar to Jehovah on the shores of Lake Pleasant."

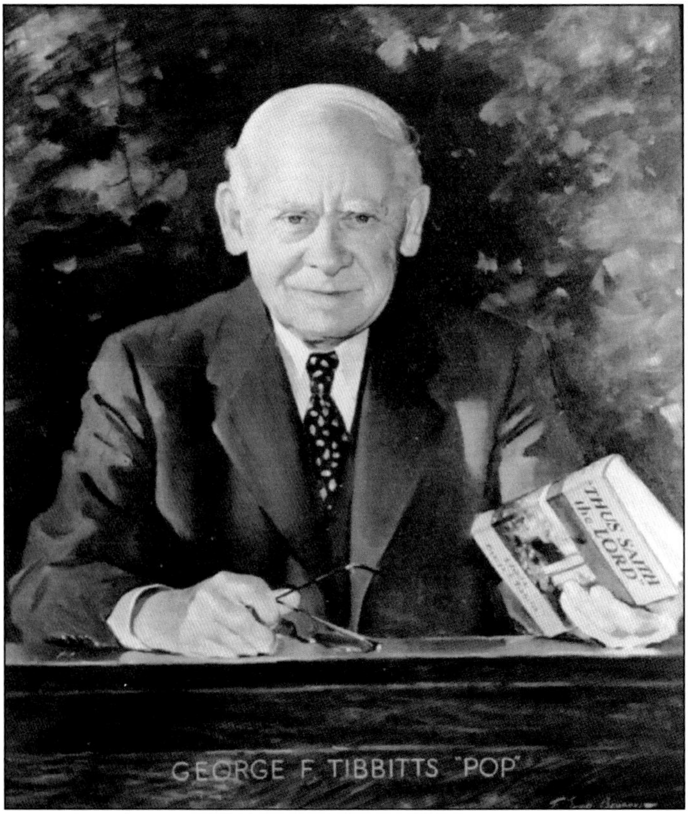

George F. "Pops" Tibbitts, founder of Camp-of-the-Woods, worked with the Young Men's Christian Association. In Cincinnati and Lynchburg, he first took young men on camping trips, and he found a kinship with the camping ministry of the gospel. He was one of the founders of YMCA Camp Dudley, the Silver Bay Conference Center, and Camp Glen Erie on Lake George.

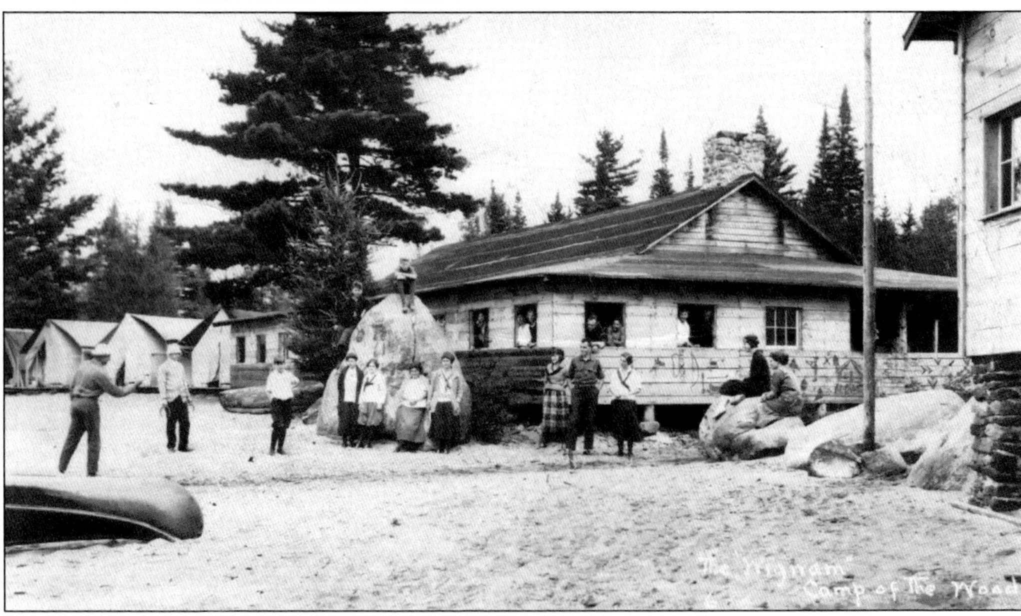

The Wigwam, a building that now houses the post office and guest service offices, and the Rock, a large rock that has been there since before Camp-of-the-Woods, are main features on the white sandy beach at Camp-of-the-Woods. A protected swimming area is provided for campers as well as boating, canoeing, and sailing.

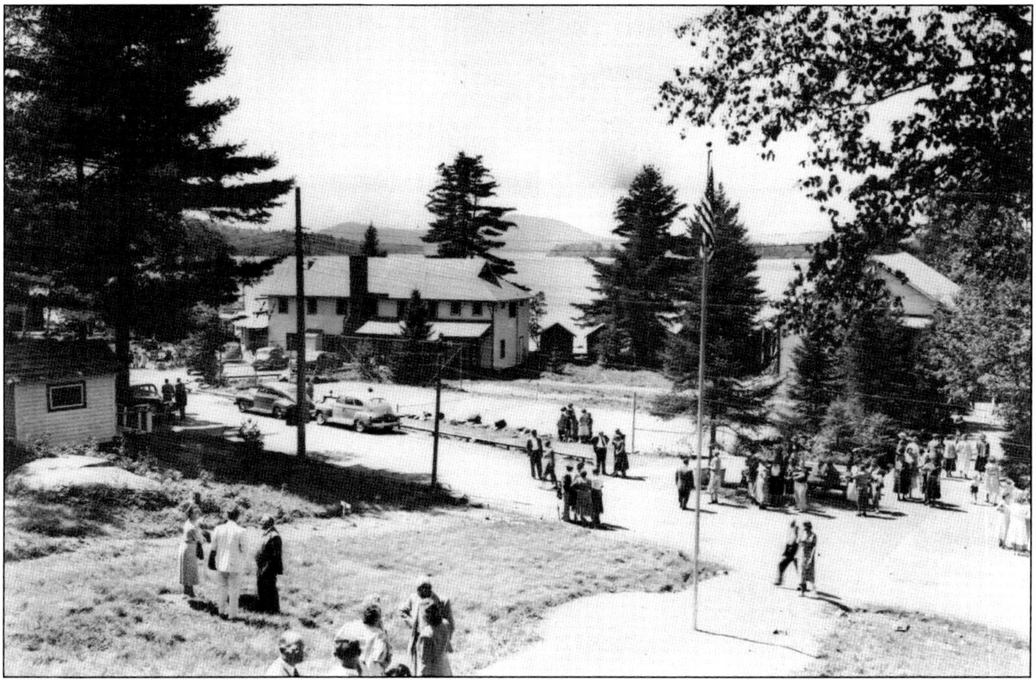

Shown are some of the Camp-of–the-Woods cabins and service buildings looking across Lake Pleasant. Today Camp-of-the-Woods consists of the addition of Tapawingo, a girl's camp on an island, and the Woodlands Conference Center.

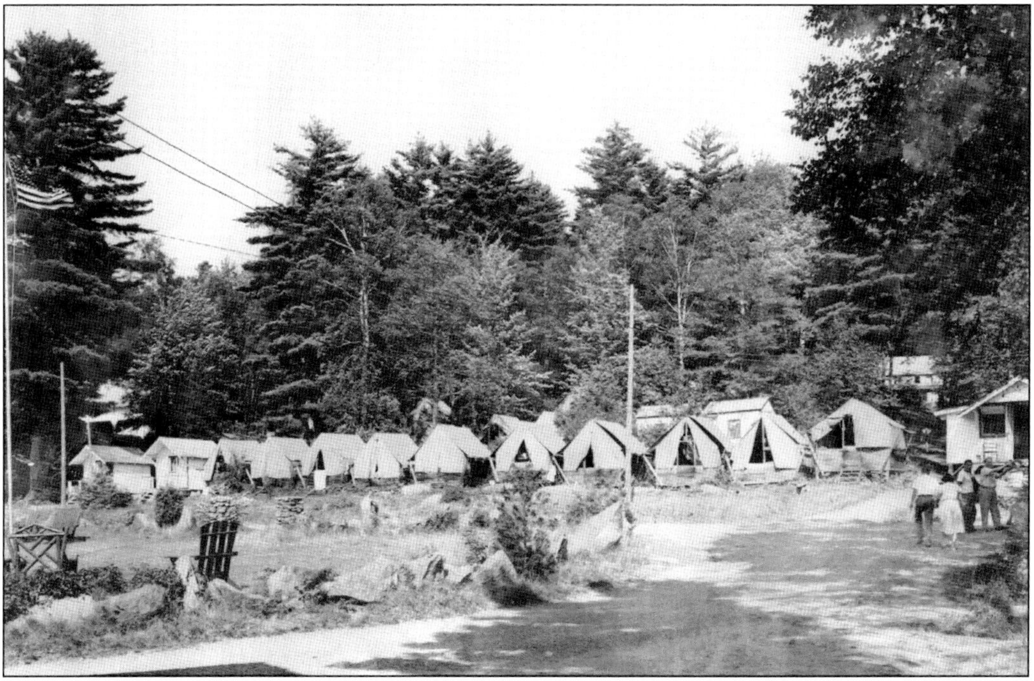

The elevation of Camp-of-the-Woods is 1,724 feet and the rear of the camp rises to 2,000 feet, overlooking Lake Pleasant and the Adirondack Mountains. At first much of the camp consisted of tents on platforms.

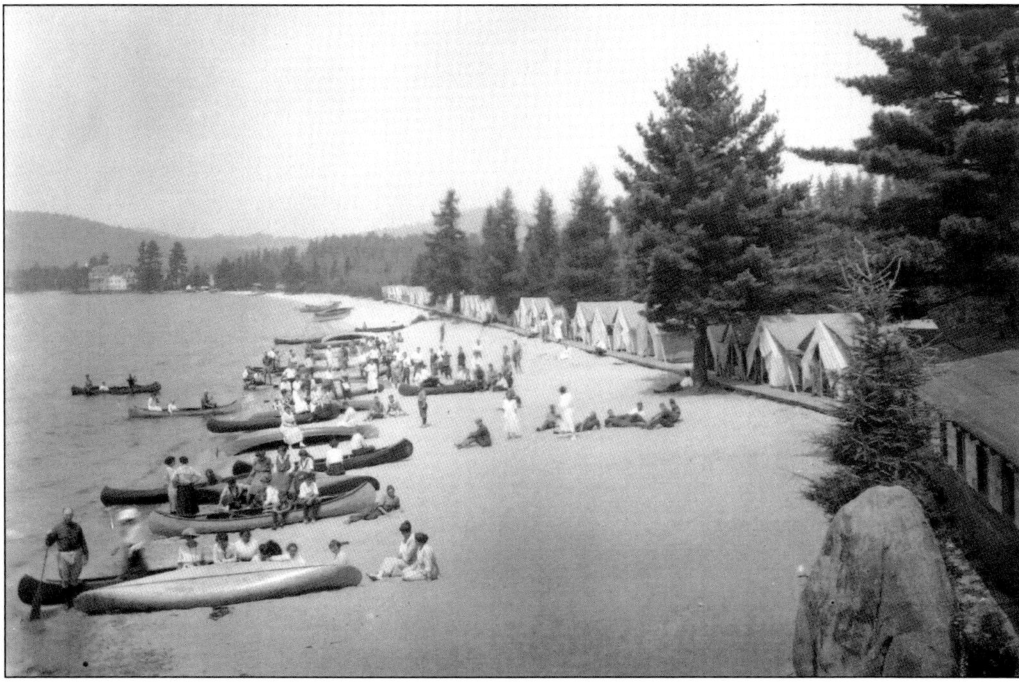

The tremendously wide sandy beach caught Pop Tibbitt's eyes first, and the beach was the perfect place to set up tents on platforms. The tents eventually were replaced by tentals, wooden buildings that look just like tents, but the beach will always remain the beauty that God provided. Camp-of-the-Woods, its theme being "Vacation . . . on Purpose," still runs all year long in Speculator, New York.

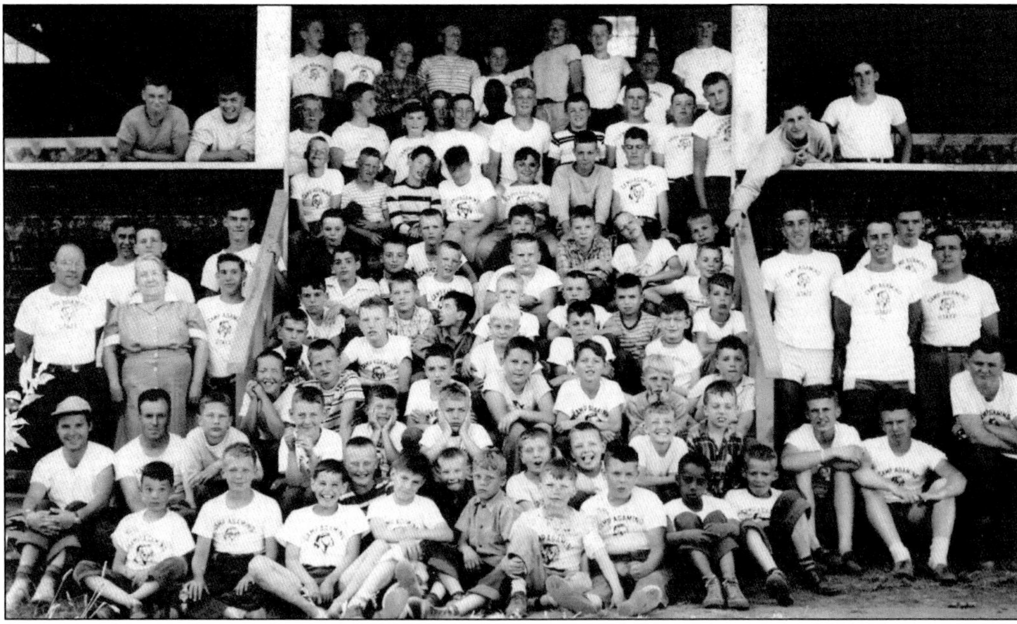

Camp Agaming was owned by the Gloversville YMCA and first started on Piseco Lake in 1915. In 1923, the YMCA purchased land on the north shore of Lake Pleasant and the camp continued there until 1966. Approximately 95 boys attended the camp the first year it was on Lake Pleasant.

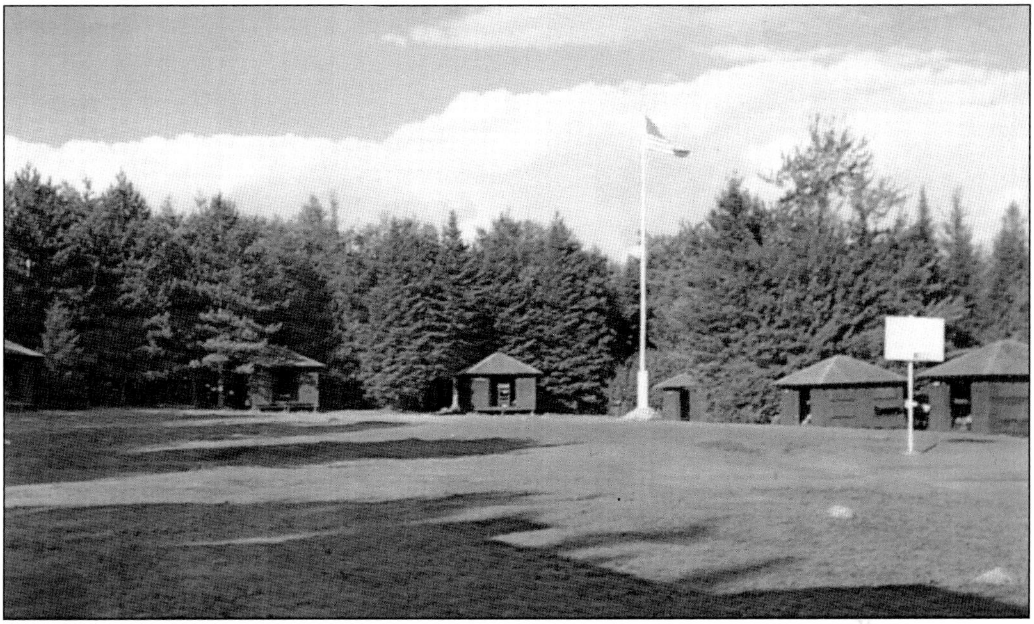

"Agaming, Agaming, we get up when the birdies sing. Where the green grass grows and it never snows. Camp Agaming!" The name of the camp was created through a contest with the Native American word meaning "on the shore." The picture above is of the camper's cabins.

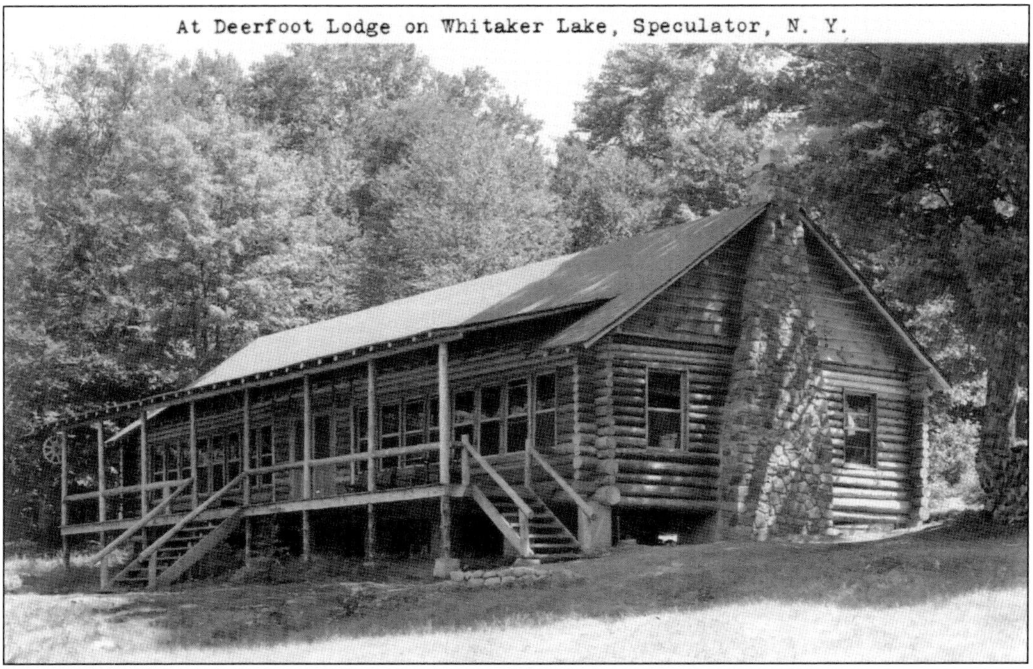

Deerfoot Lodge started at the Wilber's hunting camp on the Kunjamuk River in the Oregon territory. Eventually it was moved to Whitaker Lake where there was also a hunting camp. Harvey Kunz founded the lodge in 1929.

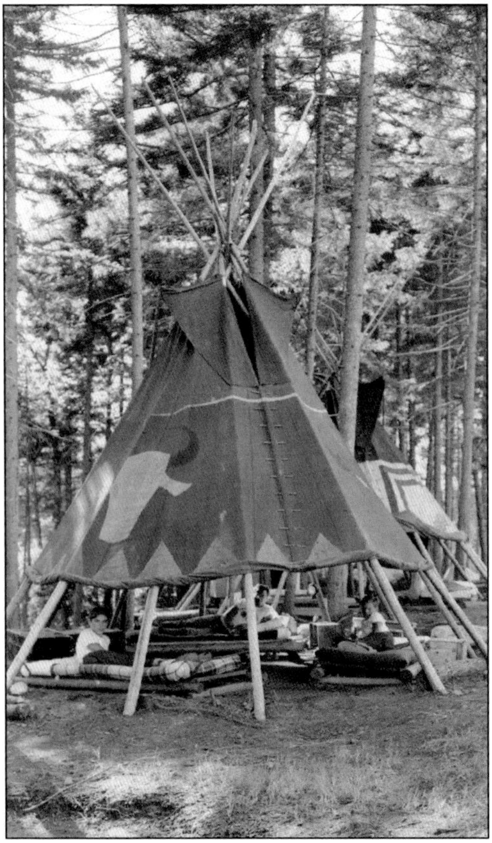

On Whitaker Lake there is an island called Indian Island where the older boys can camp out in teepees. The island can be accessed by a bridge built by the Deerfoot Lodge staff or by boats rowed from the swimming area.

Swimming, boating, canoeing, hiking, camp crafts, archery, and rifle shooting are just a few of the activities the boys can do while staying at this Christian camp for two weeks. Weeklong canoe and hiking trip adventures are also provided for the older boys. This camp still runs from June to August every summer.

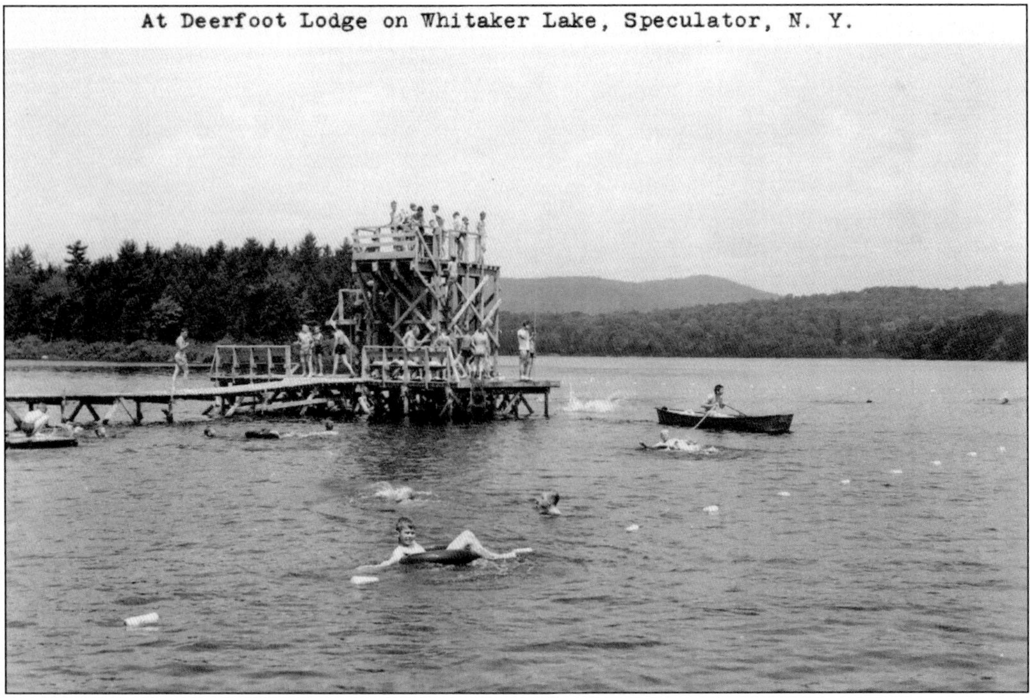

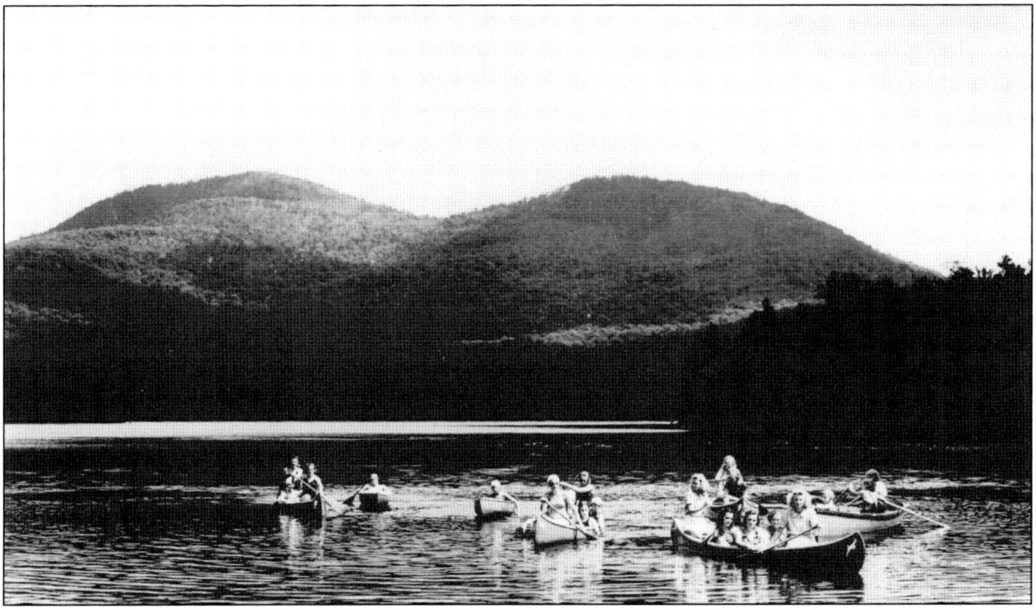

At one time there were even girls attending Deerfoot Lodge but soon only boys were allowed to attend. The purpose of Deerfoot Lodge was to provide a Christ-centered community in which men could grow to be like Him.

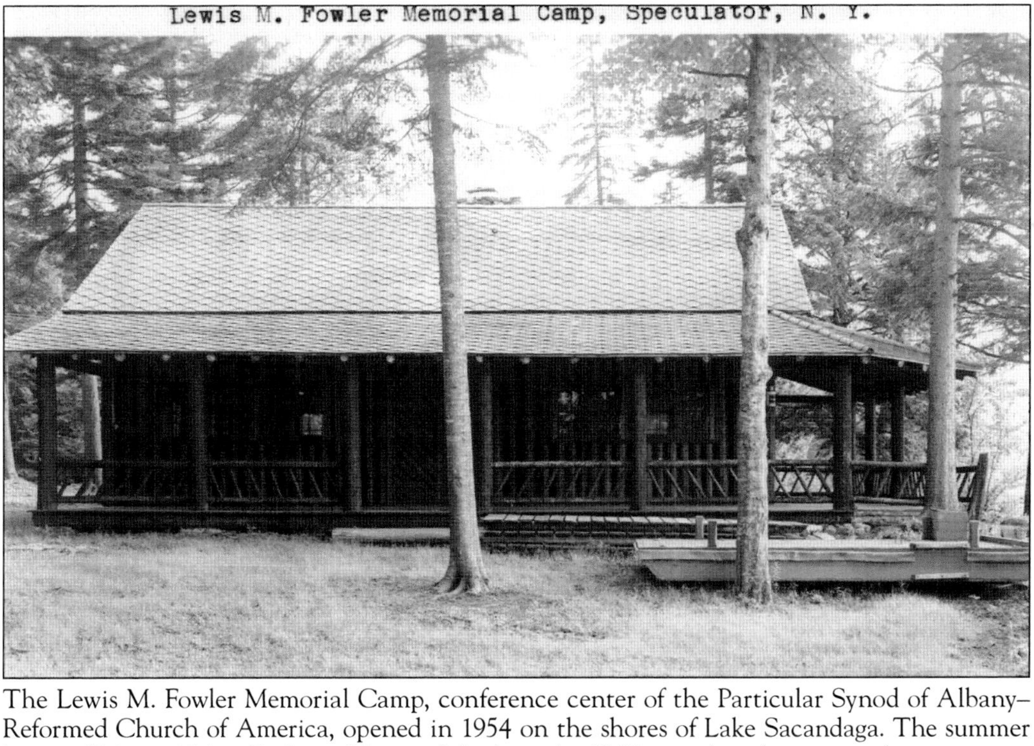

The Lewis M. Fowler Memorial Camp, conference center of the Particular Synod of Albany–Reformed Church of America, opened in 1954 on the shores of Lake Sacandaga. The summer home of Mr. and Mrs. Graham Olmstead, built in the 1920s, was bought to start the camp.

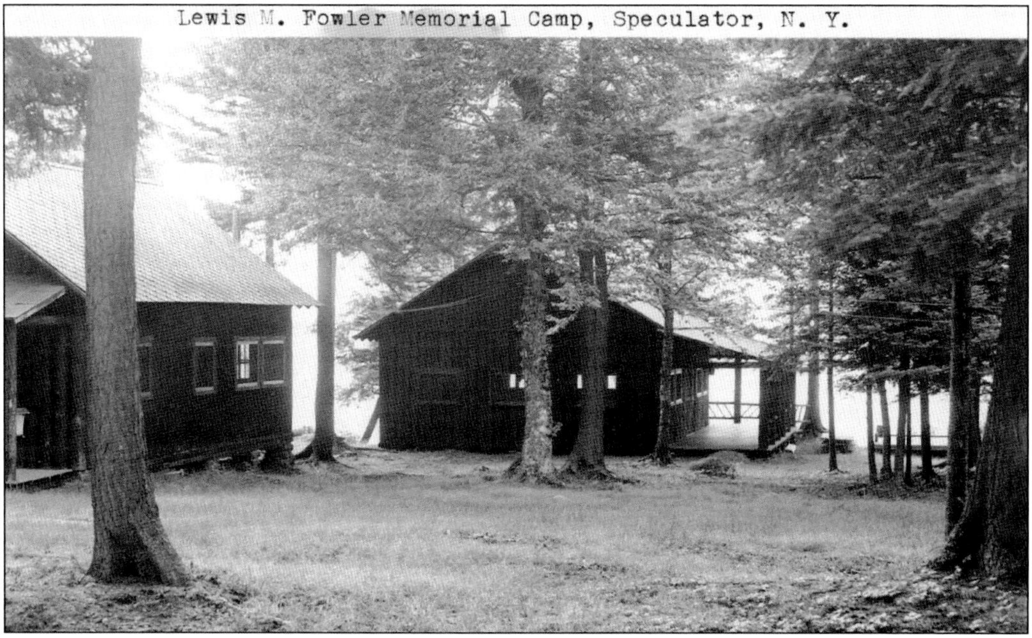

The living room lodge of the Olmsteads was used as a meeting room and the kitchen dining area was used as an infirmary. The sleeping lodge became the girl's dormitory, and the icehouse was converted into the boy's dormitory. Camp Fowler was dedicated in 1954. The above photograph is of the infirmary and lake lodge.

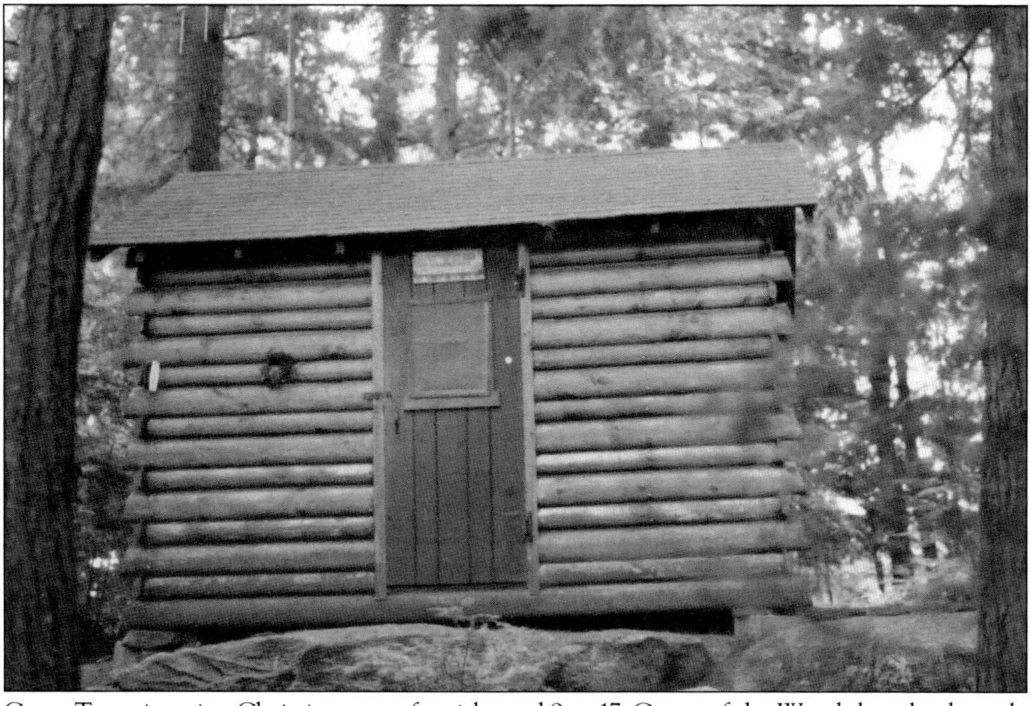

Camp Tapawingo is a Christian camp for girls aged 9 to 17. Camp-of-the-Woods bought the only island on Lake Pleasant in 1958, and Camp Tapawingo opened in 1959 with Vida Wood as director. Wickiup is one of the original buildings on the island. (Joy Huseland collection.)

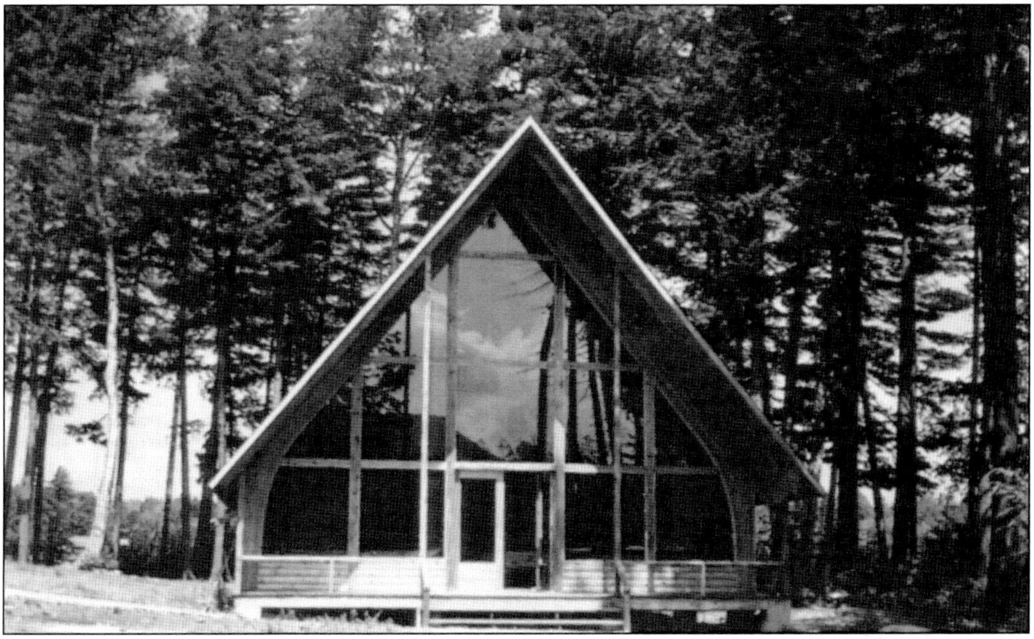

The chapel at Tapawingo is used mostly for vespers, working on badges, free time during rainstorms, and evening activities. Tapawingo means "place of joy." (Joy Huseland collection.)

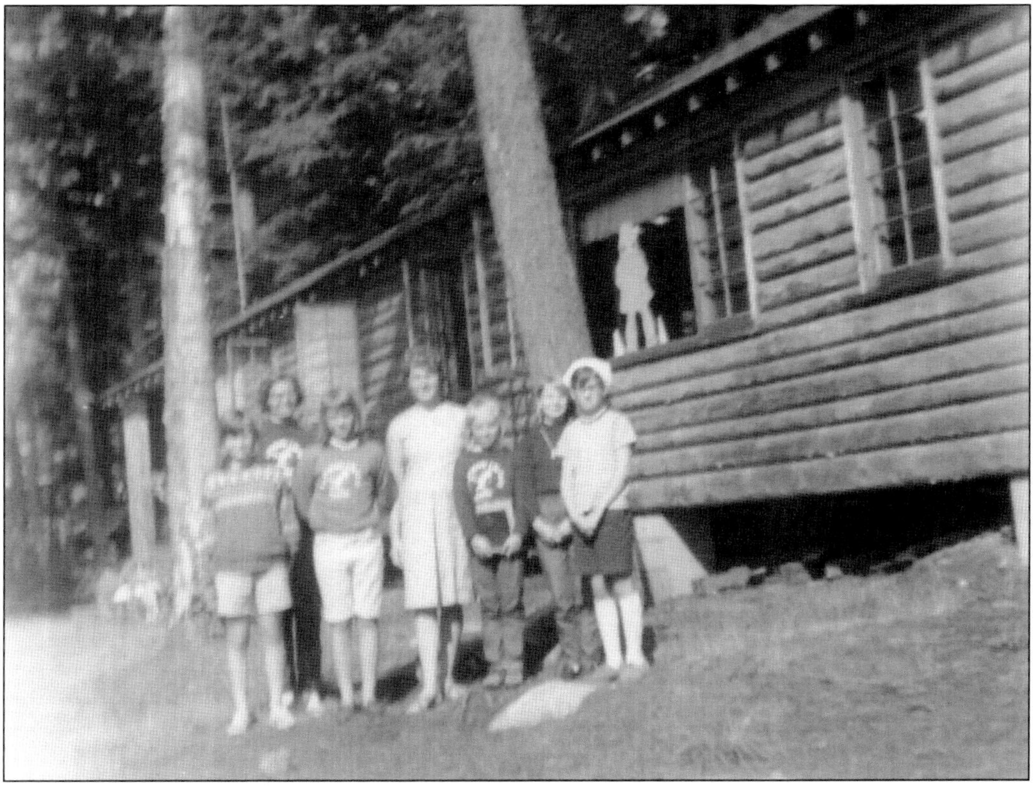

The main lodge for Camp Tapawingo holds the dining hall and offices. It was previously the summer home of the Woikes who sold the island to Camp-of-the-Woods. (Joy Huseland collection.)

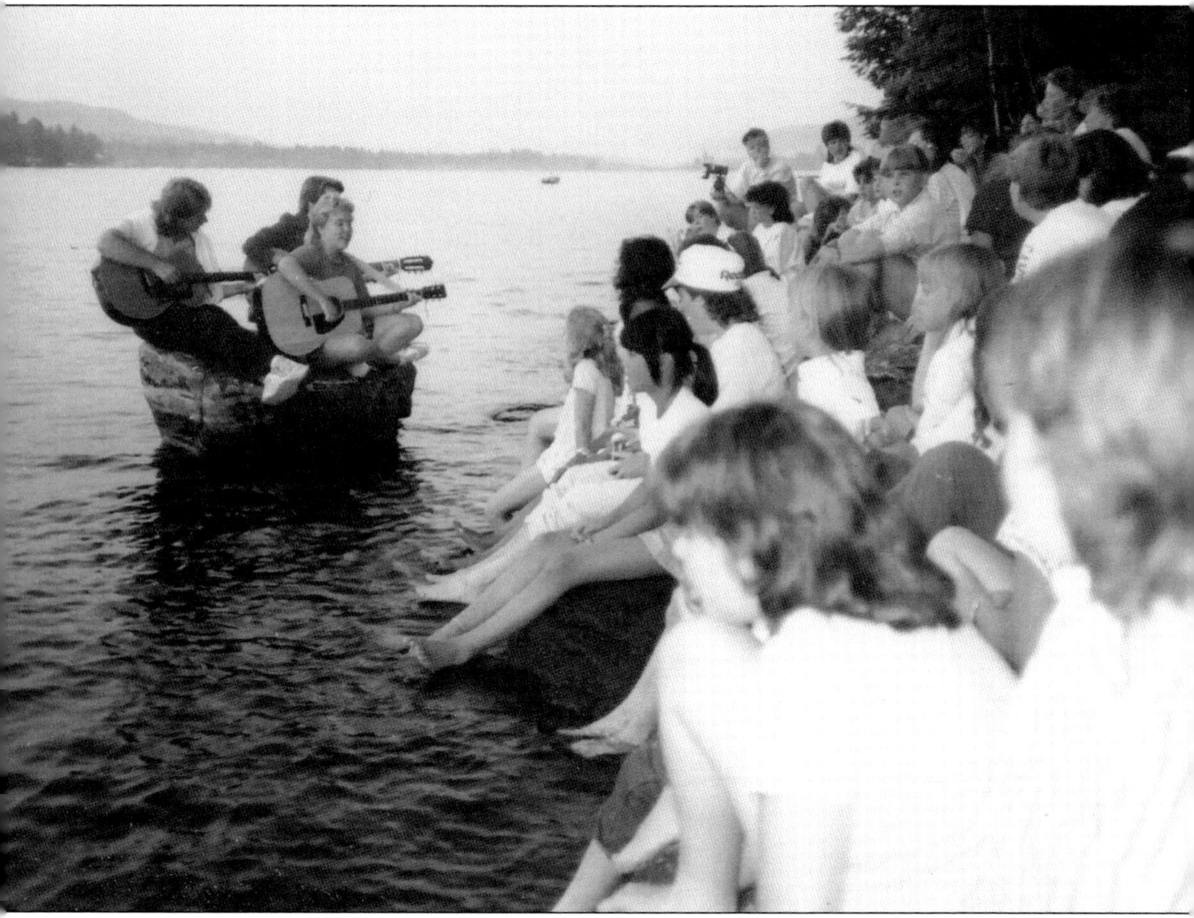

Every Sunday night at Camp Tapawingo vespers is held at the rocks and the girls sing "Go To the Rock of My Salvation." They watch the sunset and sing praise songs to the Lord. (Joy Huseland collection.)

Six

Logging, Fire Towers, and Hermits

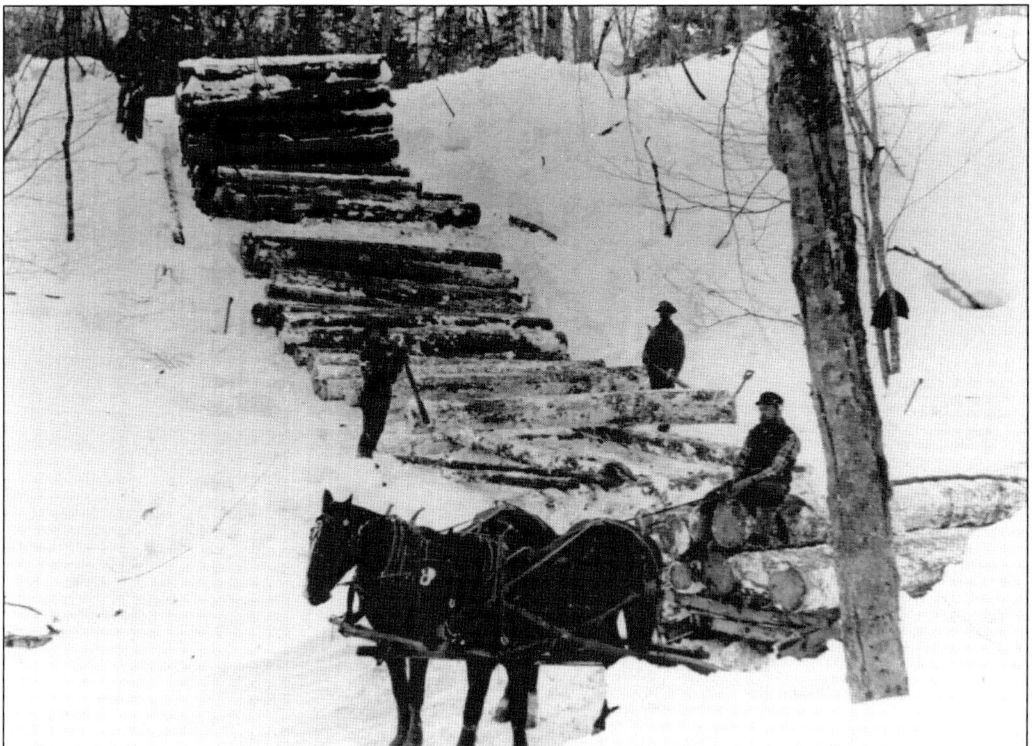

It was in the 1850s when lumber companies and private individuals moved into this area to log the virgin forest of the Adirondacks around Lake Pleasant and Speculator.

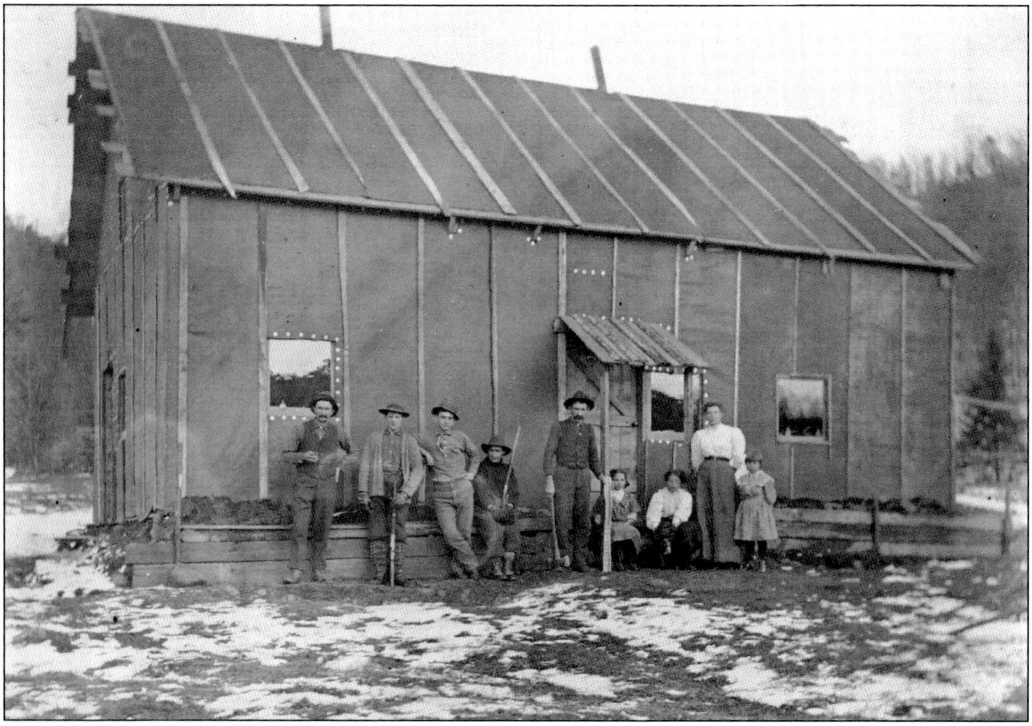

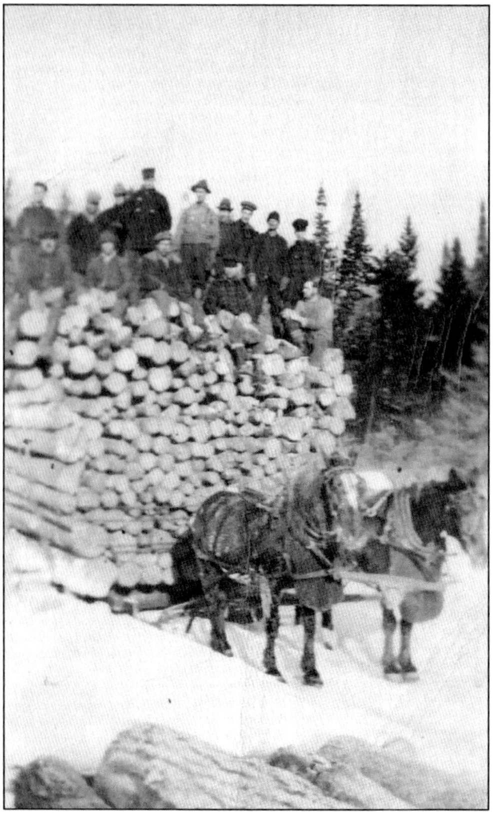

George Perkins was a lumberman from Warren County who hired men to work in the woods. His family stayed to make Speculator their home.

This photograph is of the Perkins team with a load of logs. Log bunks with steel runners were pulled with teams of horses to haul the heavy loads.

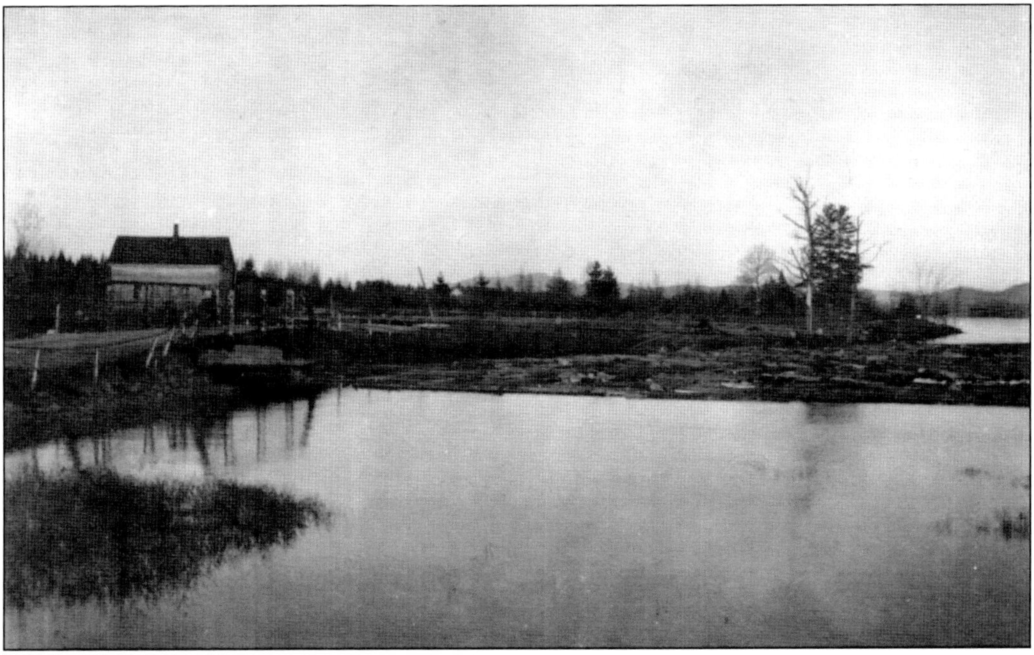

From the 1850s to the 1950s, logging was prevalent in the Lake Pleasant area. Axes and two-man saws were used to fell trees. The trees were then cut in lengths and hauled by horses to be stacked on the landings. When melting snow and spring rains swelled the creeks, the logs floated downstream with the aid of a small network of dams and sluices.

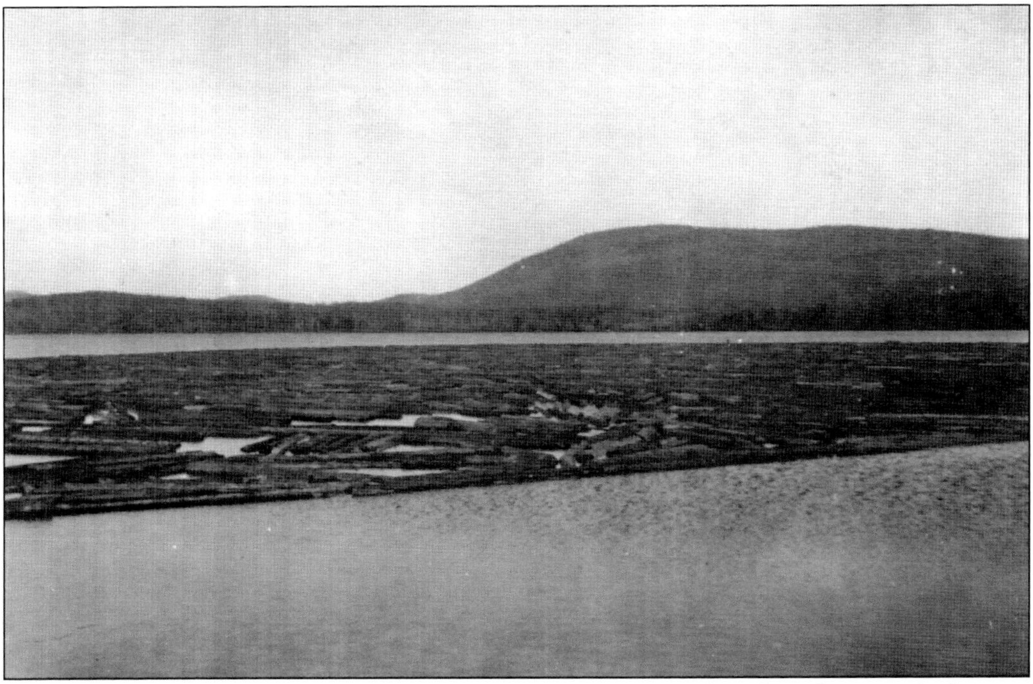

Logs were piled on the frozen lakes and ponds to be carried to market when the ice melted. It was a dangerous job with peaveys and poles to keep the logs moving. The floating logs went down the Sacandaga River to the International Paper Company Mills in Glens Falls.

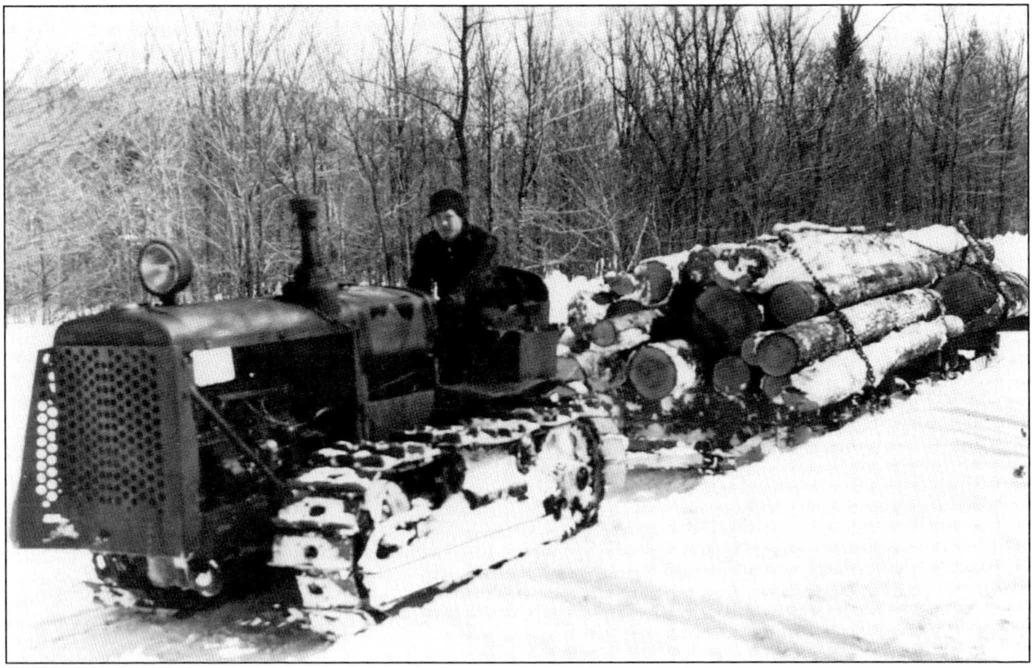

Bulldozers and tractors replaced horses to pull the heavy sleds. Several local mills existed around the area, and Tracy's Sawmill is still in business today.

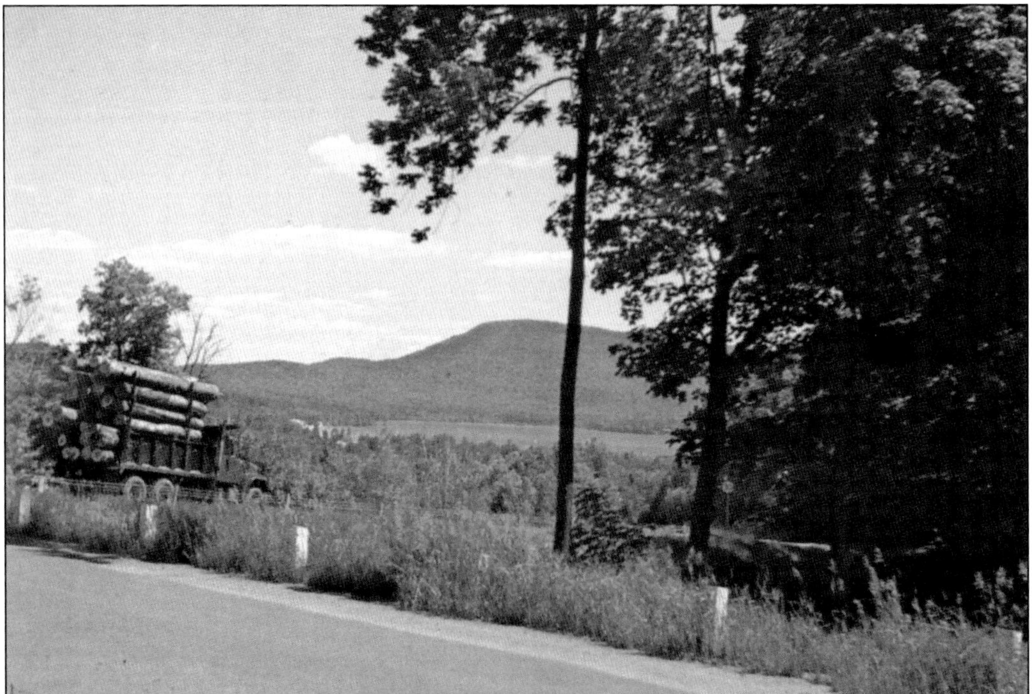

When new roads were built and old ones were improved, log trucks replaced the river drives.

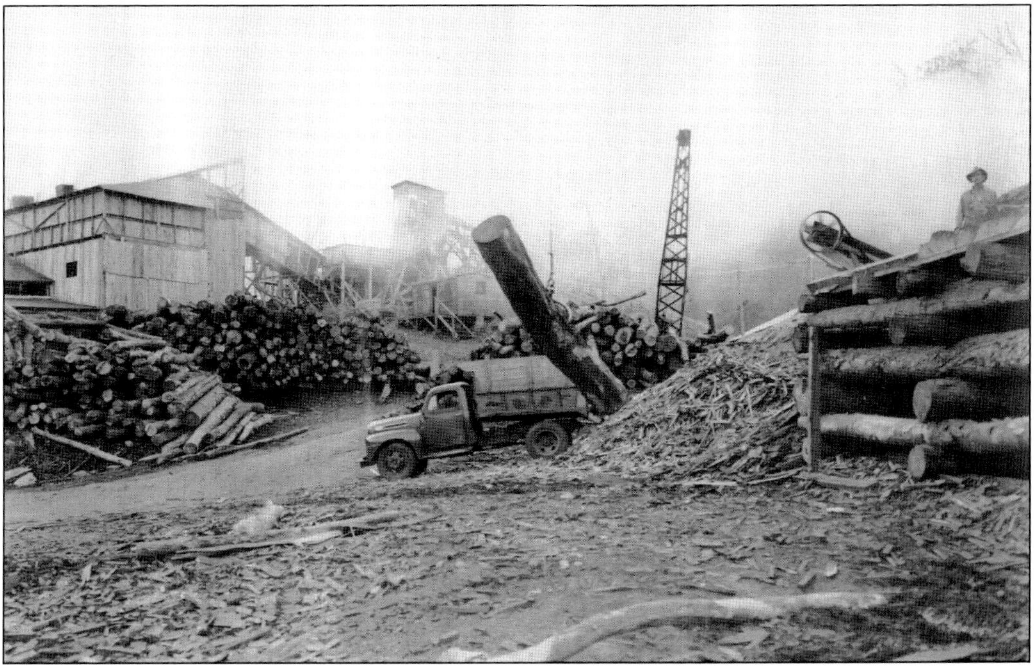

Down by the Burnham Mill Bridge, just below Speculator on the site of the former William Burnham Sawmill, Don Warner started a charcoal plant.

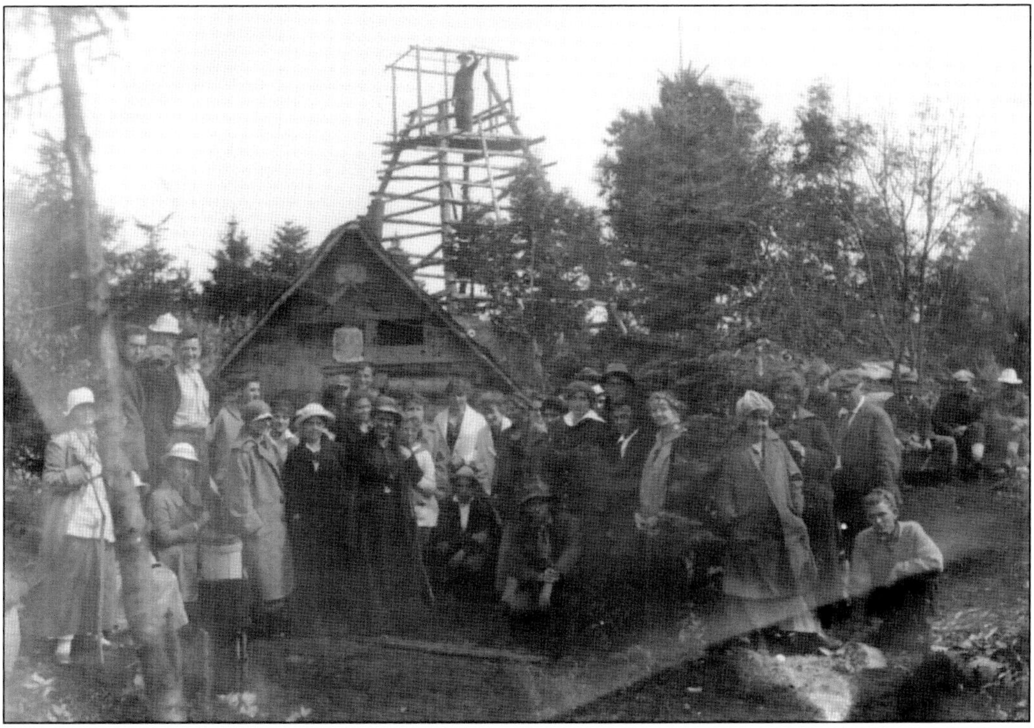

In 1912, the State of New York decided there was a need for a system to protect the forests from fires. Observation towers were constructed of wood in the beginning, such as the one pictured, manned by Alfred Pelcher on Hamilton Mountain.

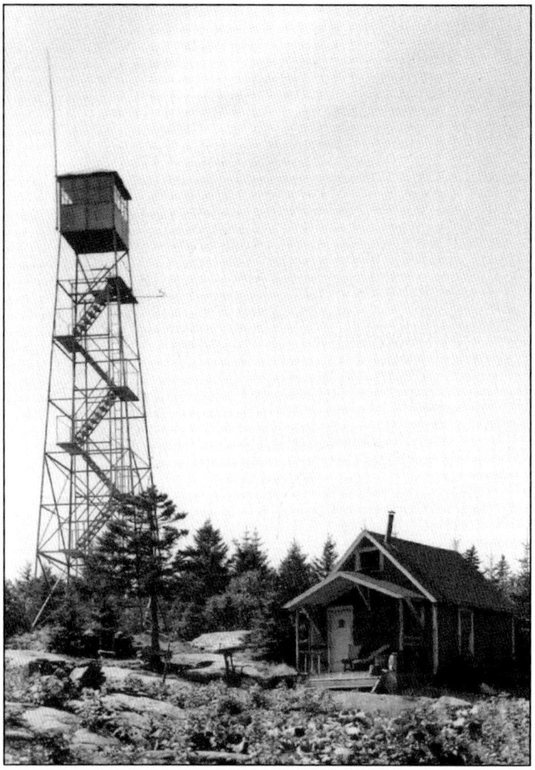

In latter years, taller and sturdier towers were constructed of steel. A cabin was built at the top of the mountain for the forest fire observer.

Several mountains in the area became sites for fire observation towers. Pillsbury Mountain, Snowy Mountain (pictured below), and Hamilton Mountain formed a network around Lake Pleasant and Speculator.

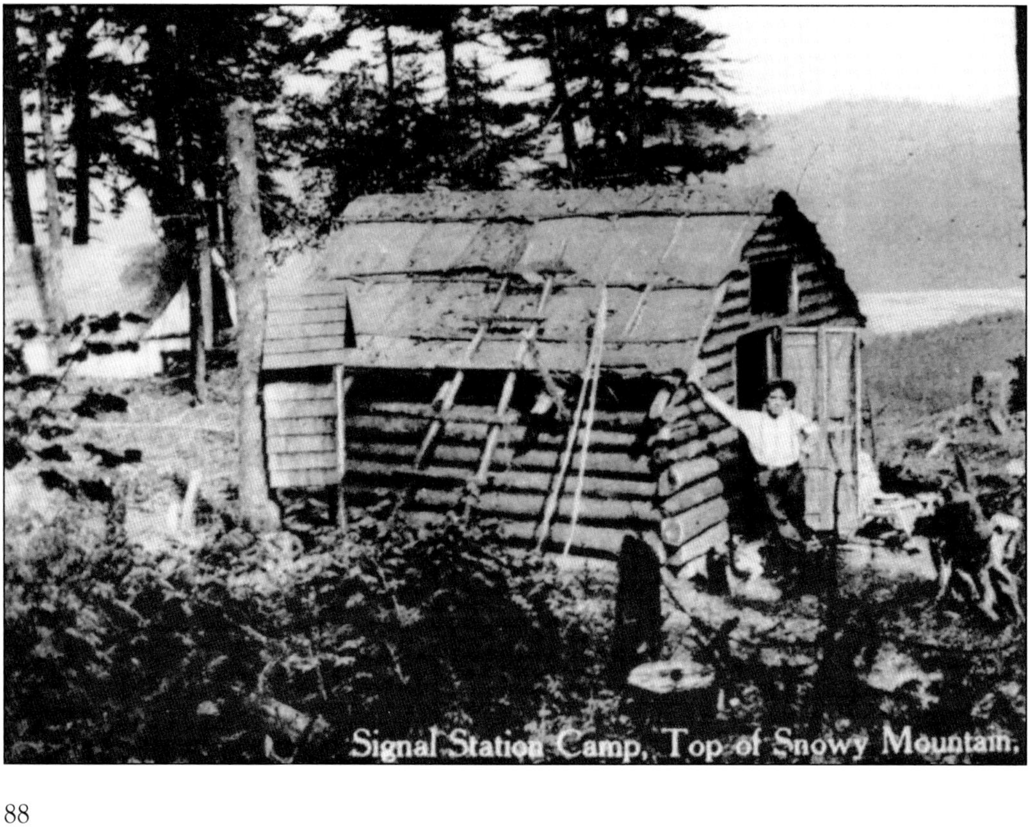

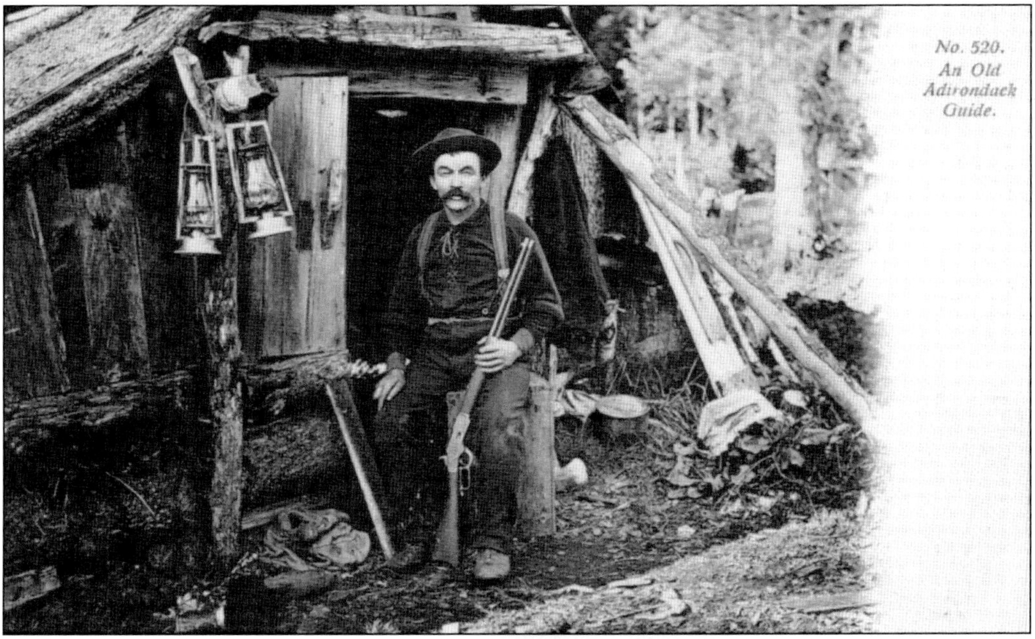

Louie Seymour was a Canadian-born lumberjack. His deep love for the solitary forest life caused him to become known as a hermit. French Louie, as he was known, had shanties and traplines all around the area and virtually lived off the land. He did however enjoy being a guide and entertaining guests at his primitive shanties and his well-built main cabin at the West Canada Lakes.

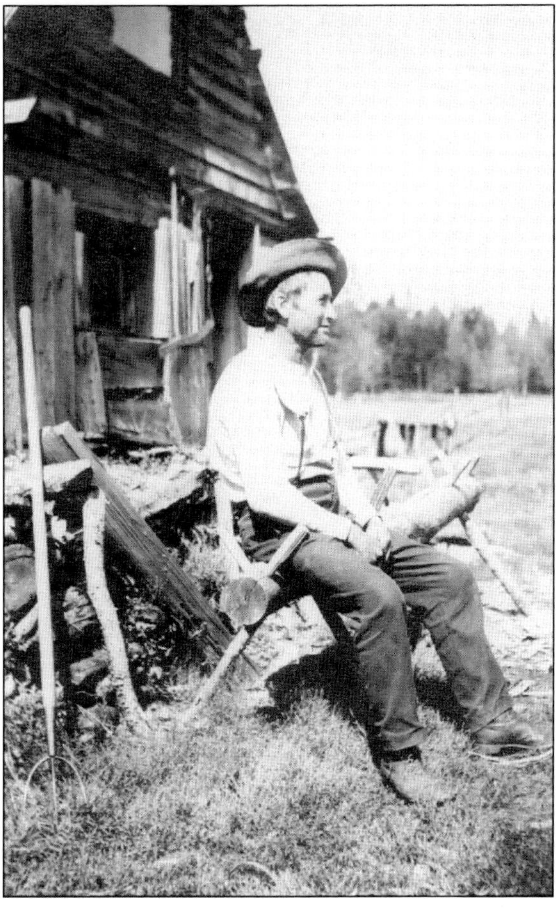

Perry Page was another man that some classified as a hermit. For the most part, he made a solitary living at his camp on Mud Lake. In the winter he would set an extreme trapline, which included staying at other cabins in the Blue Ridge Mountains. He was a guide during hunting and fishing seasons and occasionally visited his family on Page Hill. In 1914, he mysteriously disappeared and was never found.

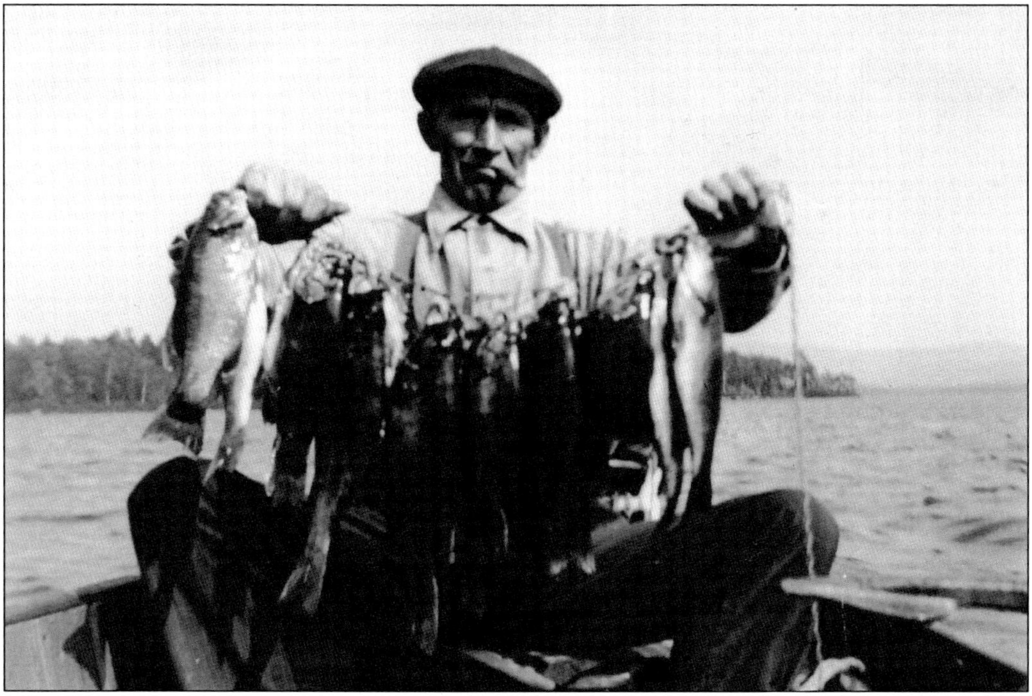

Alvah Slack is seen here with a nice "mess" of fish. The local lakes gave up an abundance of fish, including many varieties of trout and bass.

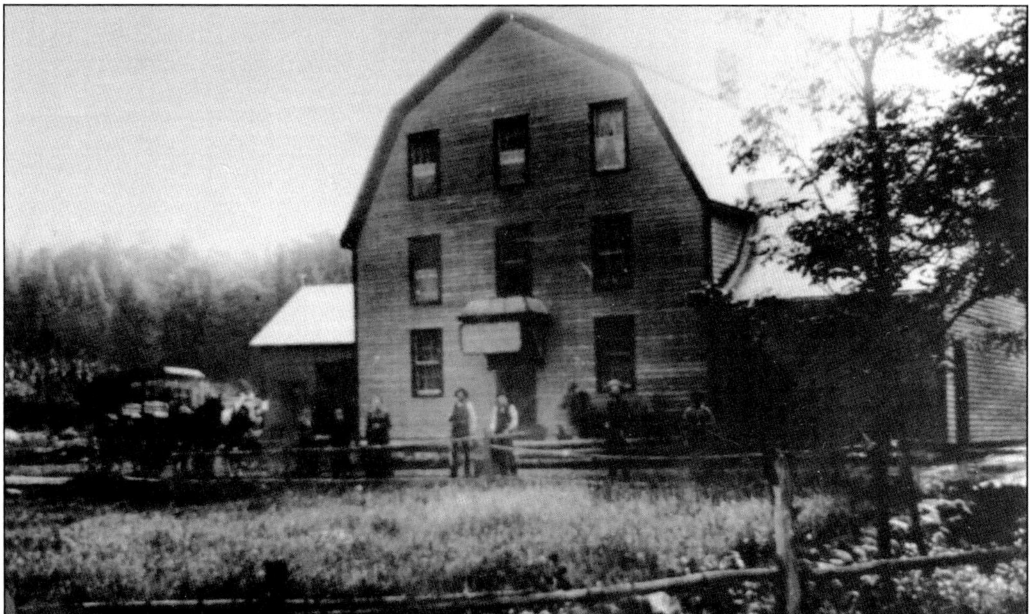

The New York State Fish Hatchery was built on Mill Stream just north of Newton's Corners (Speculator) in 1888. The hatching of trout would replenish the lakes and streams. In a few years when the hatching process had problems, cans of fish were brought in from other areas to keep the waters well stocked.

Seven

RECREATION

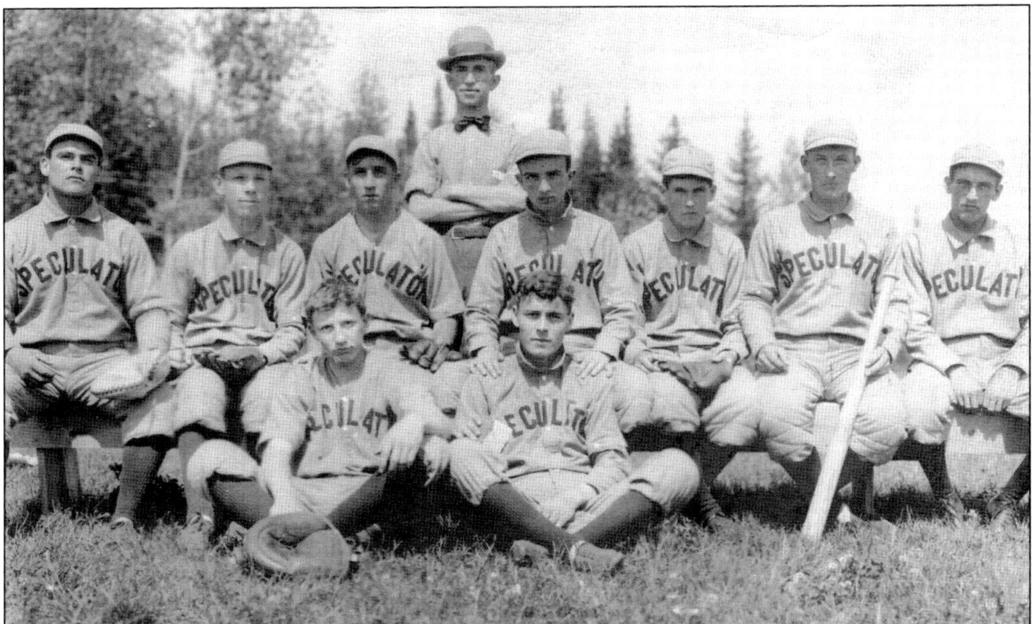

Baseball became America's favorite pastime, and Speculator was no exception. This photograph dates to around 1914 when town teams competed with each other. Pictured here are, from left to right, (first row) Dexter Slack and George Courtney; (second row) Dave Page, Lyle Courtney, Bill Wilbur, unidentified, Ashley Perkins, Truman Brown, and Elmer Page Sr.; (third row) coach James Liebenheim.

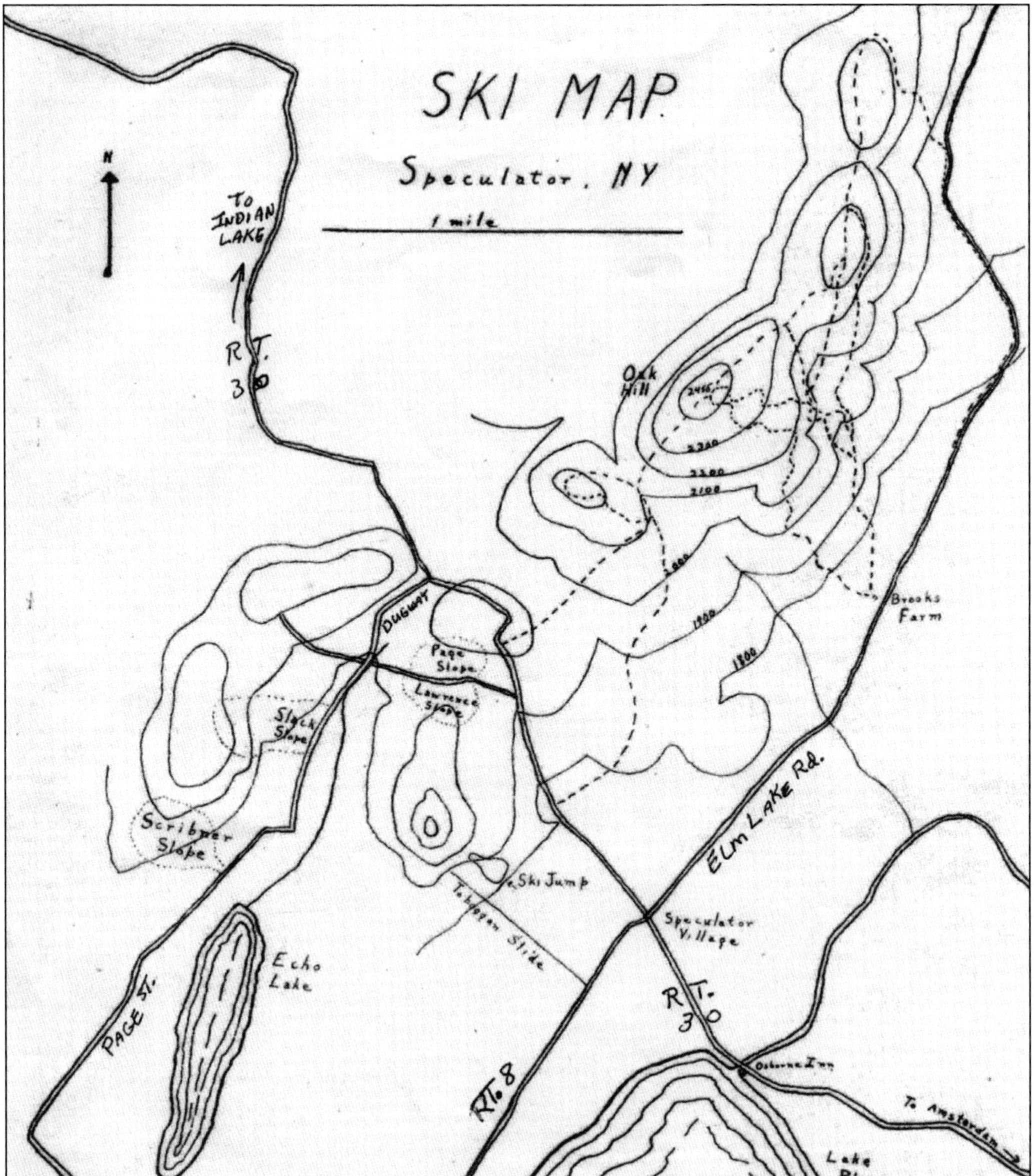

In the mid-1920s, the Winter Sports Club was organized to promote winter sports in Lake Pleasant and Speculator. There was a ski area on every slope and a toboggan run on Sturges Mountain.

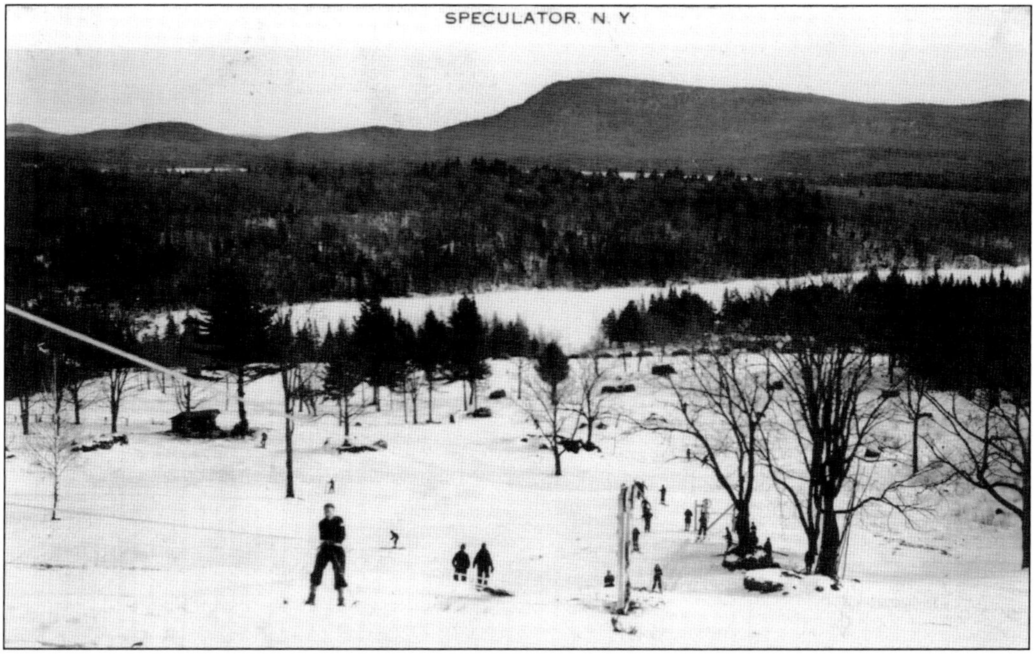

One ski tow was located on Russ Scribner's hill on Page Street. It had an engine and a rope tow to take skiers to the top and a snack bar at the bottom of Scribner's Slope. A log lean-to was part way up the hill for shelter.

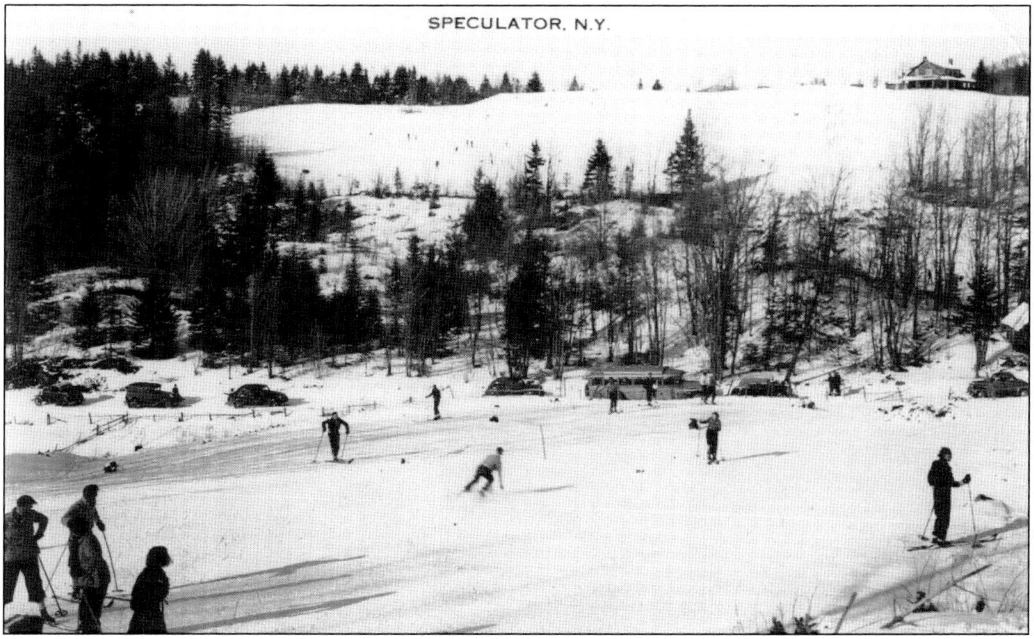

At the intersection of Page Street and the Dugway, a road dug out to connect the old Indian Lake road with Page Street, were a couple more ski areas, including Lawrence's and Page's Ski Slope. Pictured is Page Street lined with cars and ski buses and Melody Lodge on top of Page Hill.

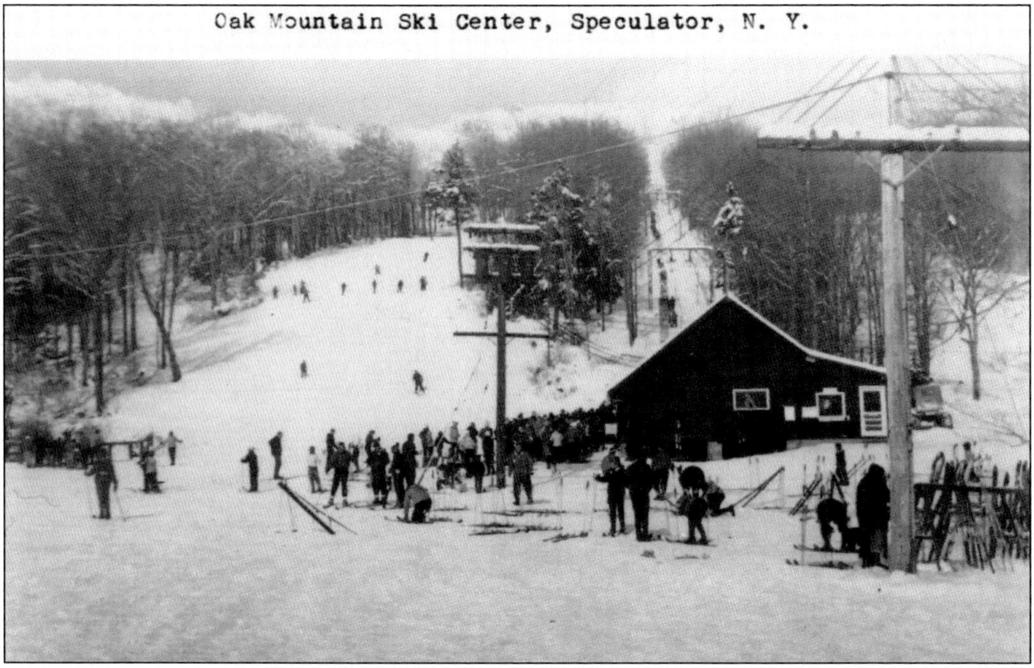

Both downhill and cross-country skiing were offered at the Oak Mountain Ski Area. By 1937, the Town of Lake Pleasant was ready to take charge of the winter sports, and in 1947 the ski tow at Oak Mountain was further developed and the other ski slopes fell to disuse. On weekends, several charter buses brought skiers from miles away.

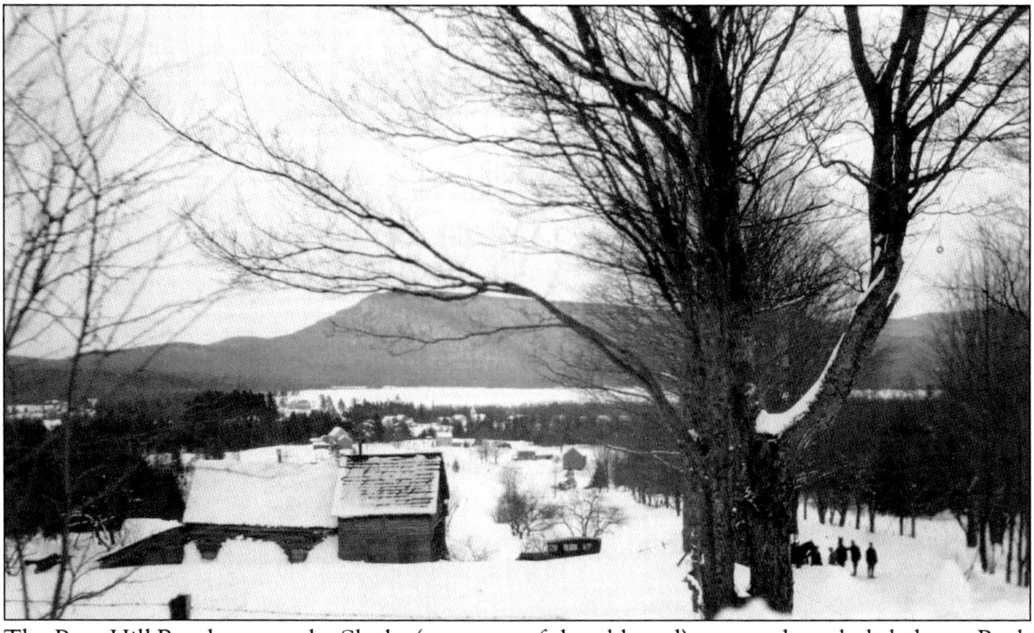

The Page Hill Road up past the Slacks (now part of the old road) was used as a bobsled run. Back then traffic was usually nonexistent on most days.

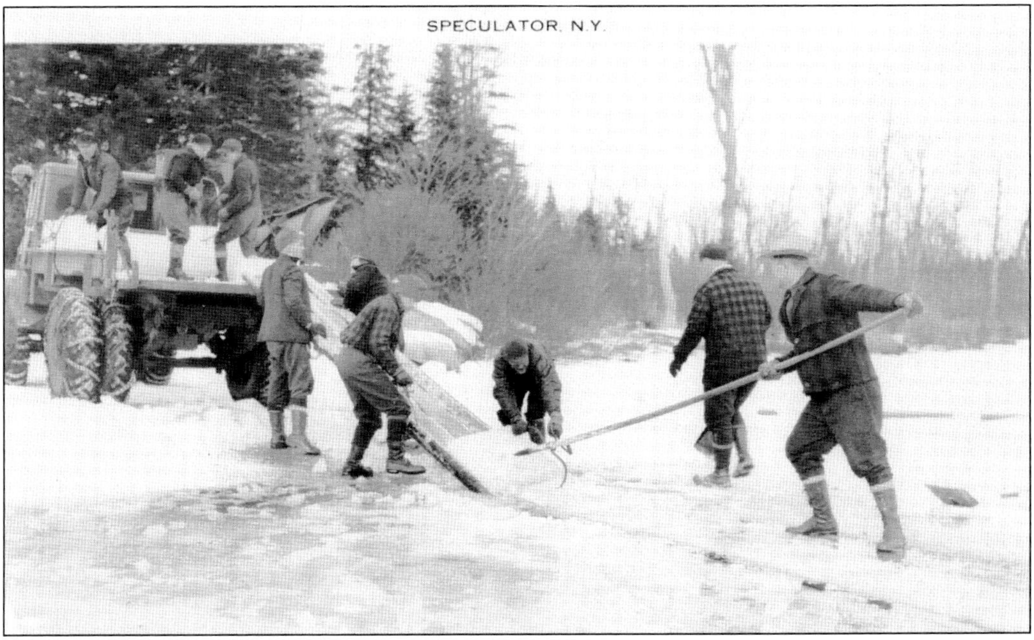

Every year starting in 1927 huge blocks of ice were cut for the toboggan slide that was built on the south side of Sturges Mountain. Huge blocks of ice, 3 feet by 5 feet, were cut. One block was placed for the bottom, two were for the sides, and it was then covered with snow. The toboggan slide was an important part of the winter sports program and drew a good crowd.

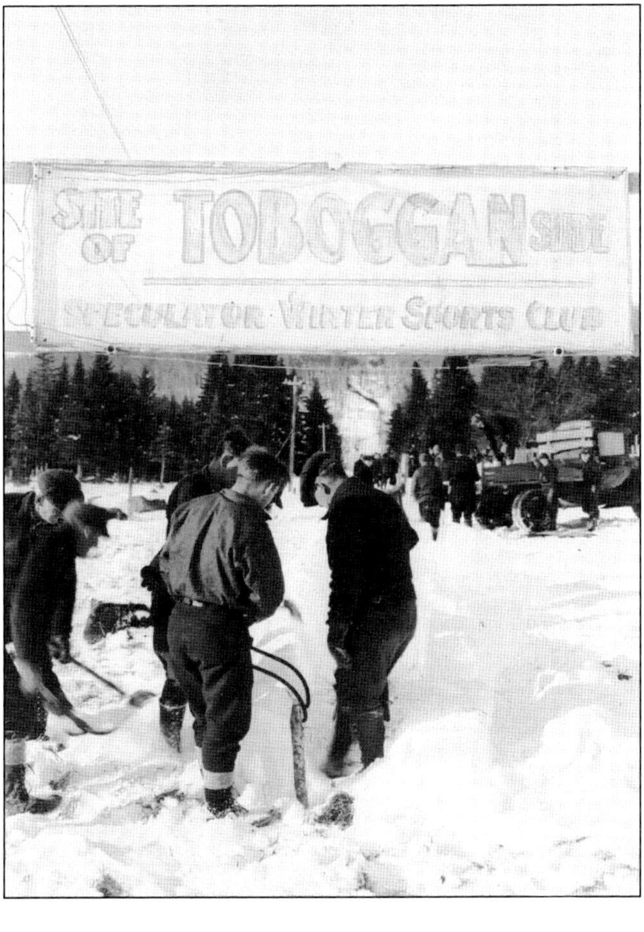

Building the toboggan run provided winter employment for many who were out of work during the Depression years.

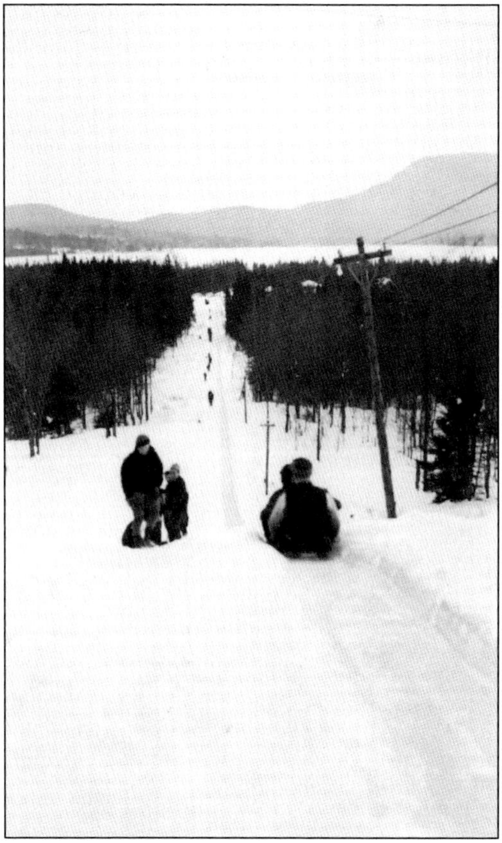

Patrons received a fast ride on wooden toboggans that had metal stripes added to the underside. Supposedly some daredevils would go down the slide on skis, skates, and even a shovel.

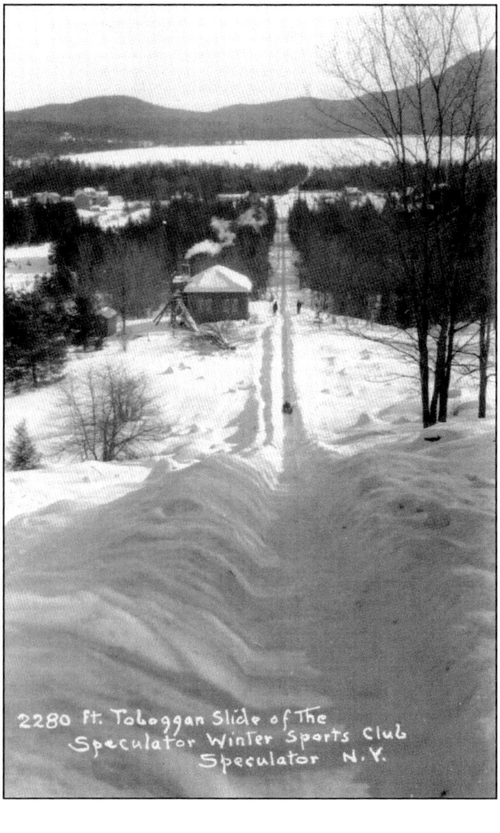

A warming hut was constructed near the top of the toboggan run. It had a huge fieldstone fireplace that made it very pleasant on cold days.

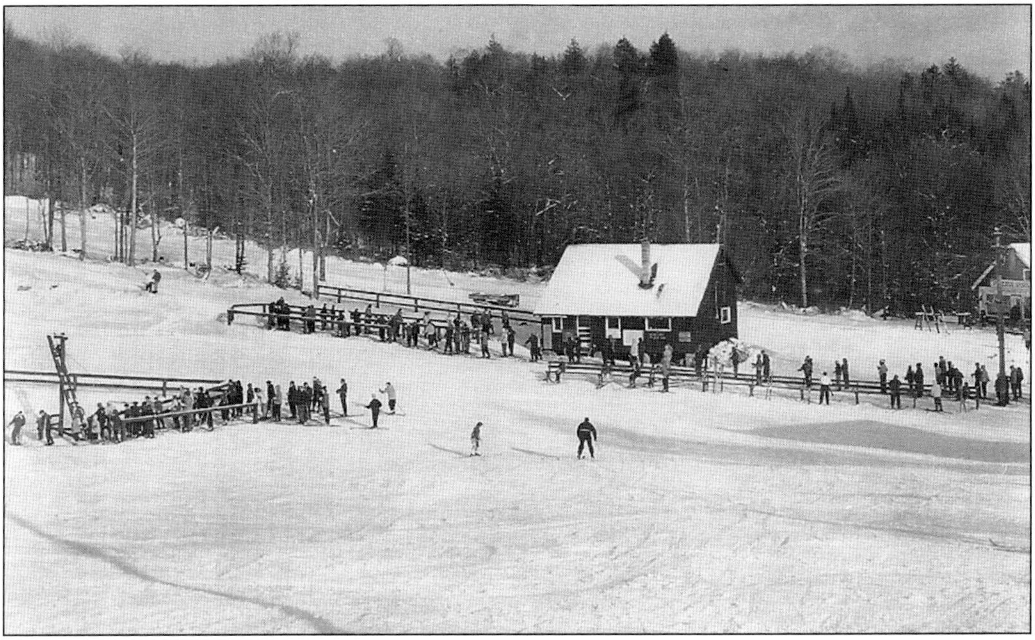

By 1947, Oak Mountain Ski area was about the only ski slope being used. With the rope tow to the Bunny Hill on the left, and the T-bar to the harder slopes on the right, Oak Mountain Ski Center became a family haven in the winters.

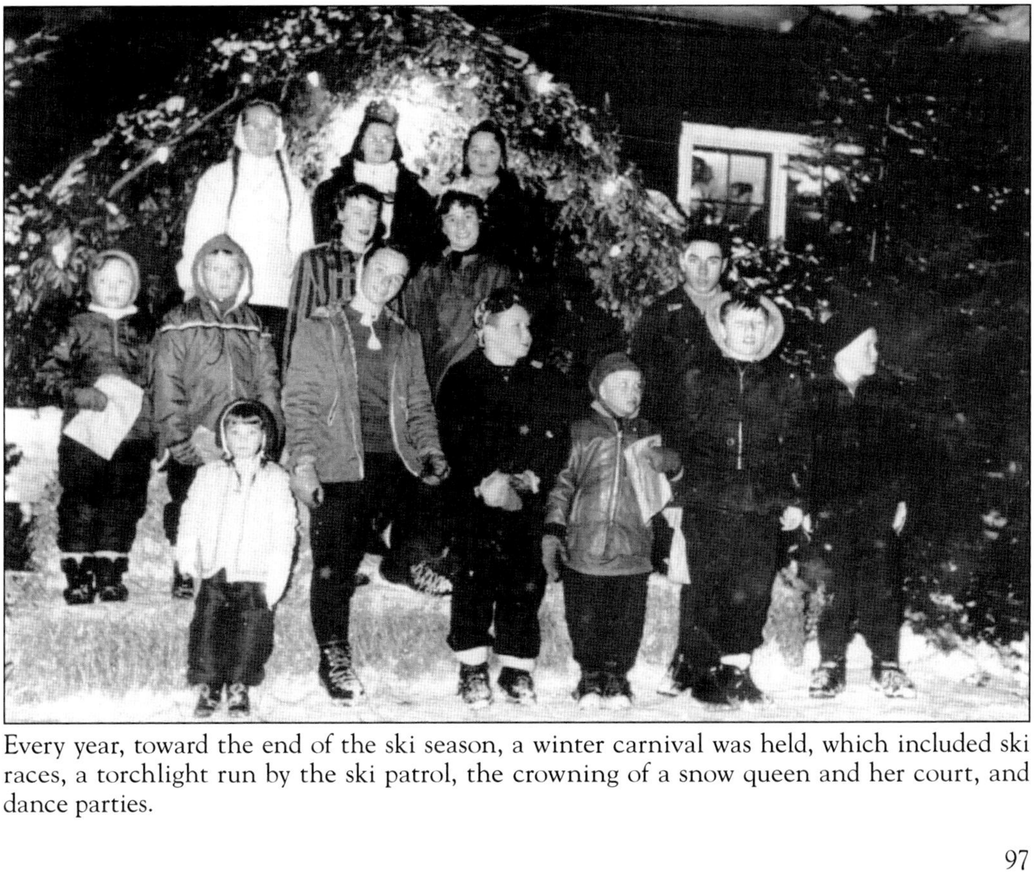

Every year, toward the end of the ski season, a winter carnival was held, which included ski races, a torchlight run by the ski patrol, the crowning of a snow queen and her court, and dance parties.

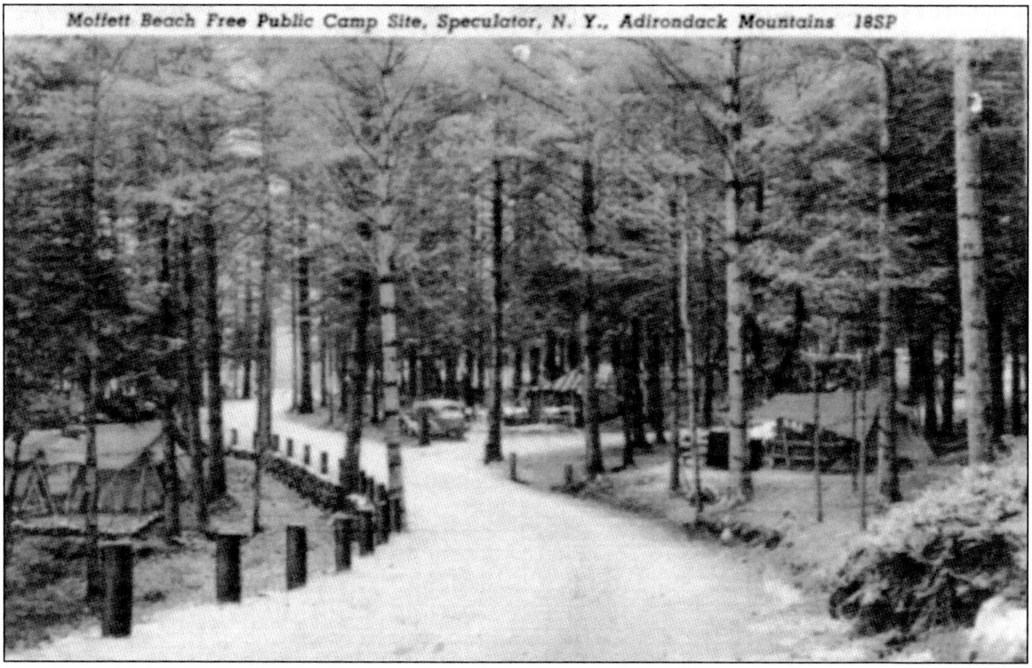

The State of New York realized that the state park could be better protected, as well as provide for recreation, by setting aside areas for camping. The abandoned Moffitt farm was already a popular picnic spot, so designated free camping sites soon followed.

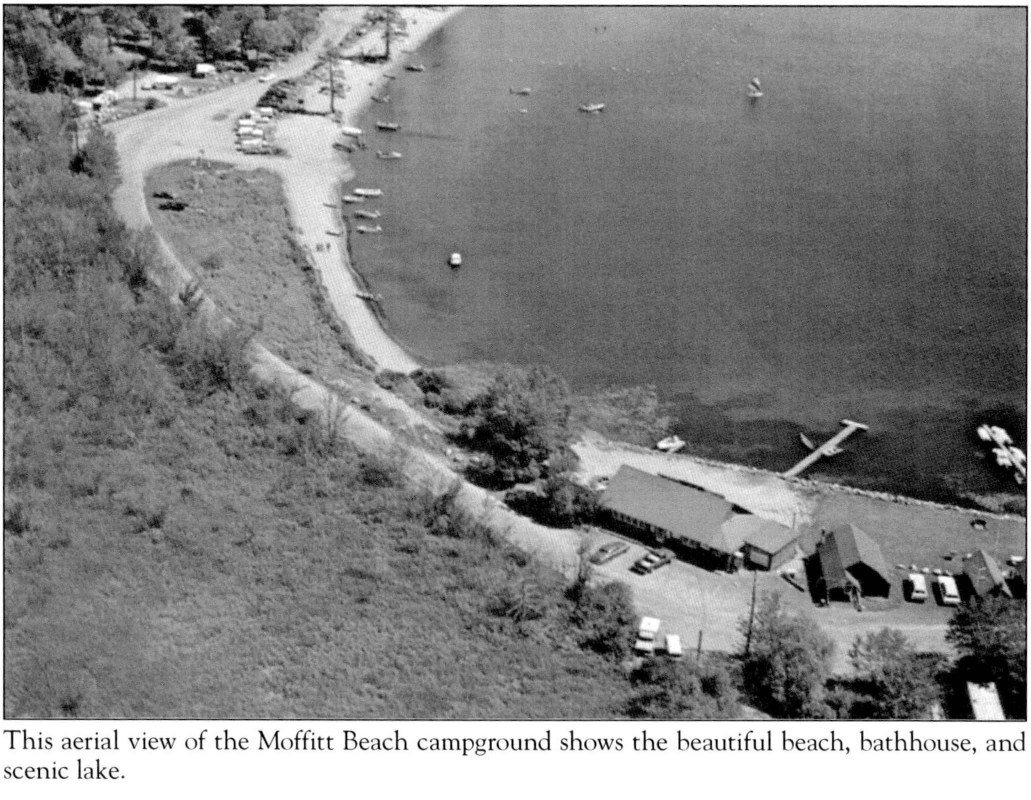

This aerial view of the Moffitt Beach campground shows the beautiful beach, bathhouse, and scenic lake.

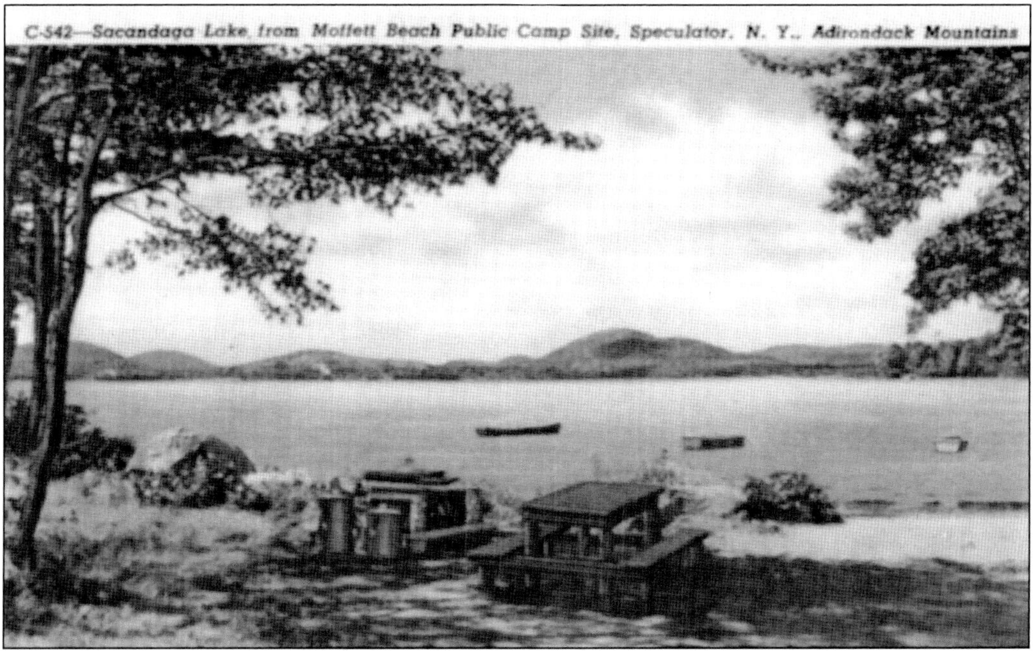

This tenting site at Moffitt Beach campground has a full view of Sacandaga Lake. Stone fireplaces were built for the convenience of the campers and also to keep the fires safely contained.

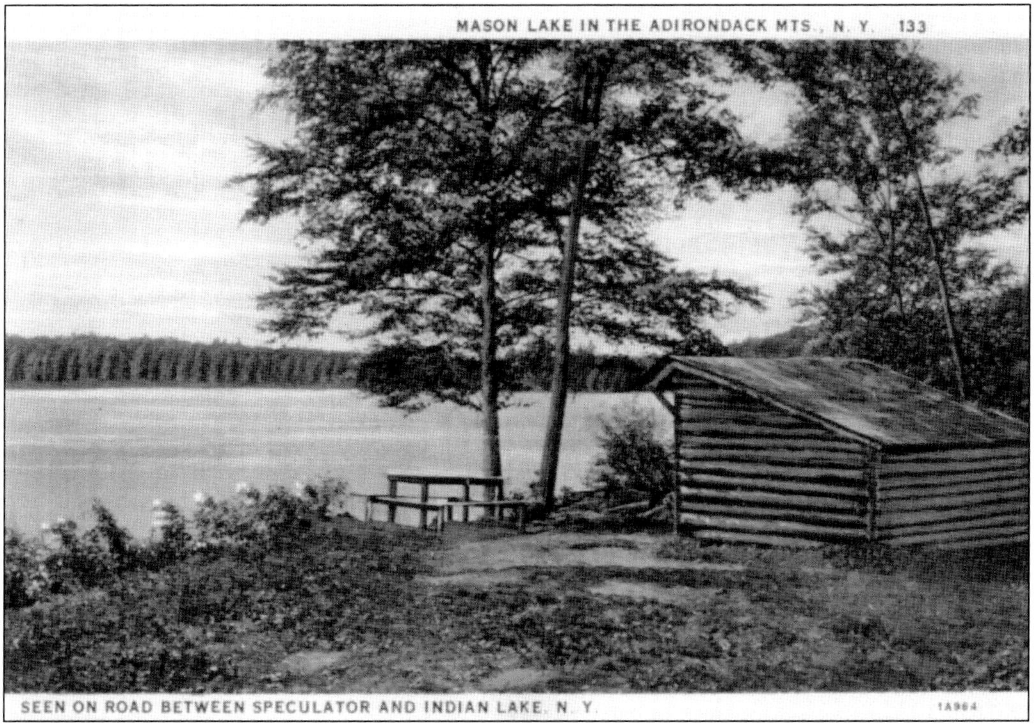

The State of New York also built lean-to shelters on popular hiking trails and occasional lakes. This lean-to was built on Mason Lake, which is located on the road to Indian Lake.

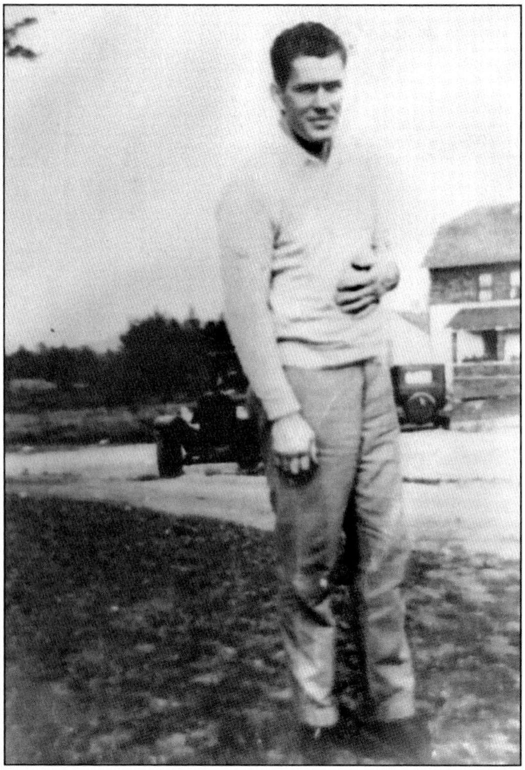

In the Roaring Twenties, prizefighting became popular among the high society crowd who followed the boxers training in Speculator. Bill Osborne, proprietor of Osborne's Inn, served in the marine corps with Gene Tunney, a prizefighter hopeful. Gene Tunney accepted an invitation from Bill Osborne in 1926 to come and train in Speculator for his world heavyweight championship title against Jack Dempsey, whom he defeated.

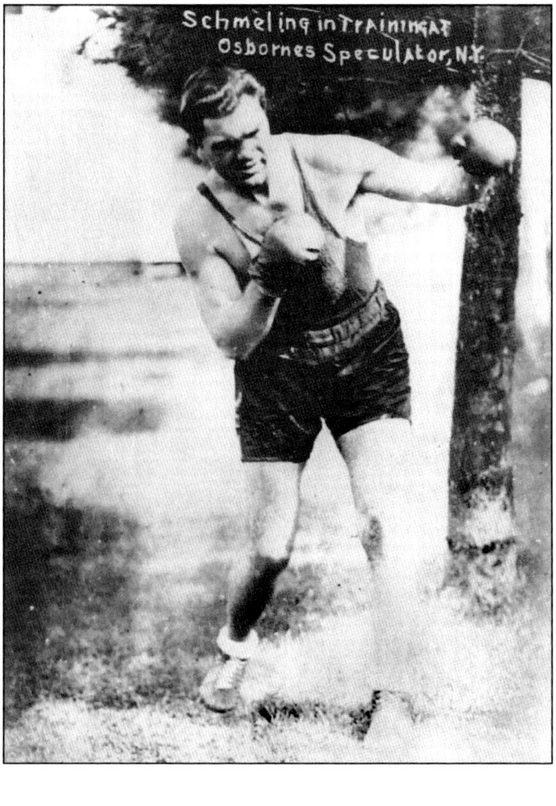

Max Schmeling was from Germany and was a world heavyweight champion in 1930. He came to train in Speculator in 1932 and defeated Joe Louis in 1936. He was called back to Germany to serve in the German Army during World War II.

Max Baer was the world heavyweight champion in 1934. Both Max and his brother, Buddy, came to train in Speculator. Max was training to fight Joe Louis. In all, at least 10 boxers came to train in Speculator at various times.

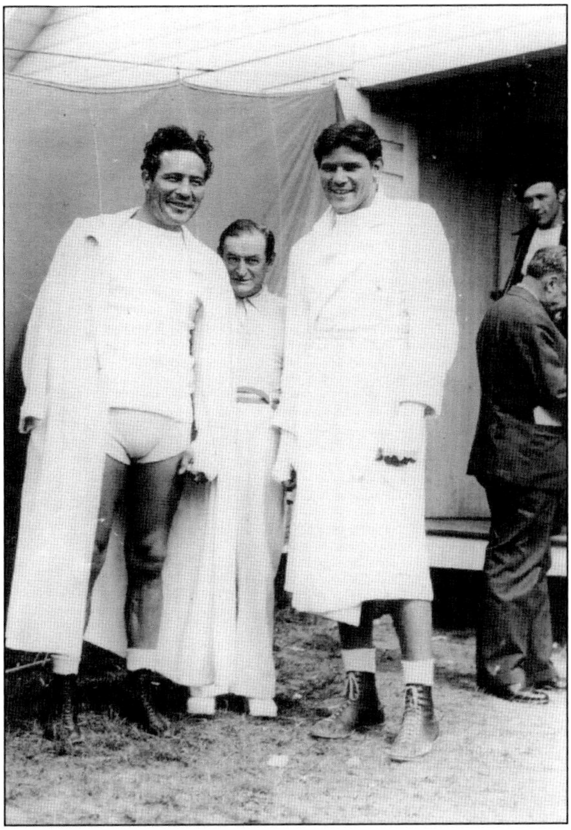

Crowds gathered to watch sparring matches and paid a fee to do so. Newspaper columnists set up shop and kept their typewriter keys flying. The whole world wanted to be informed.

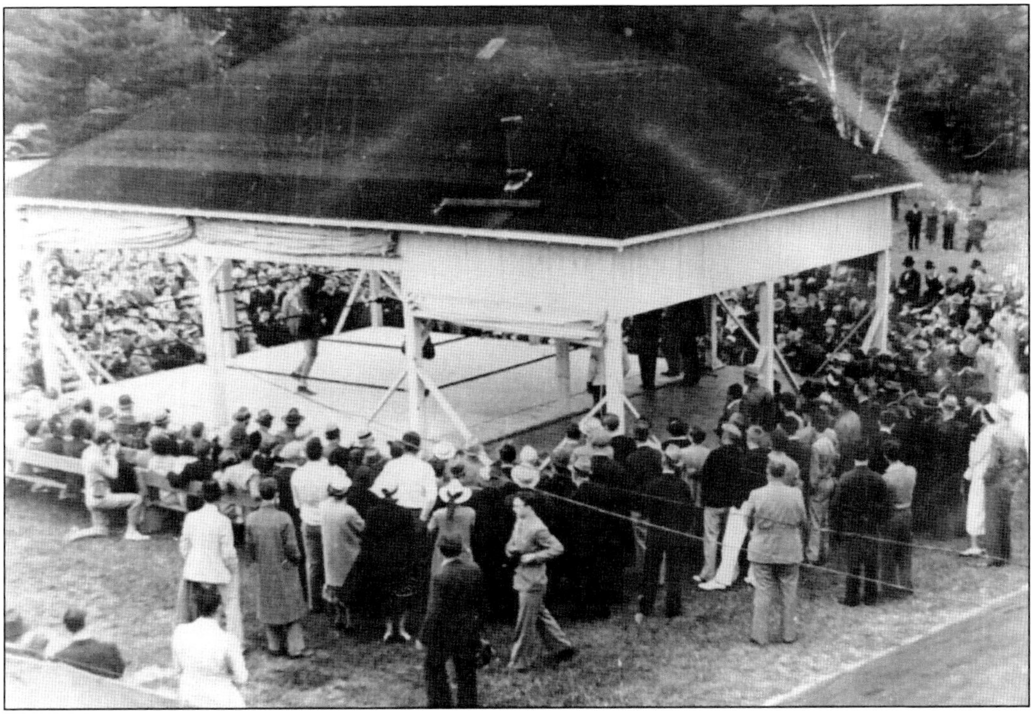

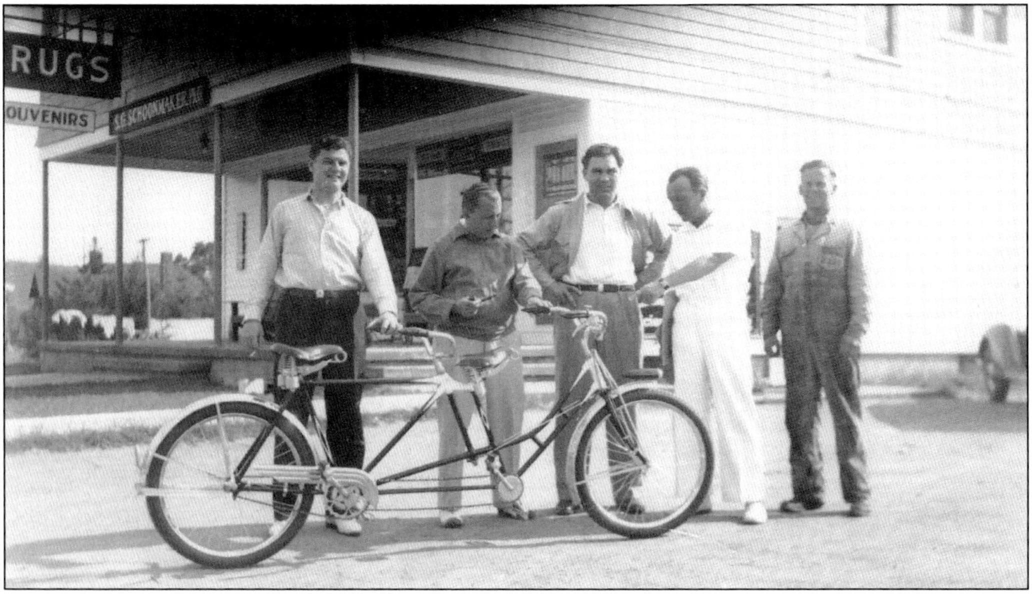

This photograph was taken in front of Schoonmaker's Drugstore. Charlie Downey is on the right in his Esso coveralls. Charlie Downey rented tandem bikes to the prizefighters.

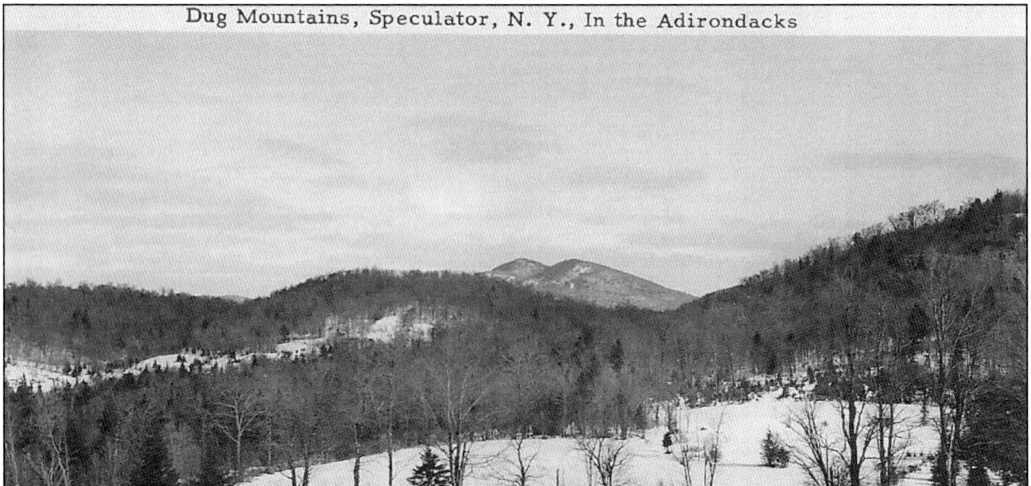

Whether on a trail to Fawn Lake, Colonel Peck's grave, or the new Sacandaga Pathways or a mountain climb up Pillsbury Mountain, Hamilton Mountain, or even the Dug Mountains, all ages can enjoy the wonders of nature on a hike in Lake Pleasant and Speculator

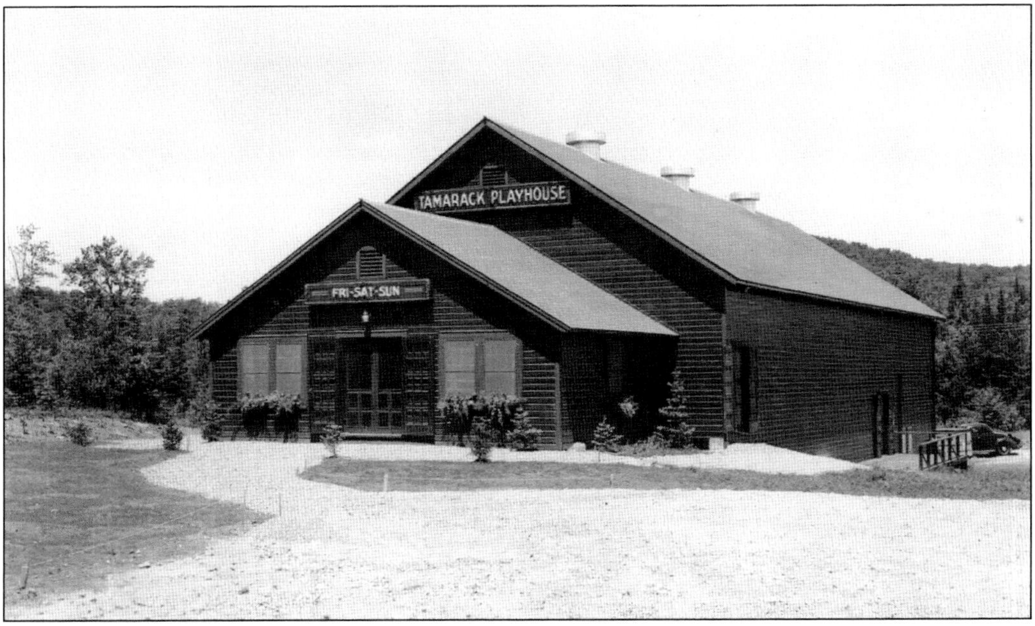

In the late 1930s, Malcolm Atterbury and his wife, Ellen Ayres Hardies Atterbury, brought their acting troupe from Amsterdam, New York. Malcolm Atterbury had the Tamarack Playhouse built and bought White's Hotel on Fish Street to house the actors. Many performers moved on to Hollywood, including Carl Malden, Carl Betz, Kirk Douglas, and Malcolm Atterbury himself.

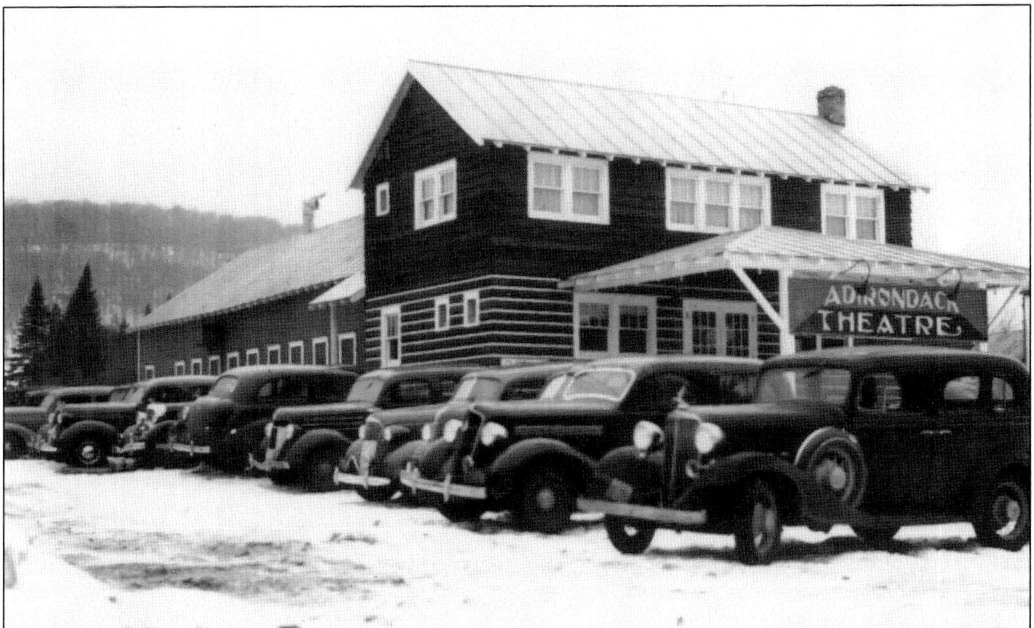

Isaiah Perkins built the Adirondack Theatre in 1914. Silent movies were shown with piano accompaniment. The theater was only open in the summer so these cars are for the patrons of the toboggan slide.

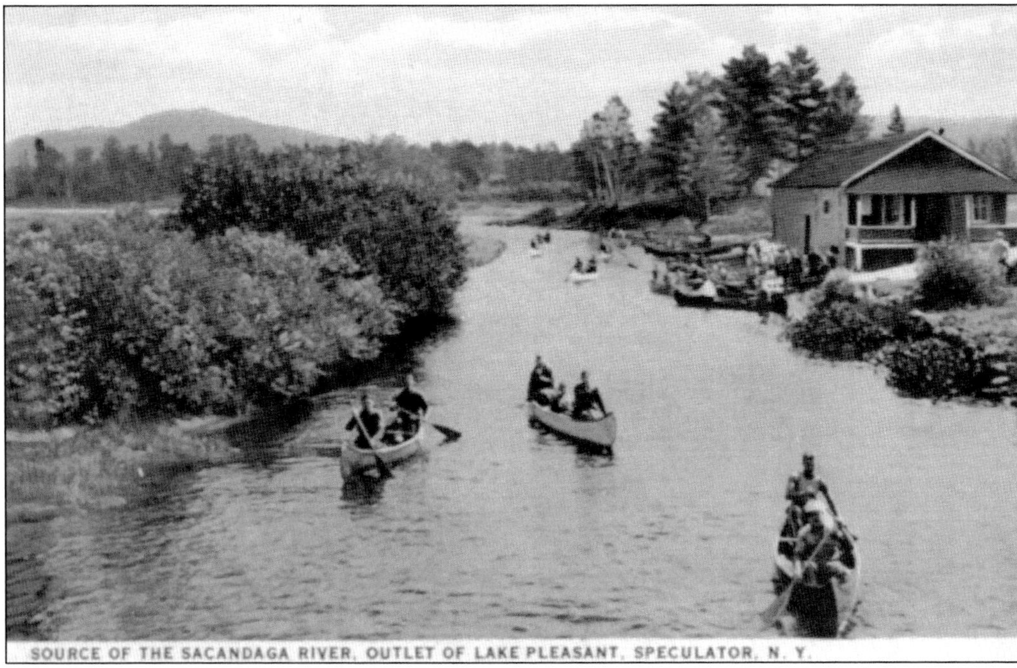

The outlet of Lake Pleasant is the beginning of the Sacandaga River. Before reaching any rapids, one would encounter Kunjamunk Bay and Duck Bay. This is also the route to Kunjamunk River and Elm Lake.

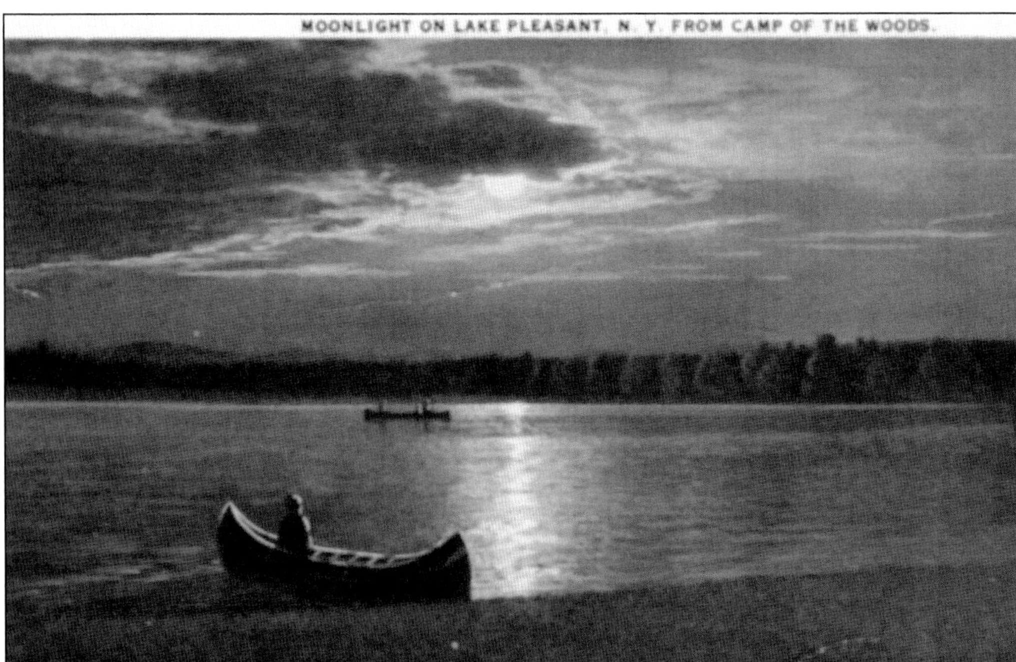

Moonlight over Lake Pleasant is unequaled in beauty on placid waters.

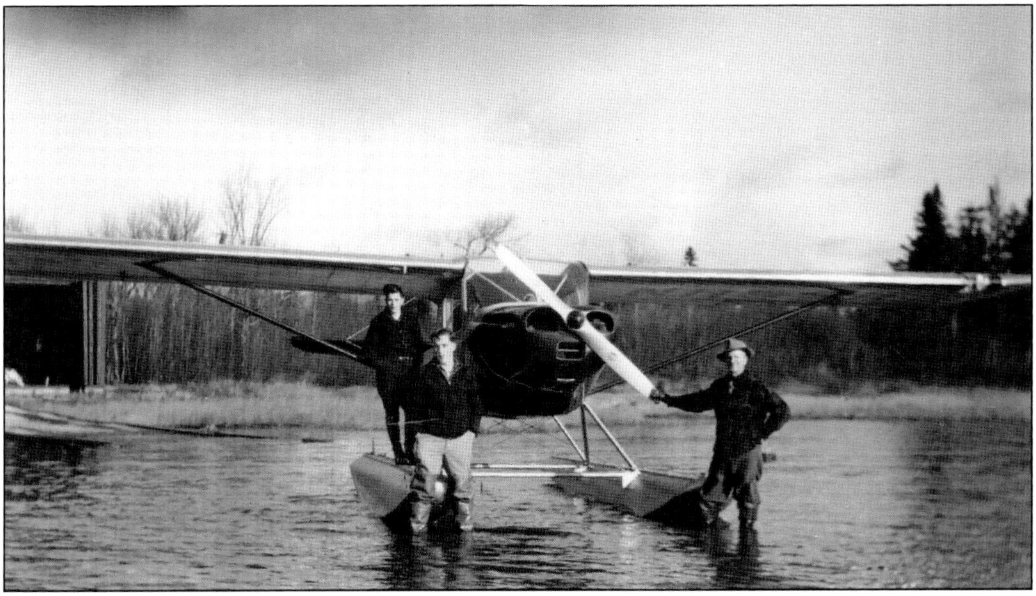

Clyde Elliott has flown many sportsmen to the small wilderness lakes in the deep woods. It took an expert to land and take off from some of these lakes.

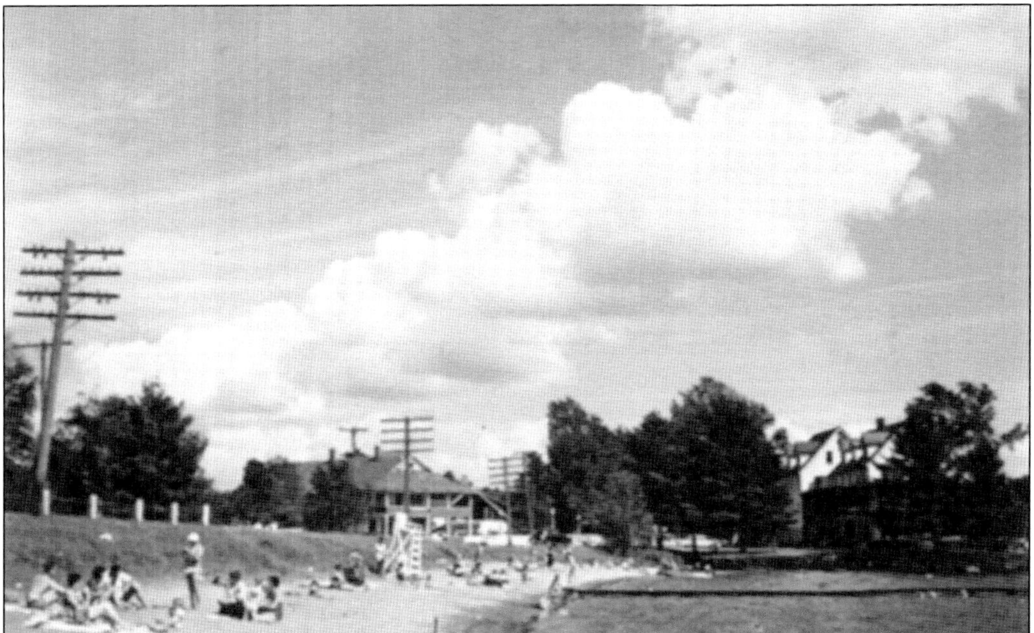

The Village of Speculator was incorporated in 1925, and in 1928 the village purchased the sandy beach by the outlet and the land across the road for recreation.

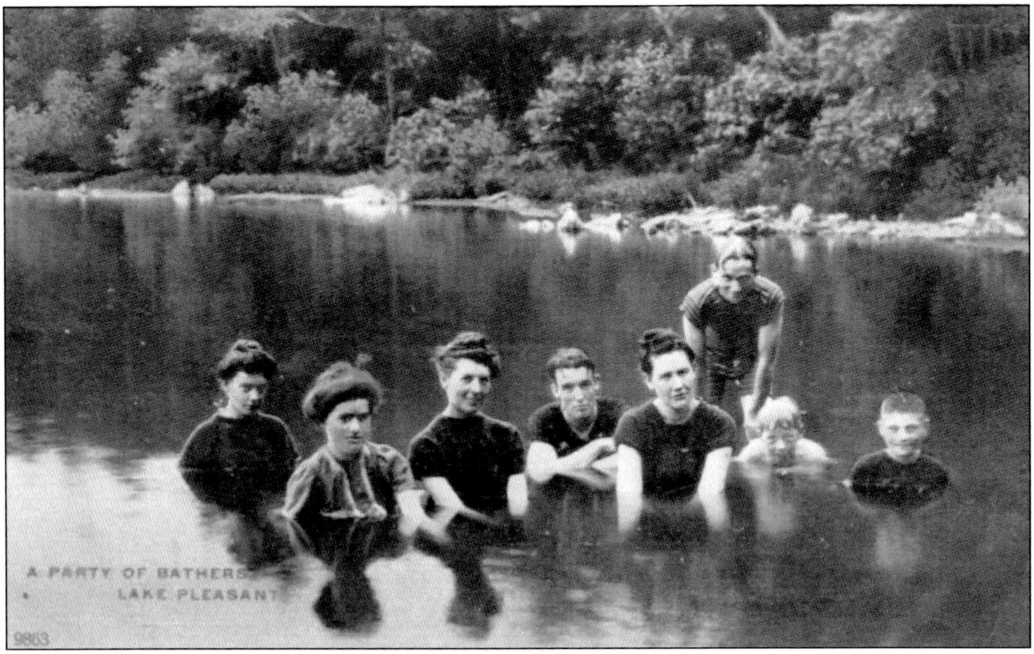

Since the 1850s, tourists have been coming to the Lake Pleasant and Speculator areas for recreational reasons, as these bathers testify in the photograph.

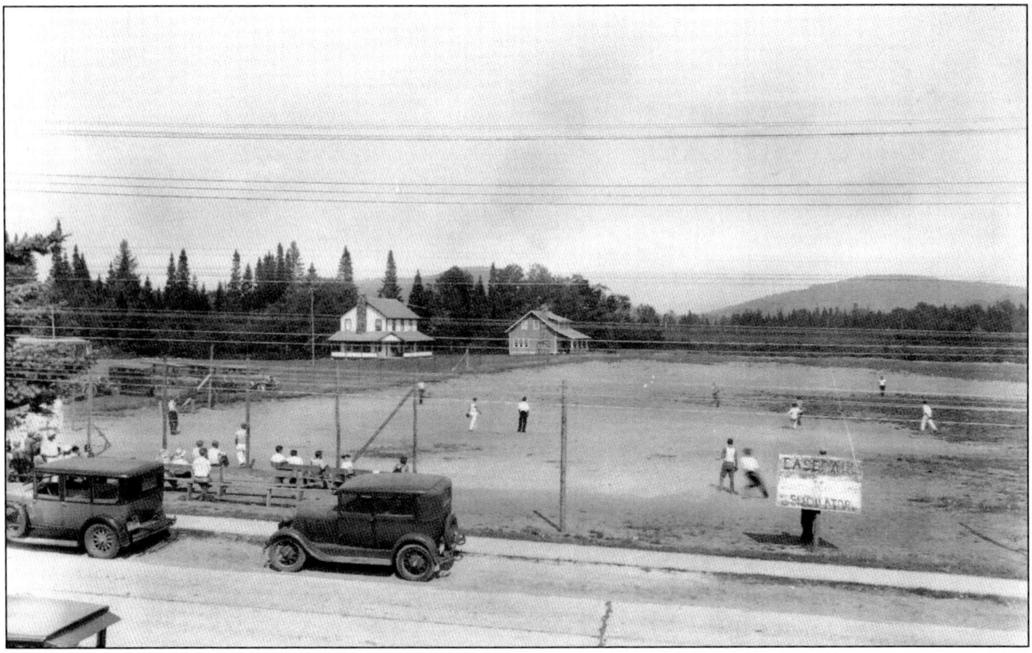
After the Village of Speculator purchased the land near the outlet of Lake Pleasant in 1928 for recreational activities, baseball began here. Home base is now part of the Speculator Fire Hall, while the baseball field moved more to the right. Now the complex includes basketball courts, a pavilion, a gazebo, a playground, and the Sacandaga Pathways.

Eight

Interesting Photographs and Facts

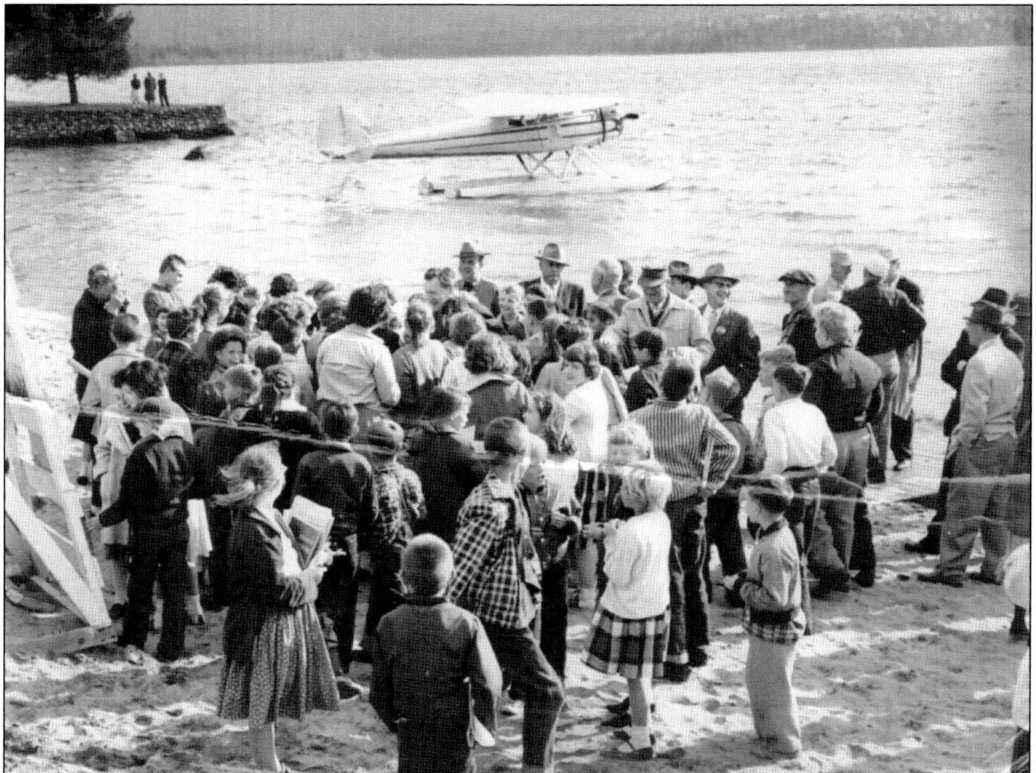

Gov. Nelson Rockefeller visited Speculator in the 1950s. This photograph shows his plane landing at the beach at Speculator. Children as well as adults came out to greet him.

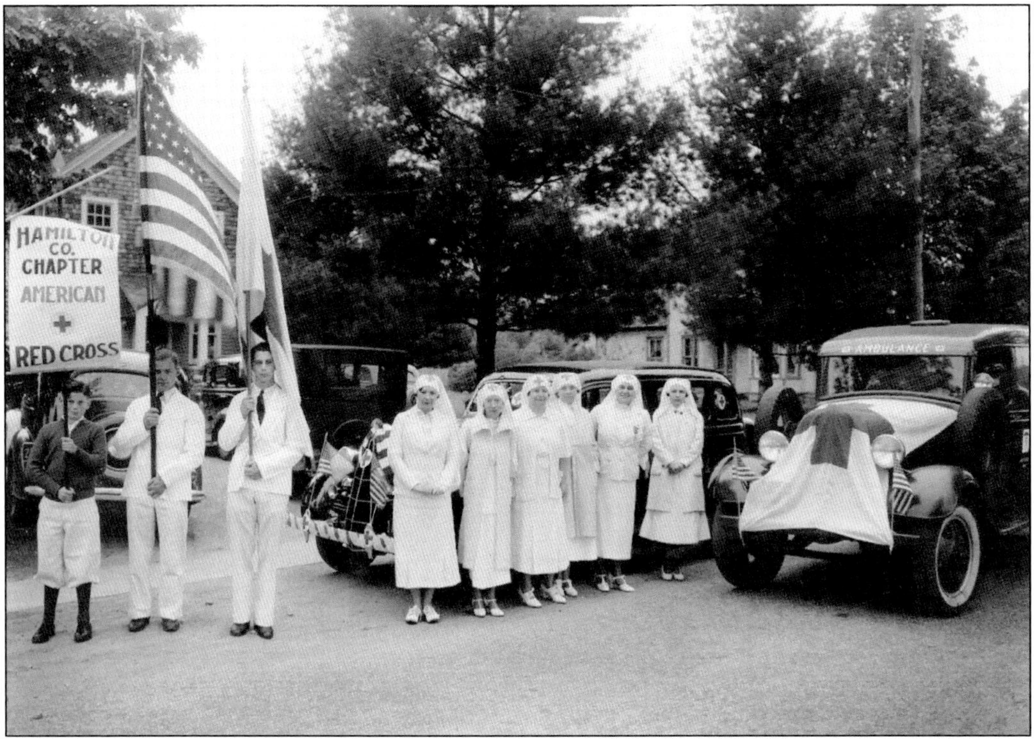

The Hamilton County Chapter of the Red Cross was formed in 1932.

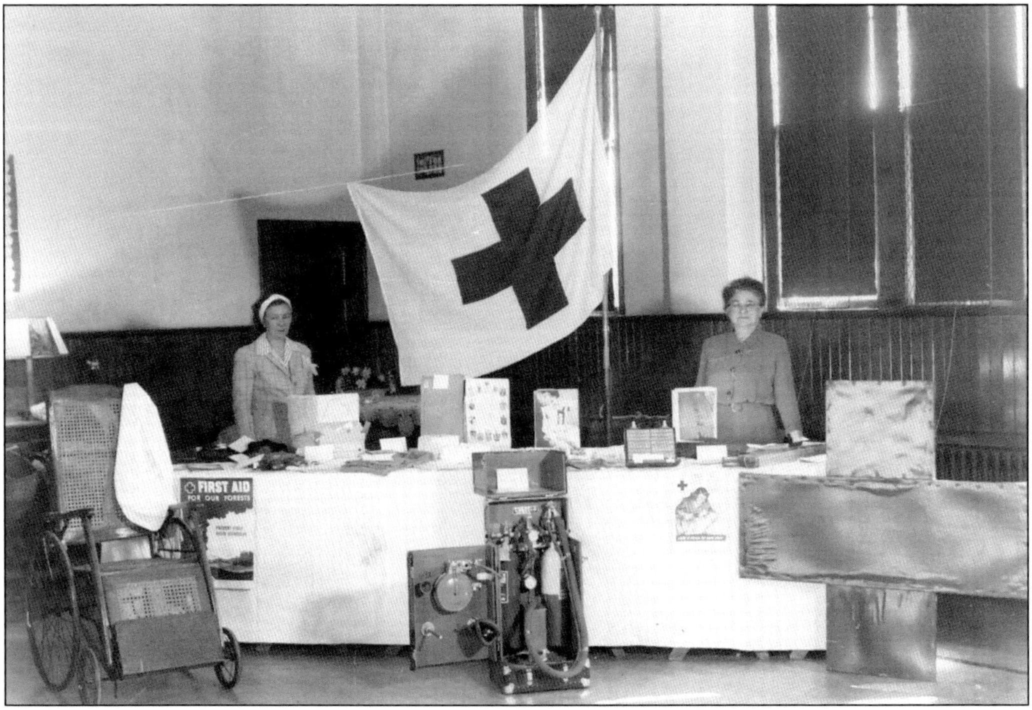

When the Red Cross was first formed, members gave first aid instruction classes. Pictured are, from left to right, Virginia Elliott and Stella King.

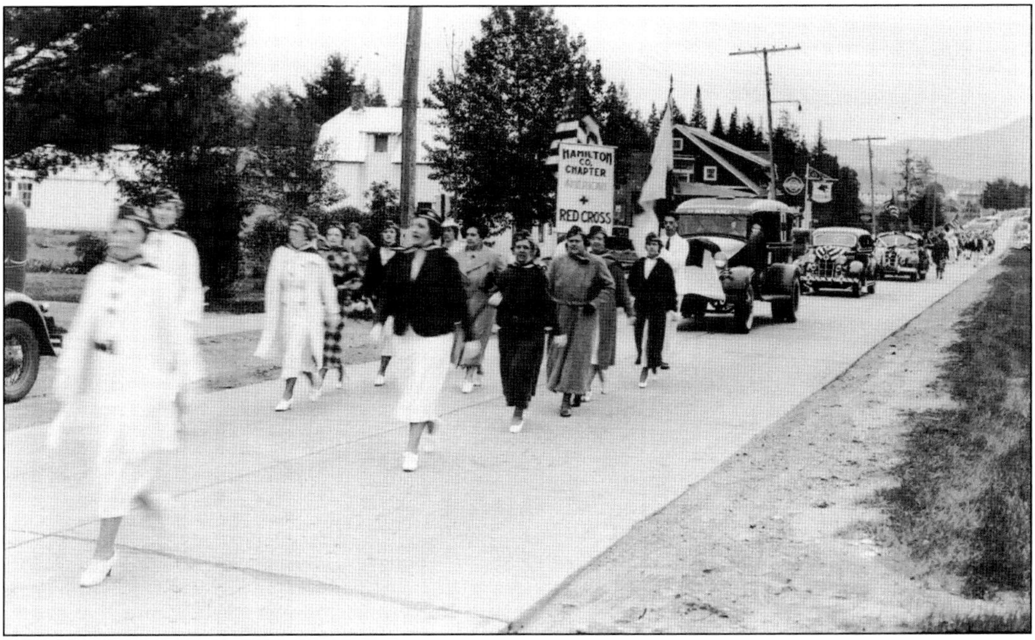

The Hamilton County Chapter of the American Red Cross is marching in the Memorial Day Parade in Speculator.

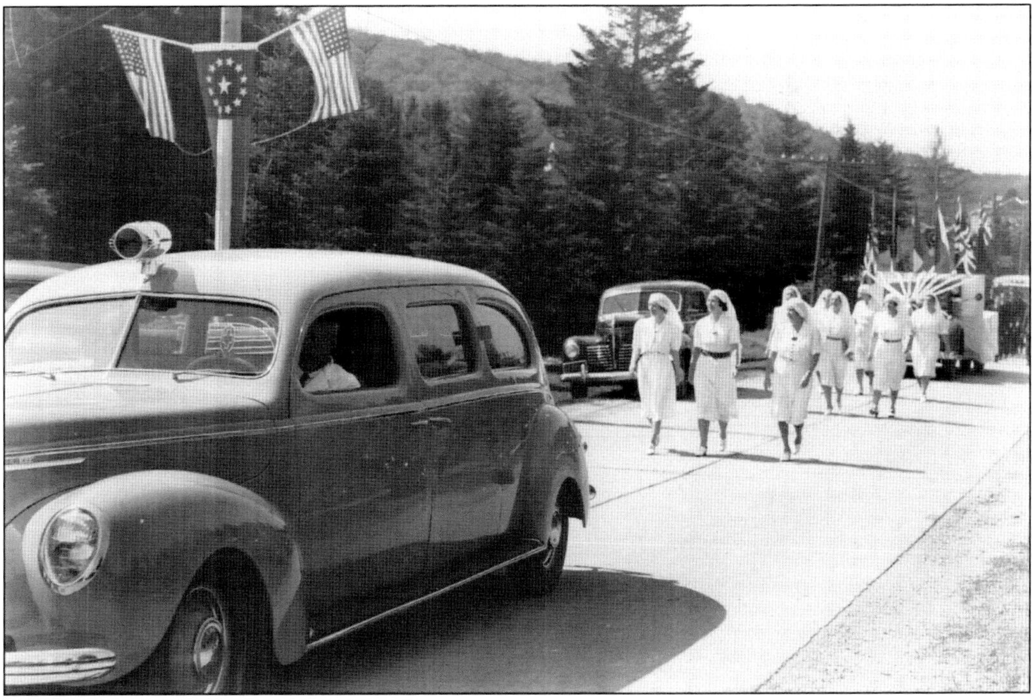
This is the ambulance purchased by the Hamilton County Chapter of the American Red Cross.

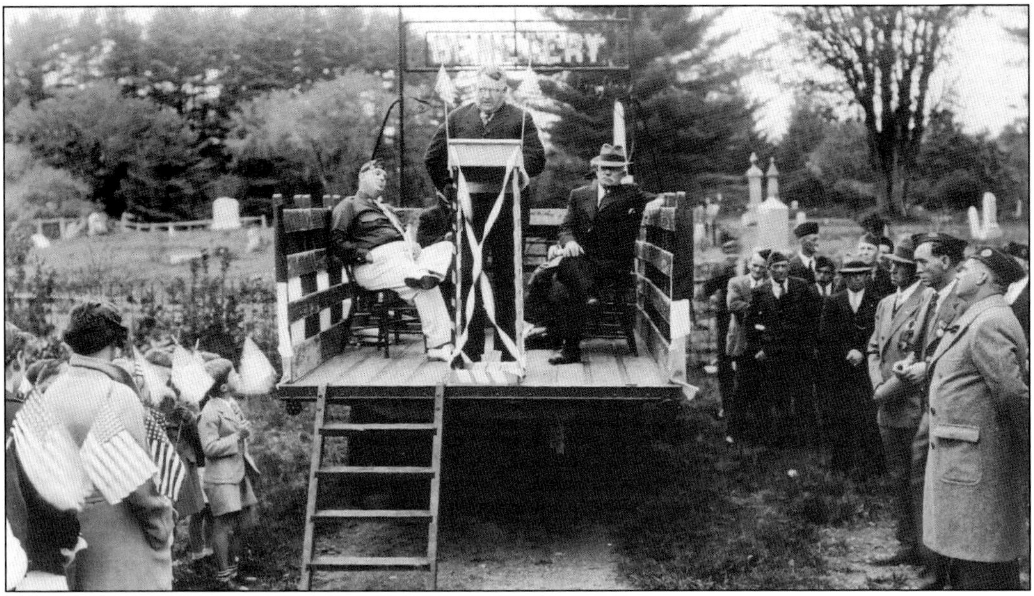

This photograph was taken in front of the Speculator Cemetery for a Memorial Day ceremony. Speakers were elevated on a truck platform.

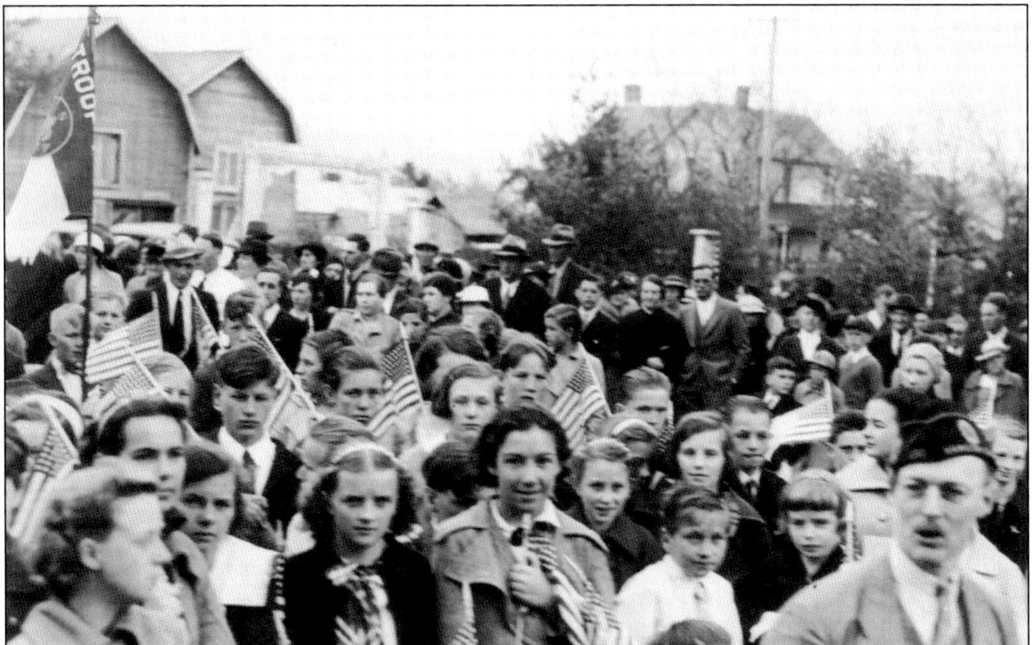

Huge crowds gathered for the special Hamilton County Memorial Day ceremonies in front of the Speculator Cemetery along Elm Lake Road.

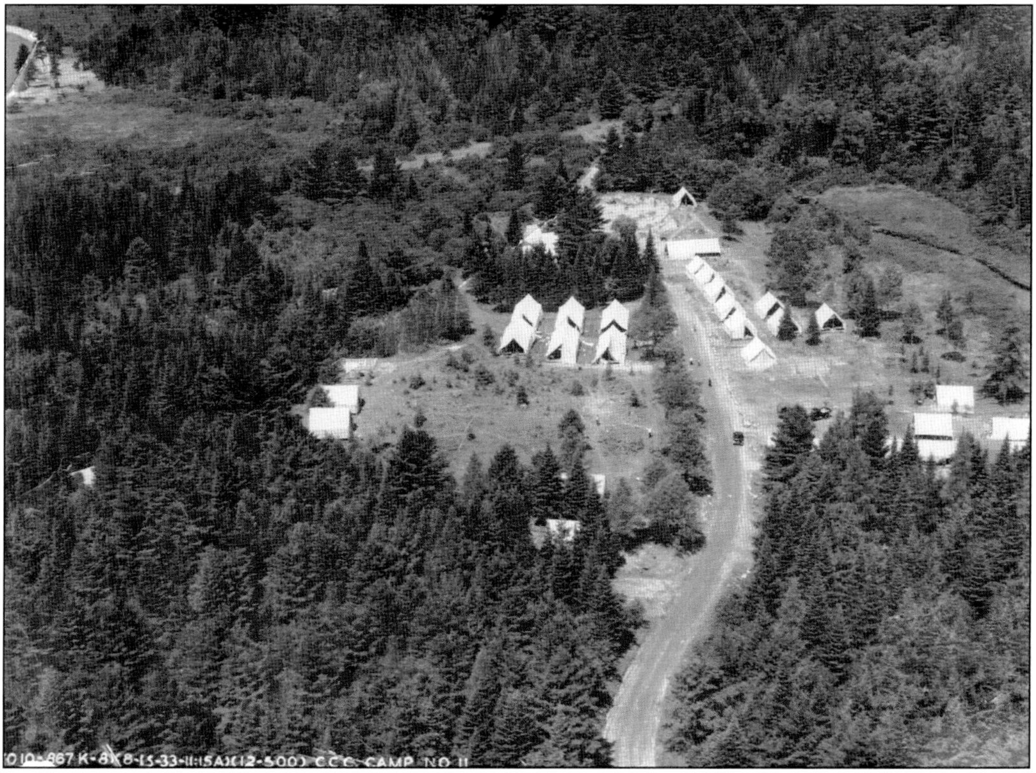

In 1934, a Civilian Conservation Corps camp was established near Speculator on the road to Sacandaga Lake. The young men, many from New York City, were put to work building and improving Moffit Beach State Campground.

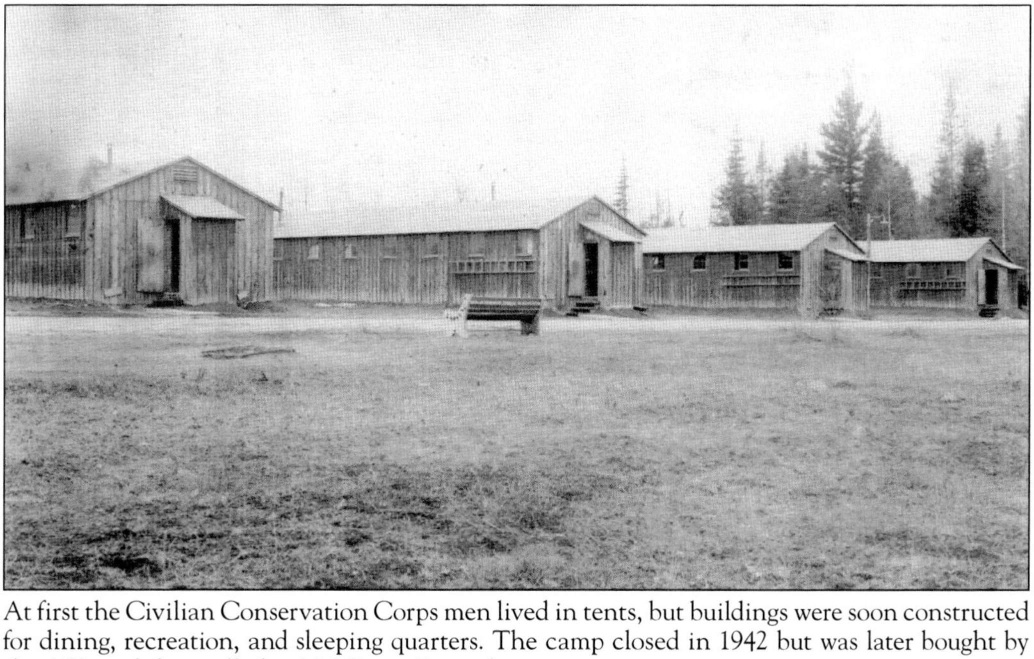

At first the Civilian Conservation Corps men lived in tents, but buildings were soon constructed for dining, recreation, and sleeping quarters. The camp closed in 1942 but was later bought by the 4-H, and they called it 4-H Camp Sacandaga.

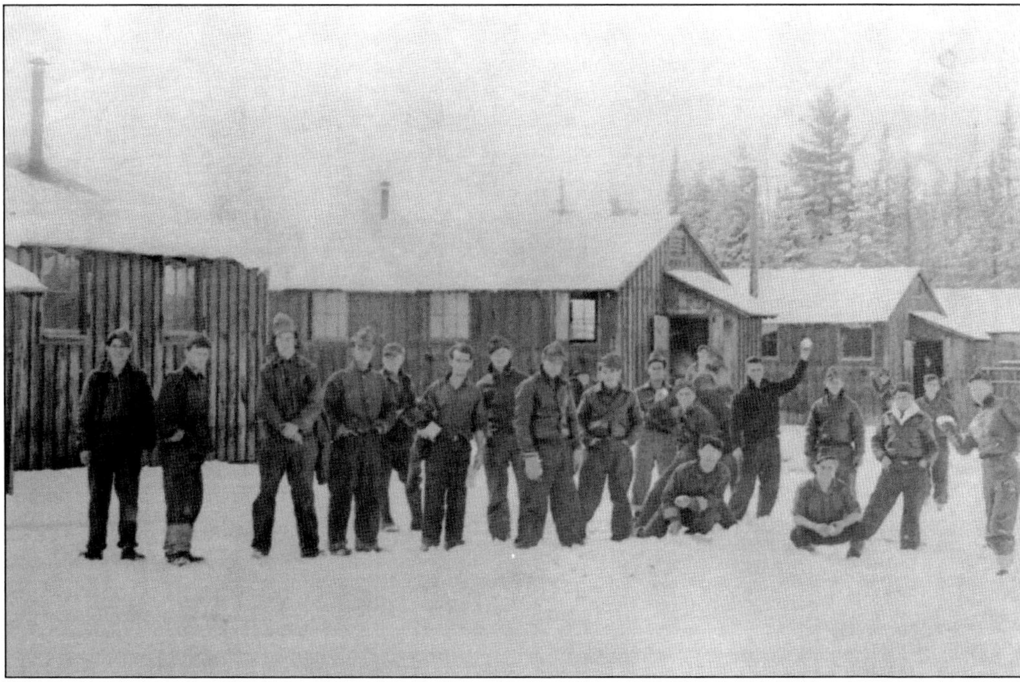

The photograph shows some of the men at Camp S-90 at Speculator. The buildings are still standing and are one of the last complete Civilian Conservation Camps left in New York State. The 4-H sold the land in 2009.

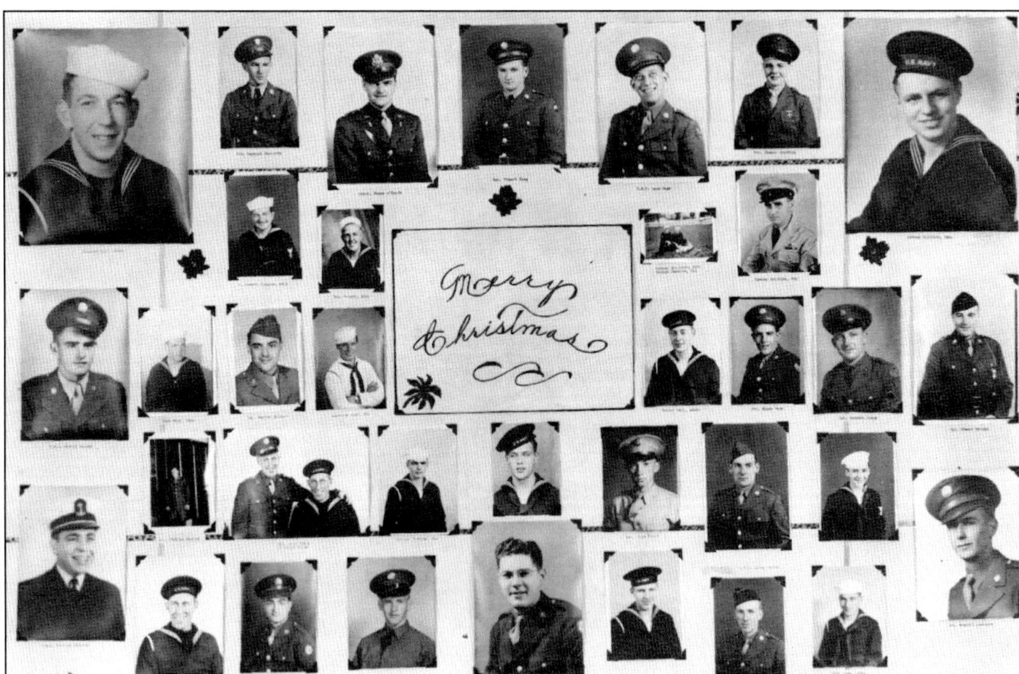

Local photographers Arthur and Lila Tefft took photographs of the men in military service one year during World War II and made a postcard. Large prints were also made.

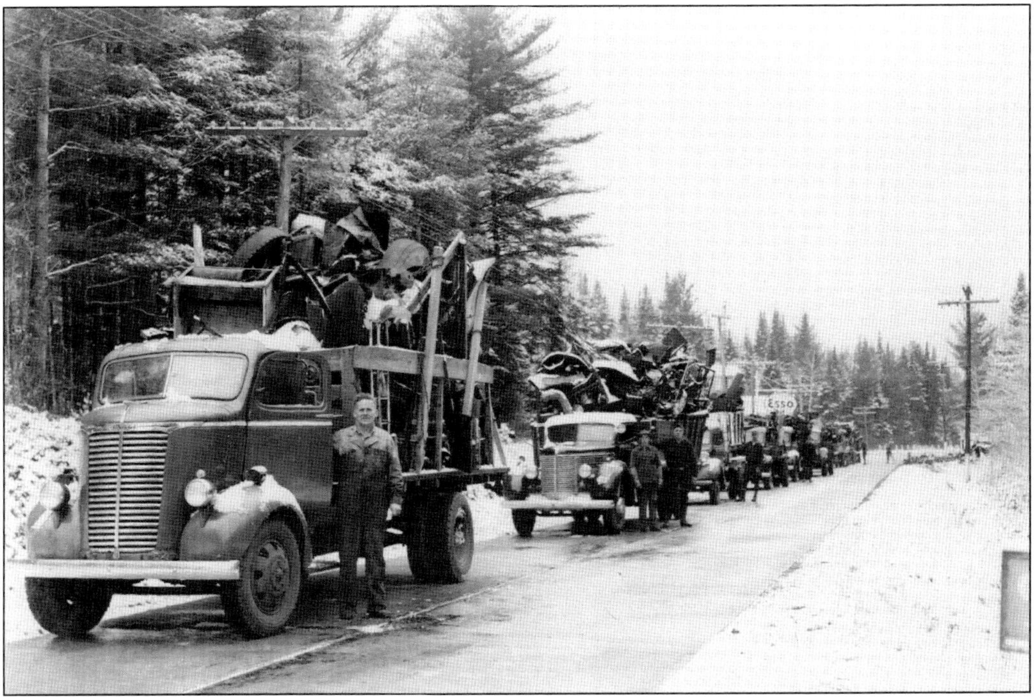

During World War II, the government asked for metal to be used for the war effort. Truckloads were collected in Lake Pleasant and Speculator.

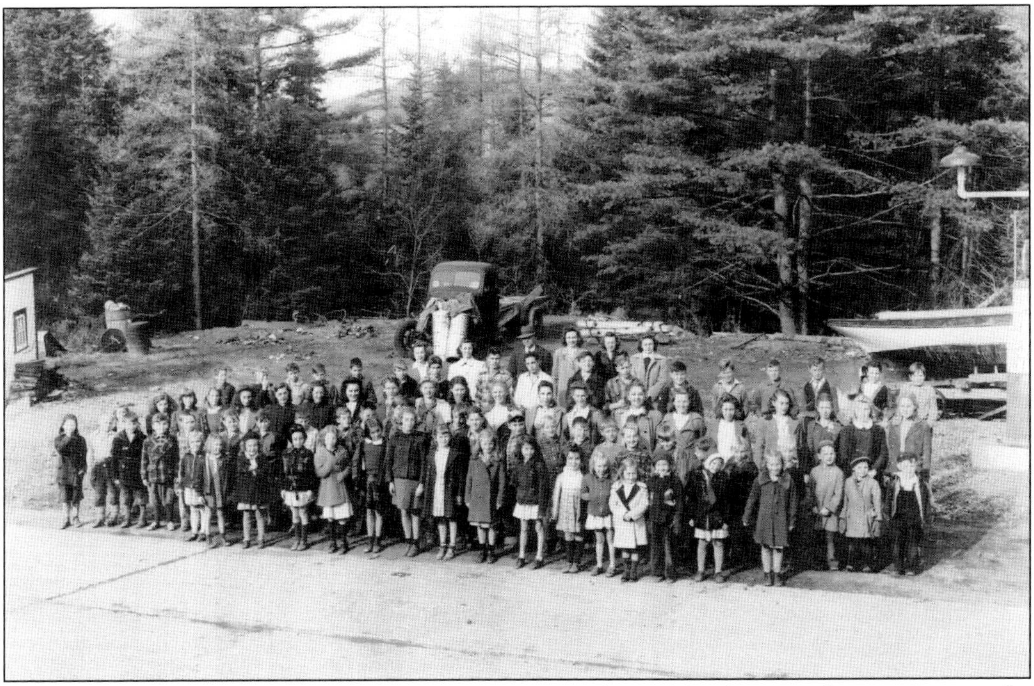

Lake Pleasant Central School children collected tons of metal for the scrap drive and received a national award for collecting the most.

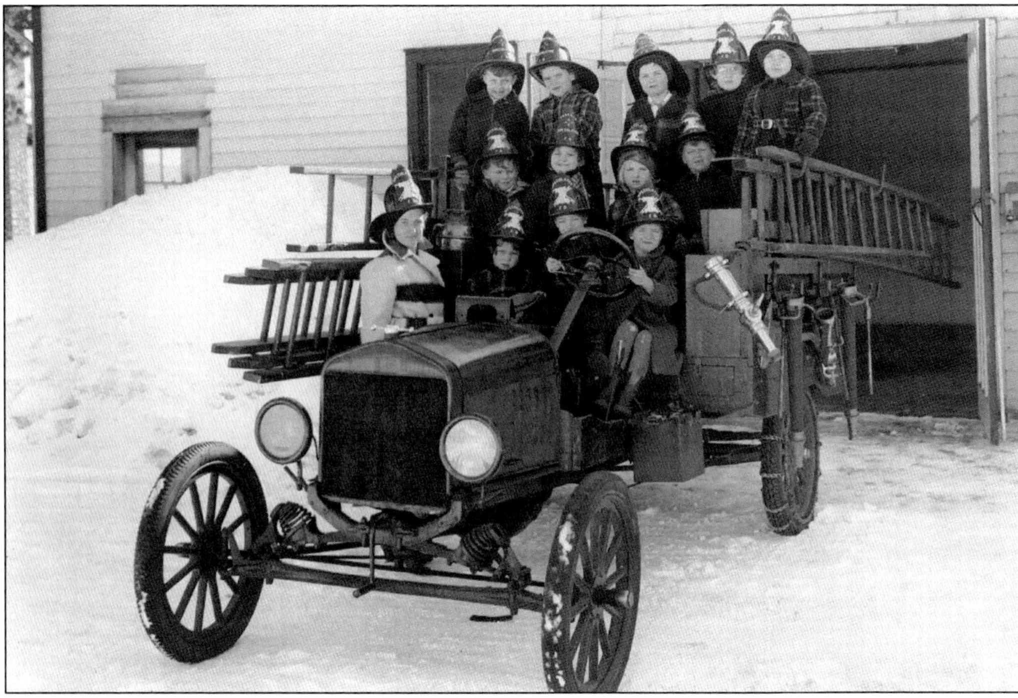

In 1927, the Adirondack Hose Company No. 1 was formed in Speculator. The firemen remodeled a 1917 Ford Model T to carry ladders, hoses, and other equipment. Local children are enjoying a ride.

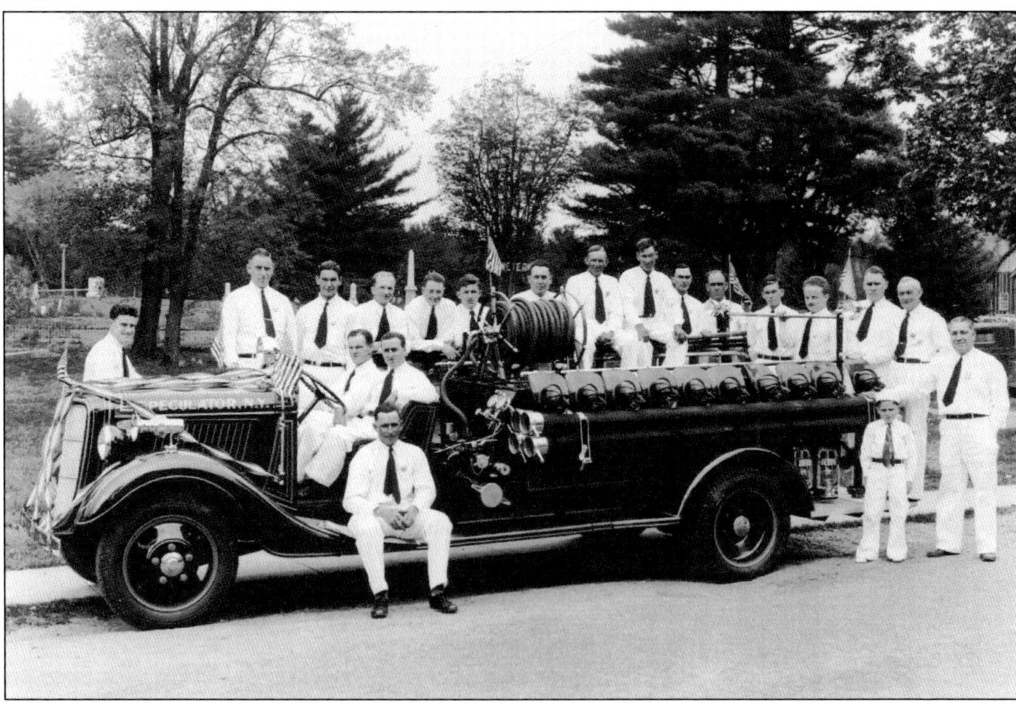

In 1929, the fire department was reorganized under the supervision of the village board. Thirty members were appointed, and in 1936 a new 1937 Ford fire truck was purchased.

When game was killed and brought to Osborne's Inn, it was photographed with anyone desiring a picture with the animal. At right is a picture of John Knox and one of his sisters.

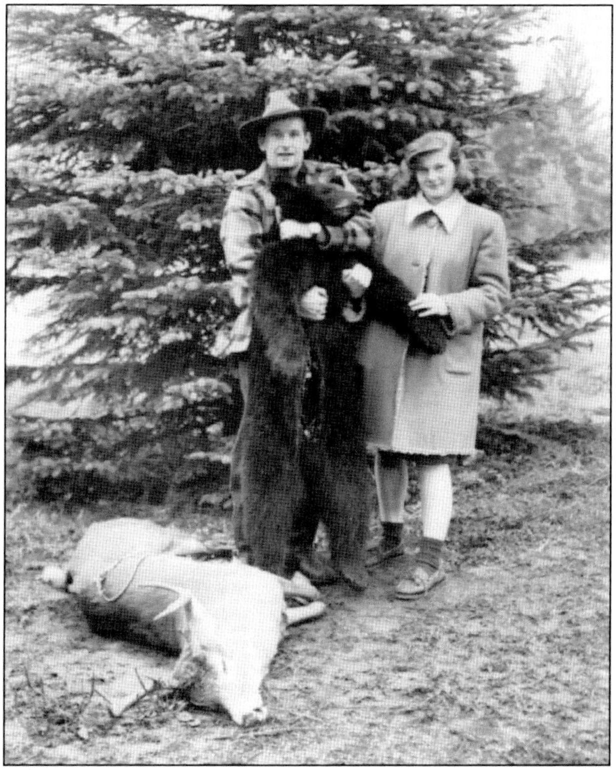

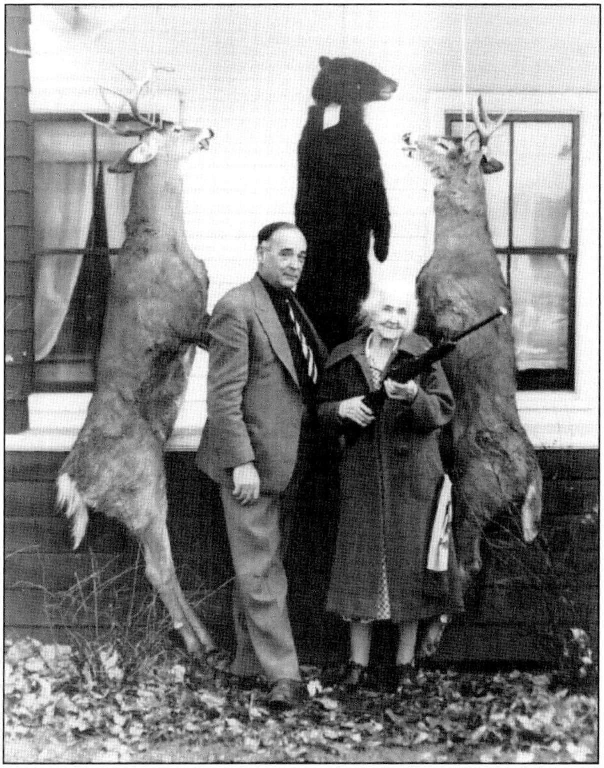

The hunter who bagged the game is unidentified but in the picture is Charlie Mullins and Nora Osborne—the proprietor of Osborne's Inn, who are both enjoying being photographed with the game.

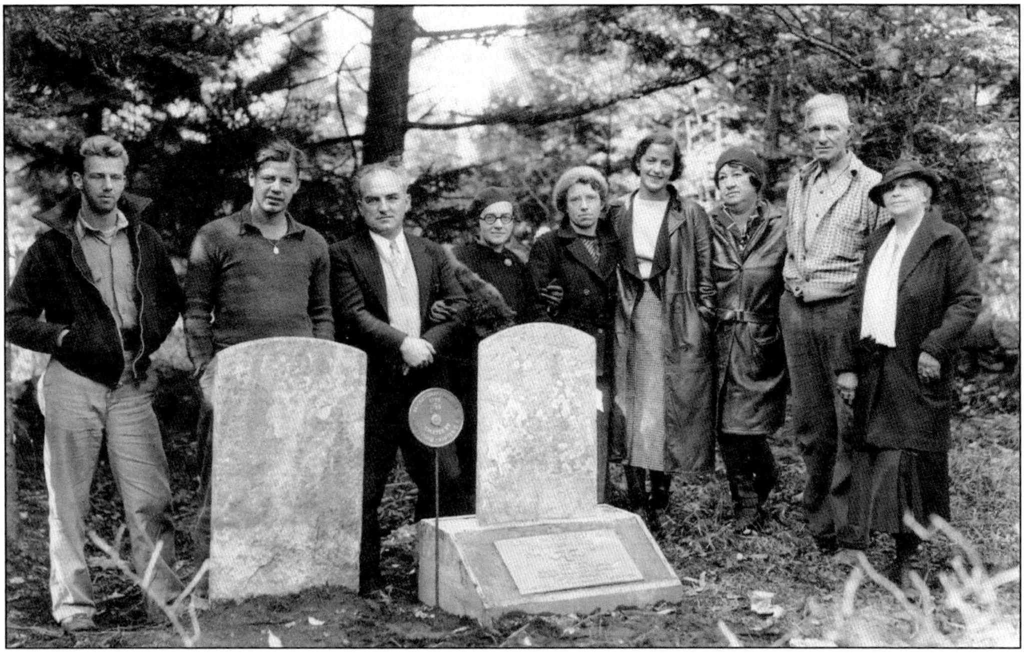

About a mile from Speculator, off the South Shore Road, is the family cemetery of Revolutionary War veteran Col. Loring Peck; his wife, Jane; and their son, Loring Jr. A bronze commemorative plaque was added about 1935. While all in the photograph are not identified, included are Lila Tefft (fifth from left), Mildred Aird (seventh from left), and Agnes and Halsey Page (at far right).

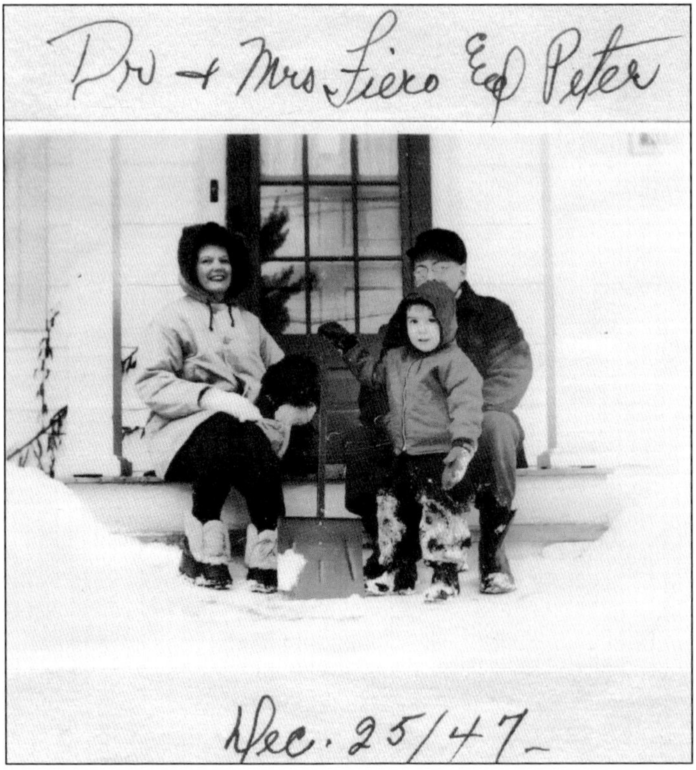

One of the resident doctors around the 1950s was Dr. Rollin P. Fiero, pictured in this Christmas card photograph with his family.

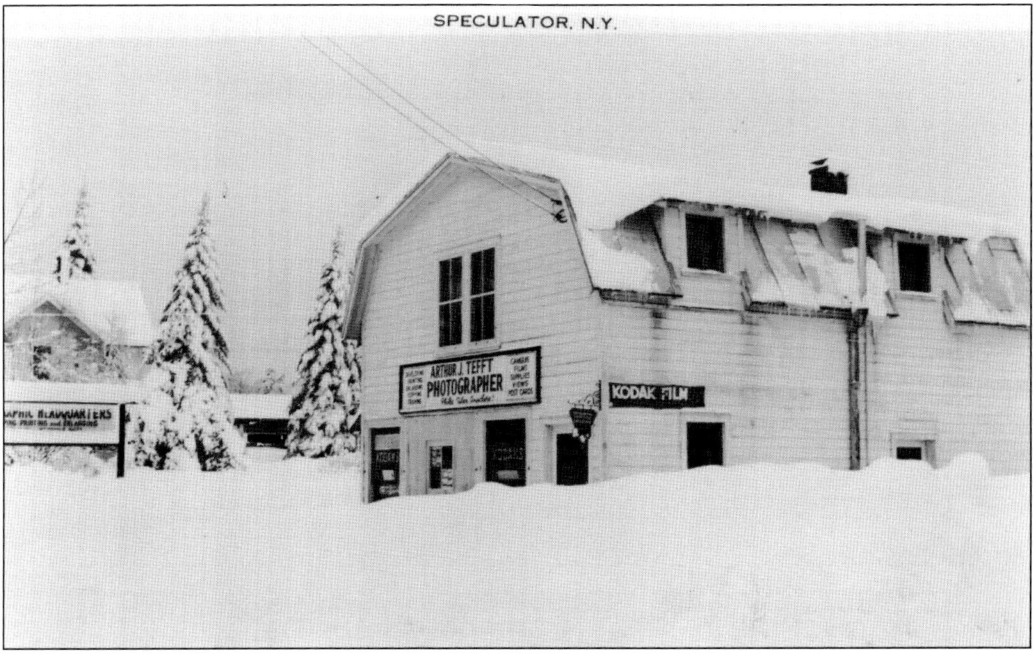

Arthur and Lila Tefft travelled from Connecticut as photographers for Camp-of-the-Woods. Like many, they fell in love with the area and stayed. They rented a vacant building and set up their first studio.

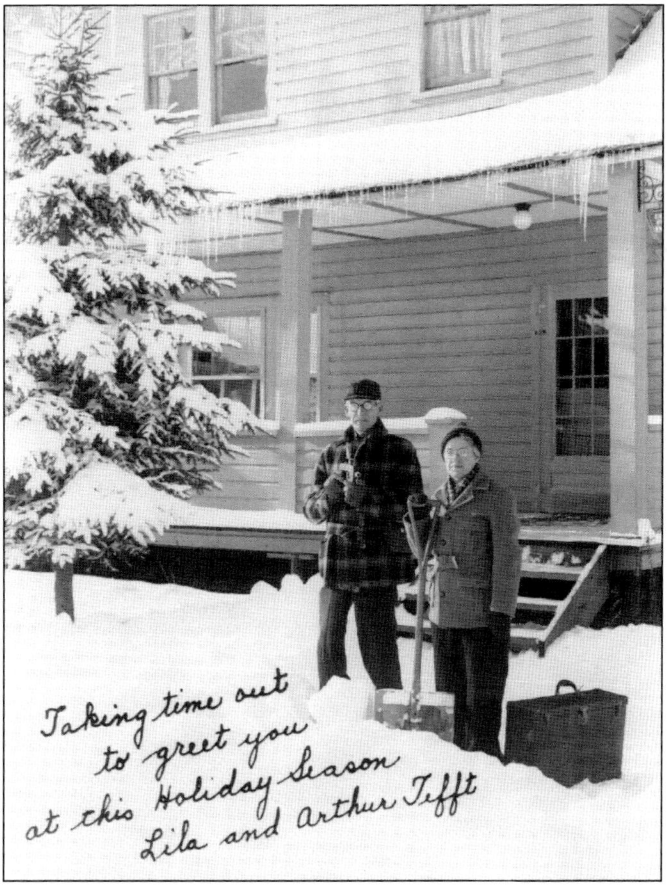

Many of the photographs and postcards that people own today of Lake Pleasant and Speculator can be attributed to the Teffts.

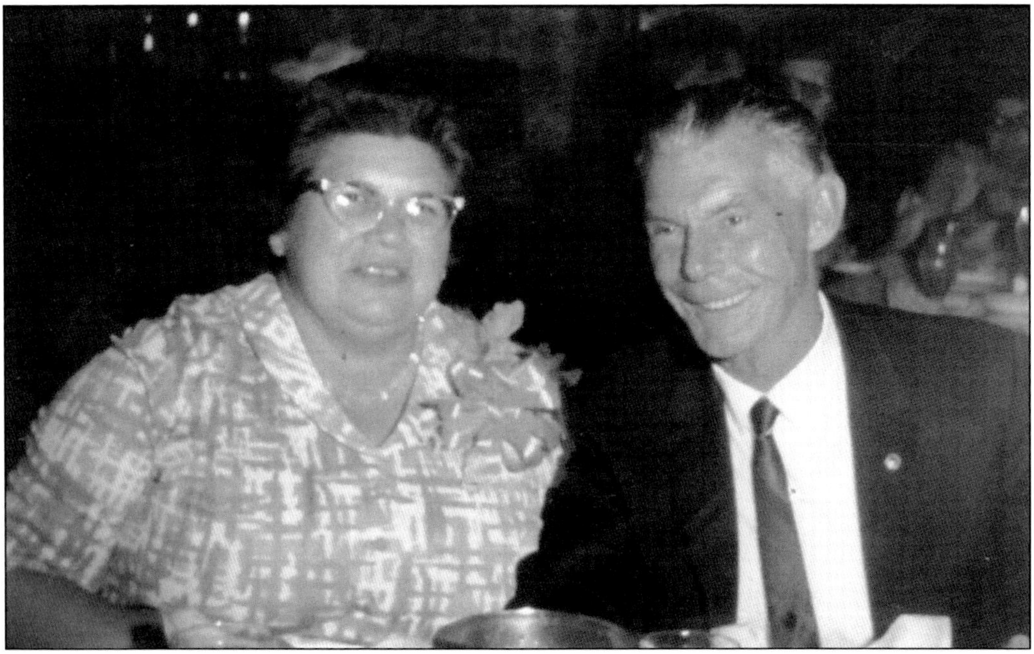

In 1931, Charlie Wickes came to Speculator with the professional hockey team the Hershey Bears who agreed to play hockey wearing the name of Speculator on their uniforms. Charlie stayed in Speculator, married Doris Slack, ran a contractor and building supply business, was elected in 1940 as town clerk of Lake Pleasant serving for 16 years, and elected town supervisor in 1958.

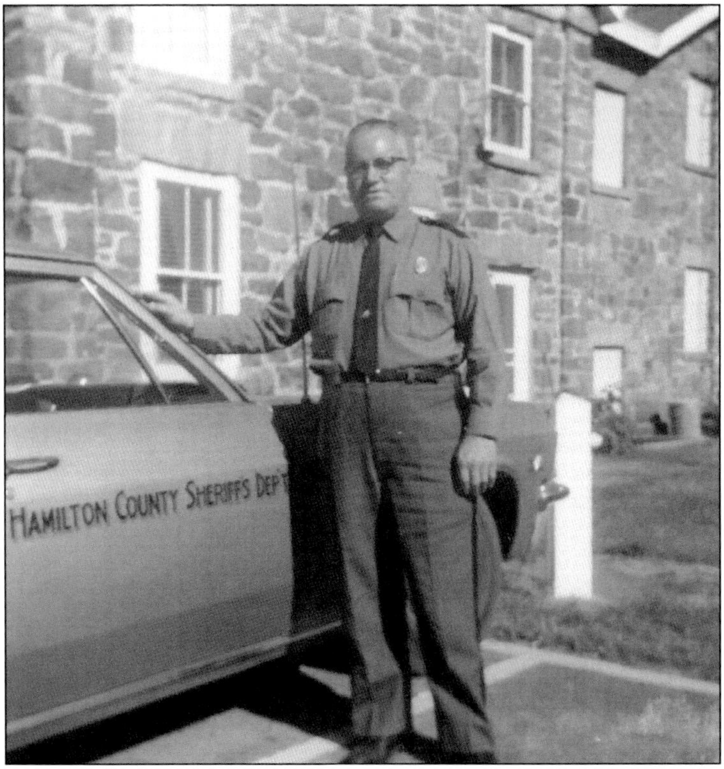

Arthur Parker was elected Hamilton County sheriff in 1964 and served until retiring in the 1980s.

Ann Telfer owned the Mammoth Garage in Speculator in the 1920s and later Hillcrest cabins in Lake Pleasant. She was also a licensed guide and started a hunting camp near Pillsbury Mountain.

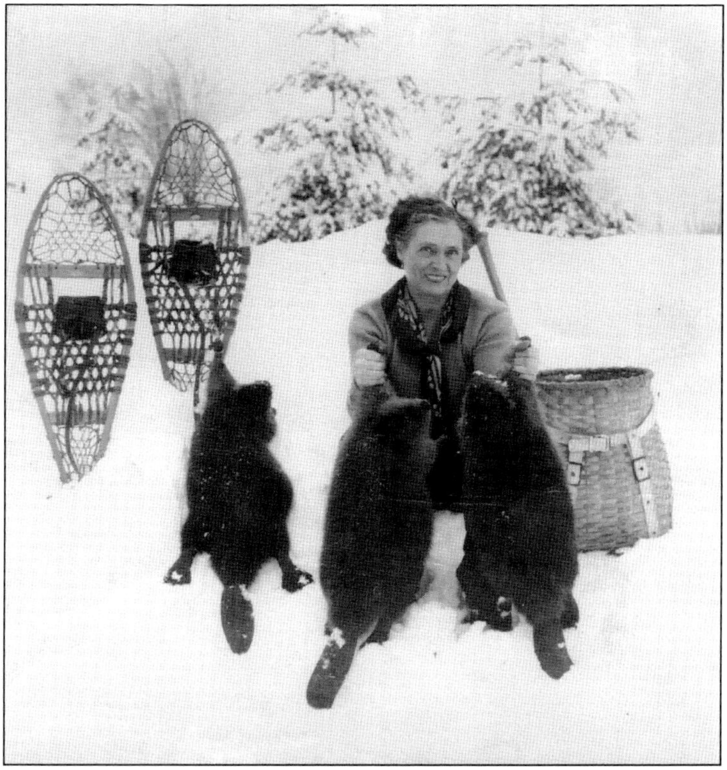

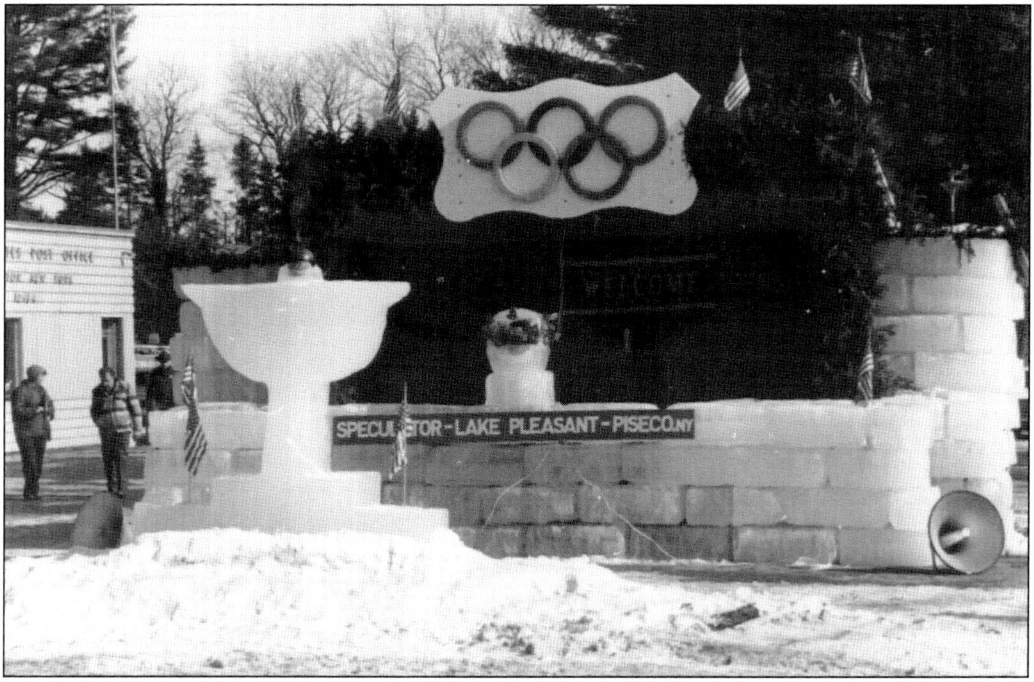

When Lake Placid was chosen to host the 1980 Olympic Winter Games, the route taken to carry the torch passed through Speculator. Local people could run with the torchbearer if they could run 3 miles in four minutes. Ice sculptures were erected at the four corners in Speculator.

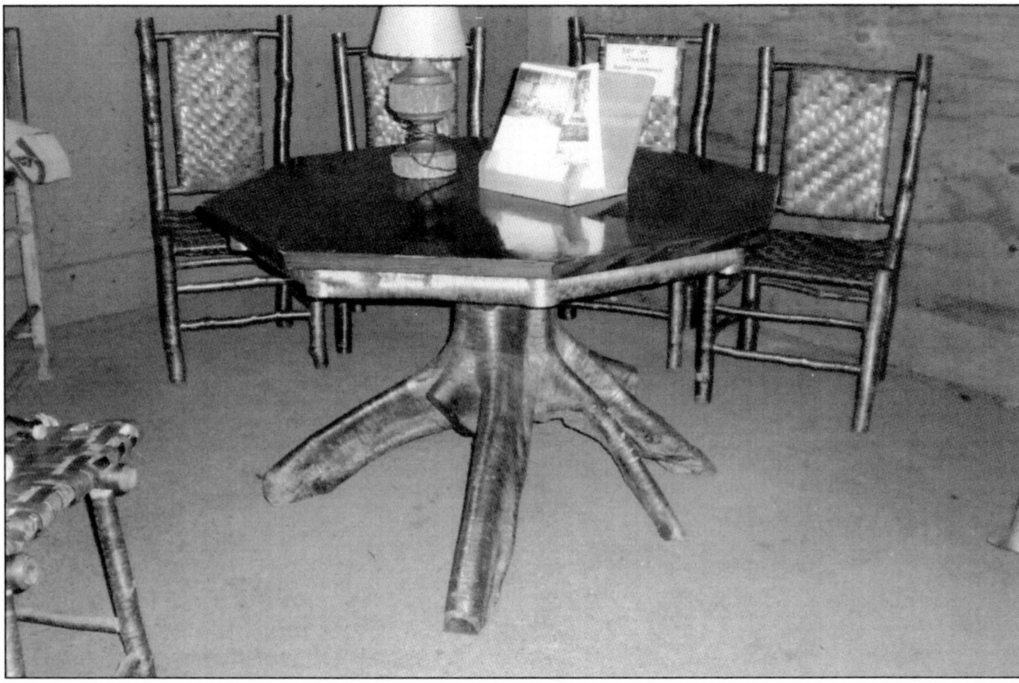

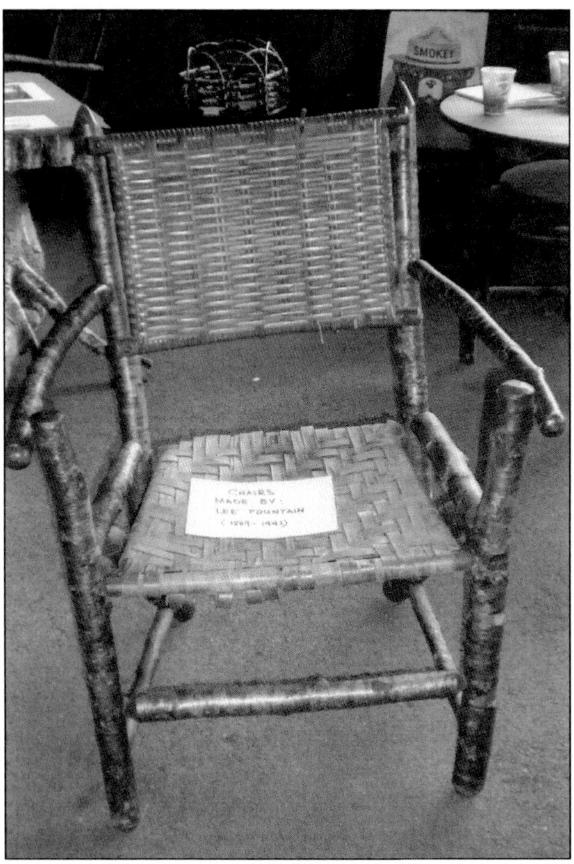

In the early 1900s, Lee Fountain ran the Lake Pleasant House in Speculator. He had a workshop in the back where he crafted his unusual rustic furniture and sold it. (Photograph by John D. Drullard.)

This is another example of Lee Fountain's work. This furniture is highly prized. Lee Fountain spent most of his life in Wells. (Photograph by John D. Drullard.)

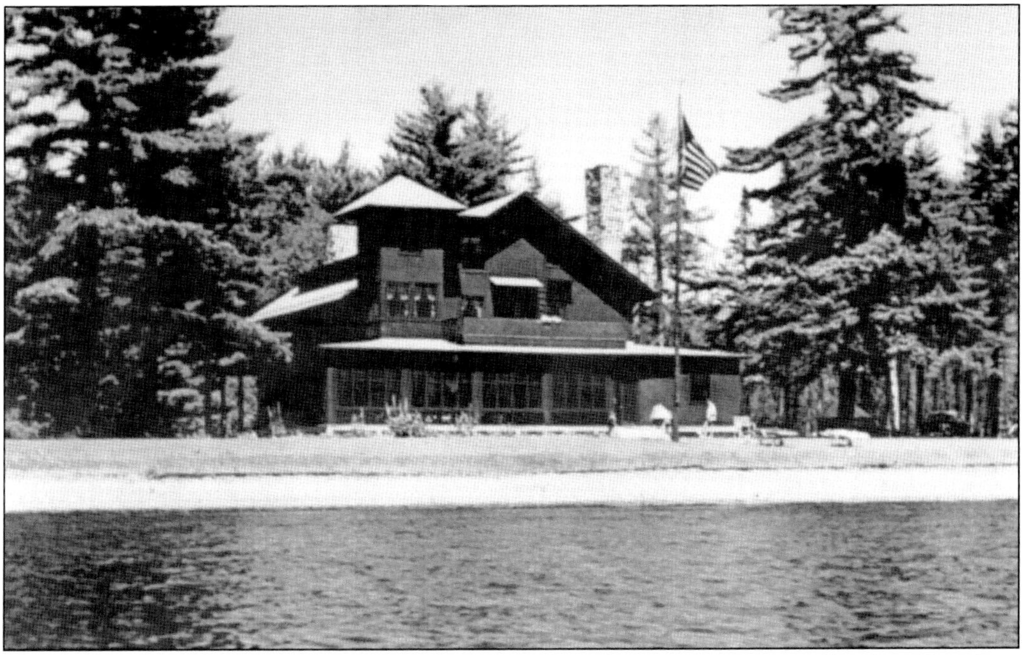

John Storin of Fultonville and New York City purchased over 2,000 acres of land at Hamilton Lake about 1894. It was the former headquarters of the Waighback Club, a hunting and fishing club. In 1917, sometime after Storin's death, his land was sold to Frank J. Bell of Glens Falls and the International Paper Company, who have used it for many years as a conference center.

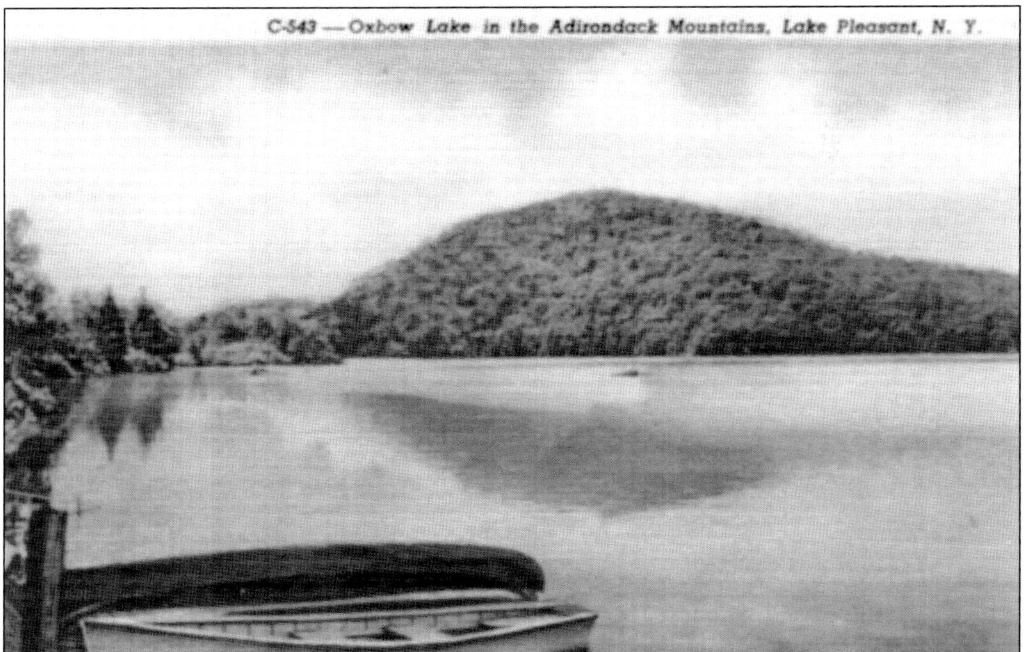

Oxbow Lake is a charming, small lake that is shared with the towns of Lake Pleasant and Arietta. It is known for its great bass fishing.

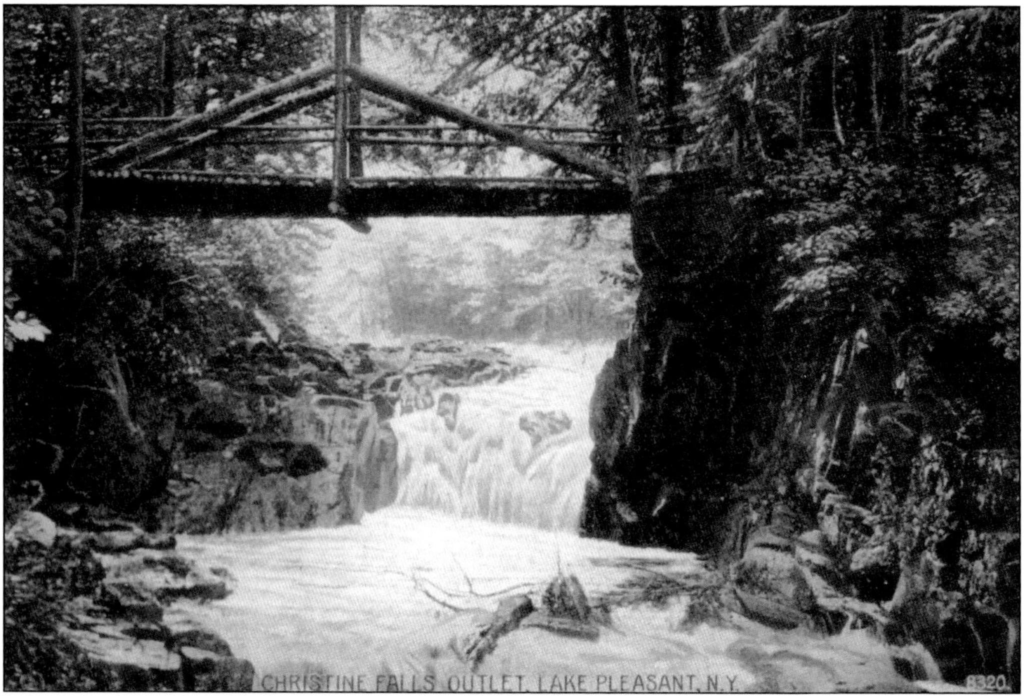

Christine Falls is located on the Sacandaga River, a short distance below Speculator.

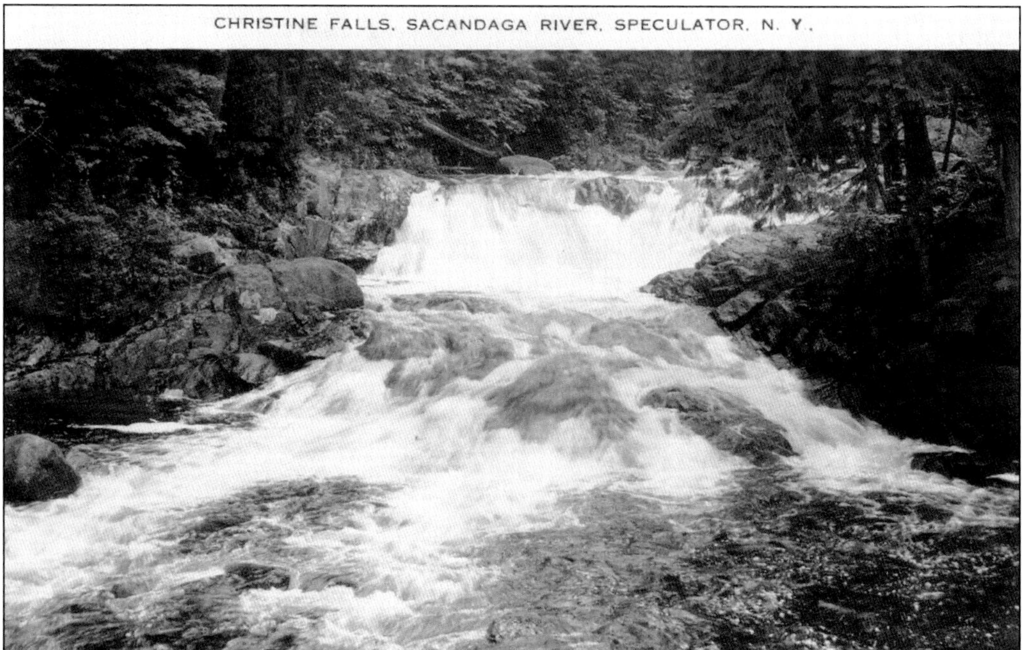

Christine Falls was named after John Hill's daughter, Christine. The Hills built the large summer home Derloch at the head of Lake Pleasant.

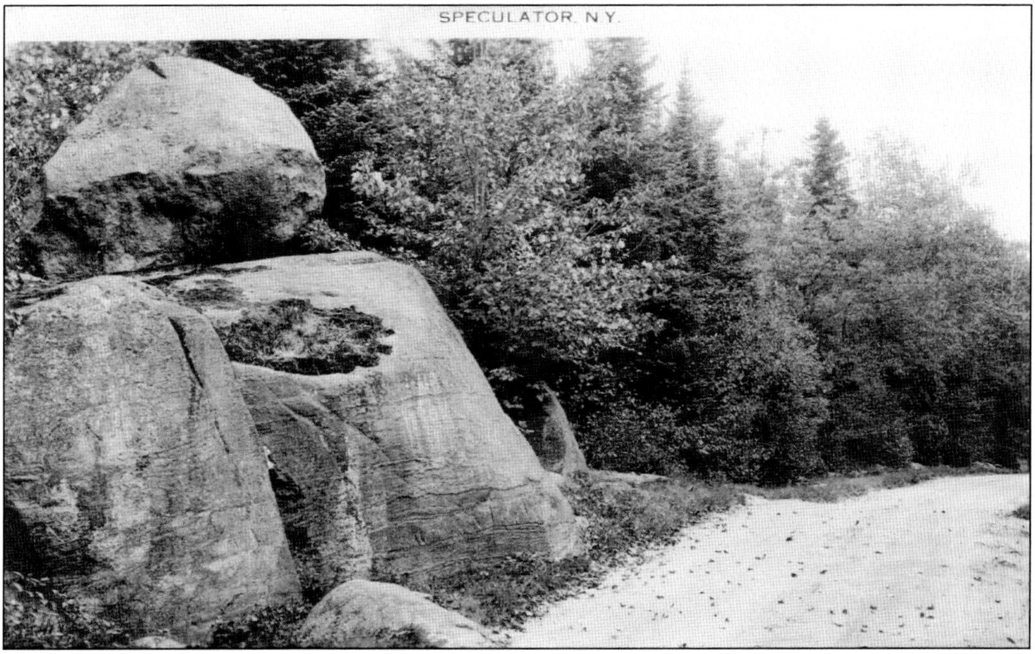

A short distance below Speculator, on the old Gilmantown Road, a large split rock can be seen. According to history, mail carrier Charlie Bidwell was returning from Wells when he was caught in a blizzard. He sought shelter in the cleft of the rock for his horses, and some versions of this tale say the horses died and others say the horses lived. No matter which tale you want to believe, the split rock is called Bidwell's Hotel.

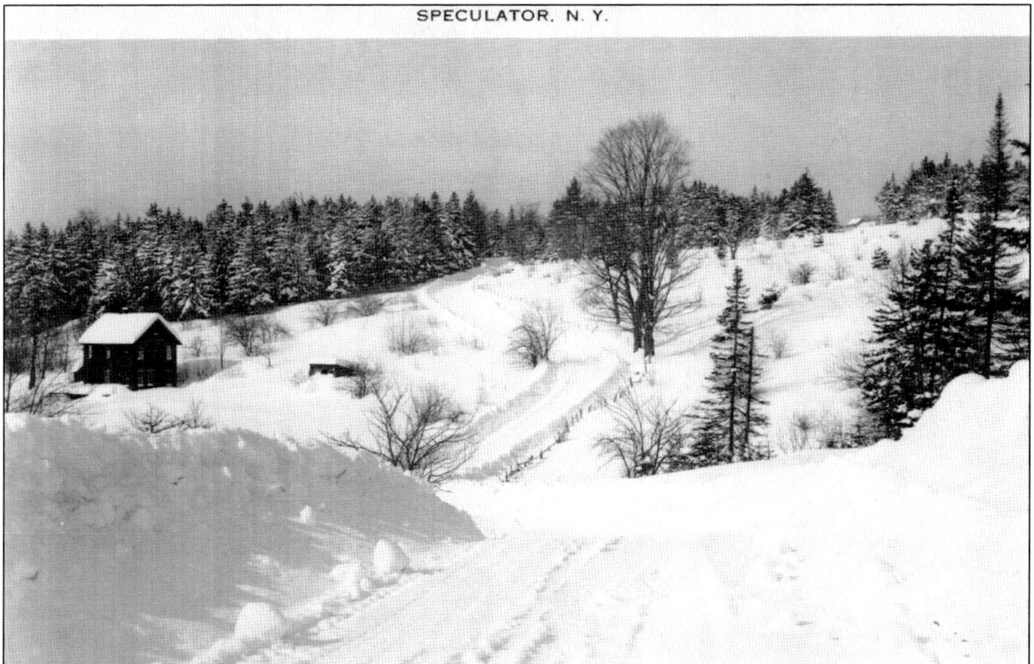

This is a typical winter road scene of Page Street looking toward the summit. Irvin and Mary Yennard's house is on the left.

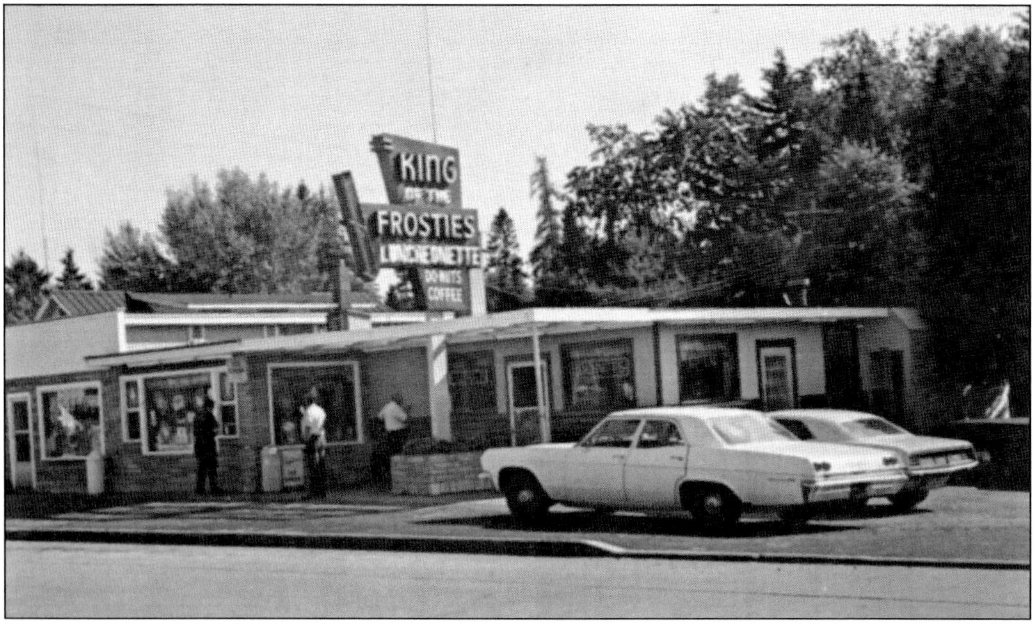

Sidney Griffith was a World War II veteran from Speculator. He opened King of the Frosties as an ice cream parlor and lunch counter. Today King of the Frosties is larger but still serves ice cream and meals to the local and tourist clientele.

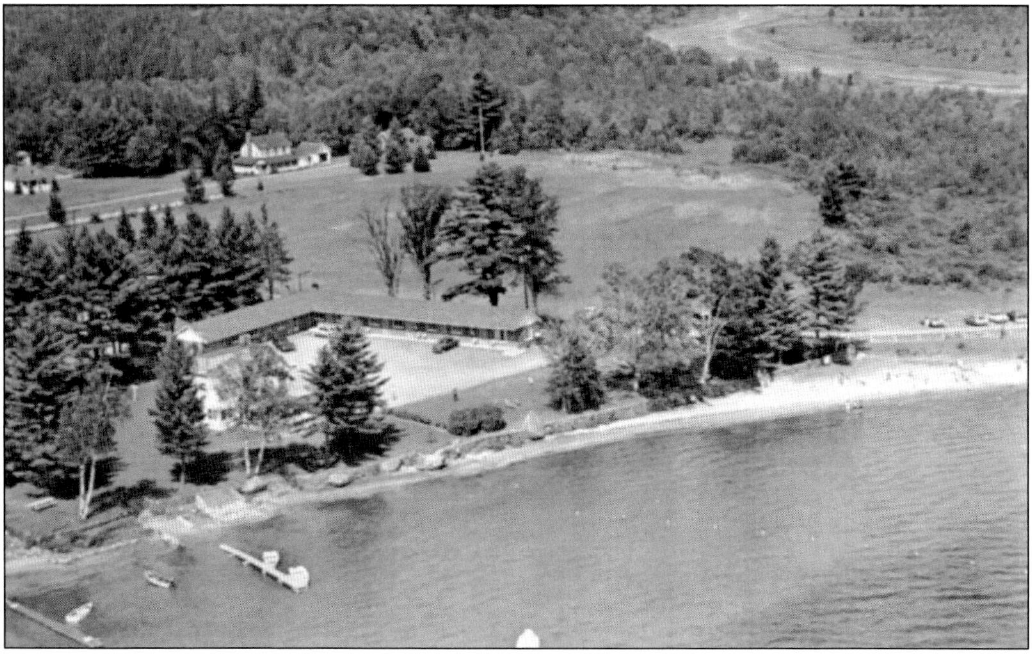

Kay Gifford bought the former Nisbet cottage by the public beach in Speculator. In the 1950s, she had the motel built. Gables Motel was named after the classic story, *The House of Seven Gables*, because of the cottage's architecture.

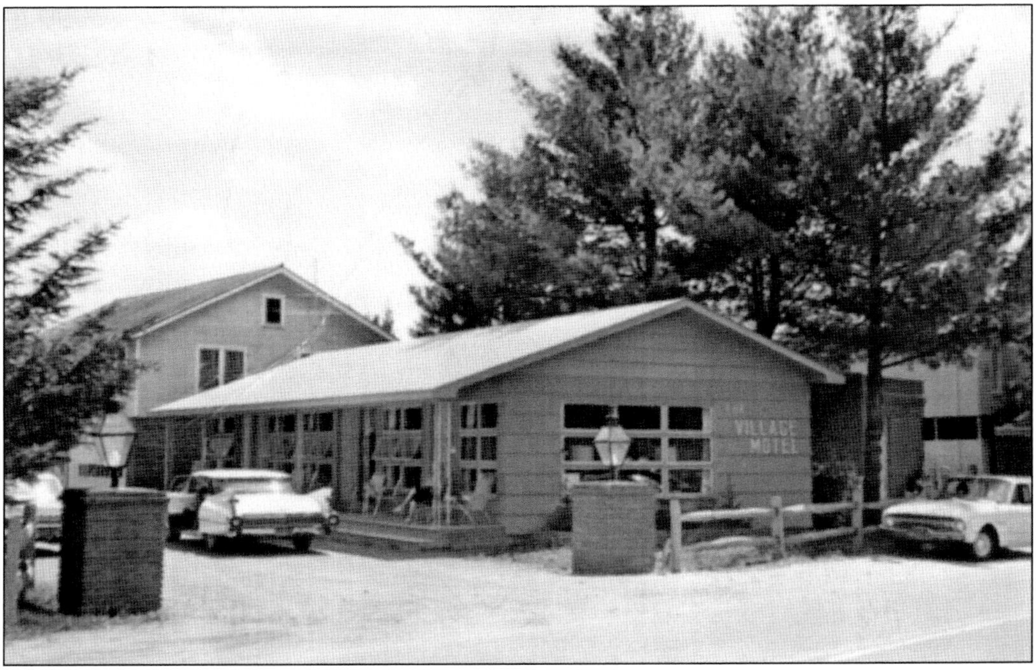

Clyde and Virginia Elliott built the Village Motel in the 1950s. Clyde also operated the Mobile Service Station at the four corners. The Village Motel is still in operation today.

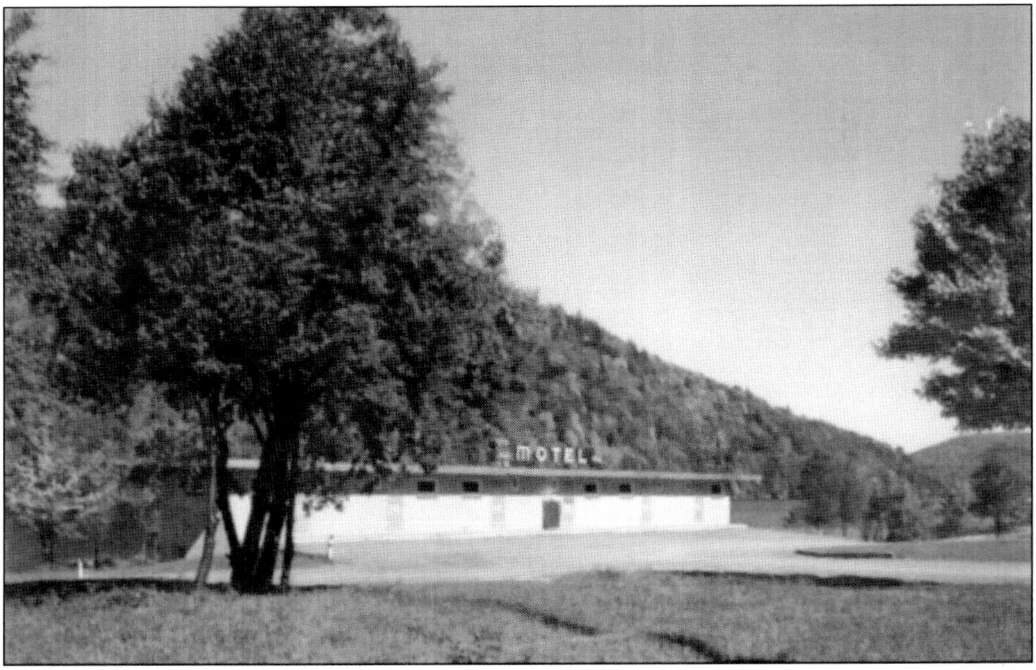

Raymond and Helen Rogers built the Oxbow Motel in 1953. It is located just over the line on Route 8 into the town of Arietta on Oxbow Lake.

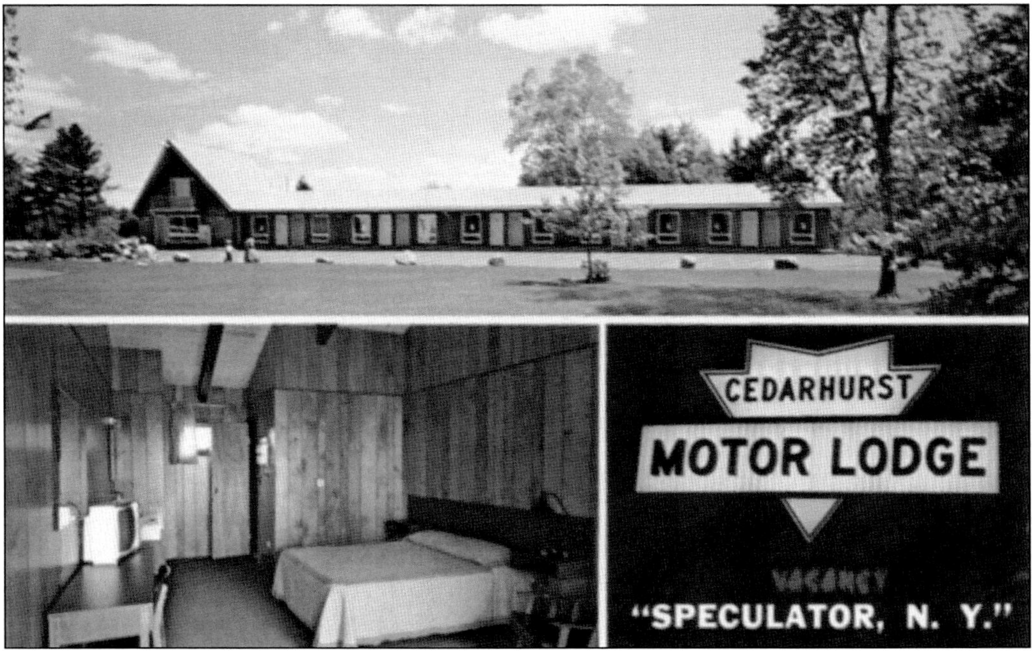

Hans Ruttmar and David Braunius built Cedarhurst around 1970, and the Ruttmar family ran it. Bob Kuiken now owns it.

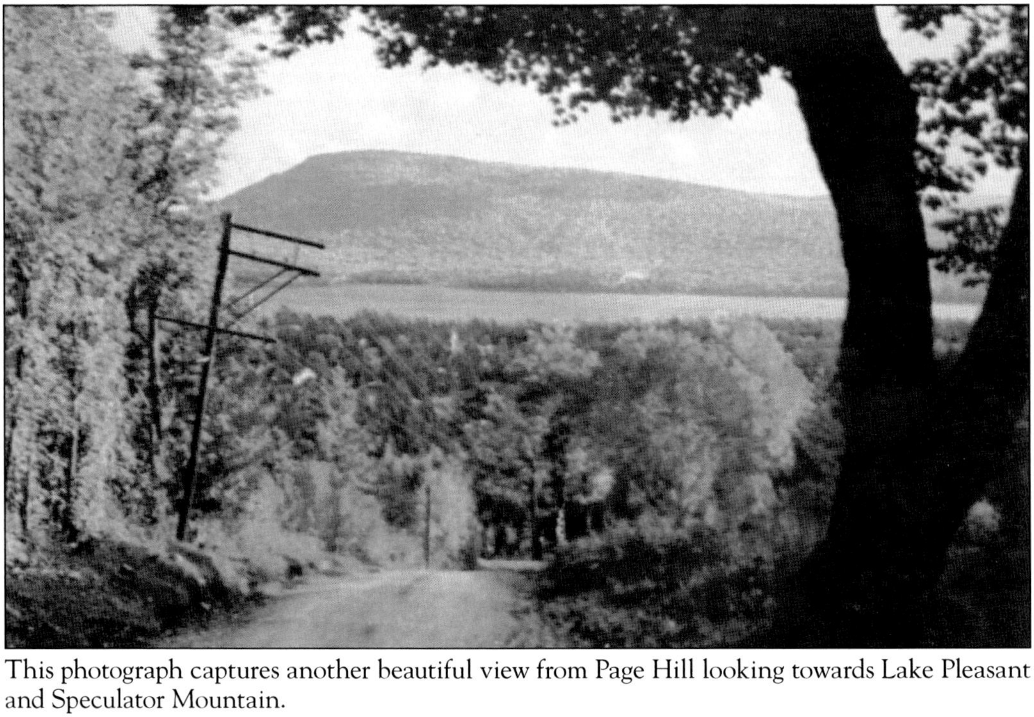

This photograph captures another beautiful view from Page Hill looking towards Lake Pleasant and Speculator Mountain.

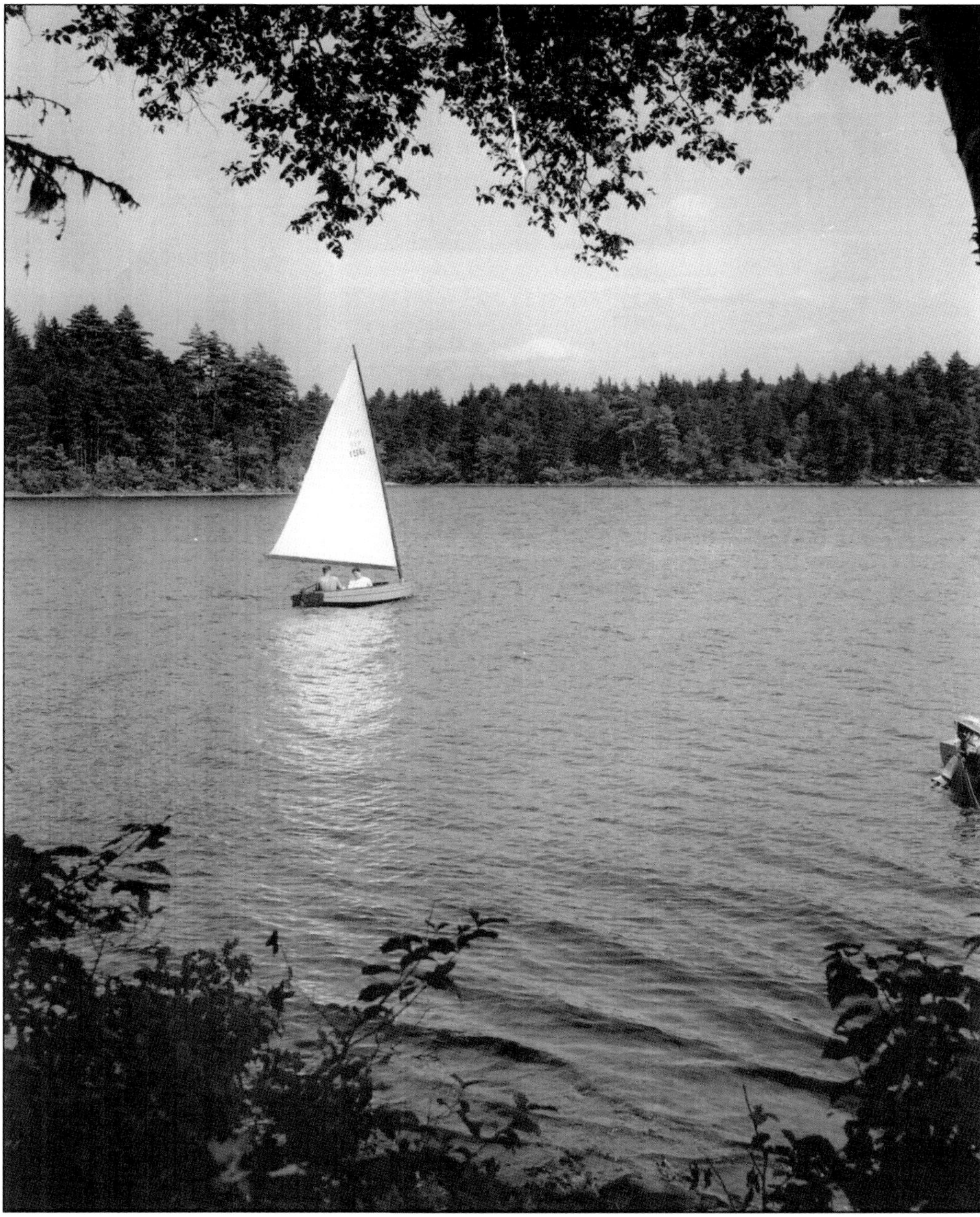

Many lakes make up the town of Lake Pleasant such as Lake Pleasant, Sacandaga Lake, Echo Lake, Fawn Lake, Oxbow Lake, Mason Lake, Whitaker Lake, and Elm Lake to name a few. The above photograph is Sacandaga Lake.